بسم الله الرحمن الرحيم

"The house of al-Arqam is the house of Islam"

Al-Ḥākim (d.405 h.) in *al-Mustadrak ʿala al-Ṣaḥiḥayn* (6185)

شَرْحُ

المَنْظُومَةِ البَيْقُونِيَّةِ

فِي عِلْمِ مُصْطَلَحِ الحَدِيثِ

A COMMENTARY ON THE POEM

AL-BAYQUNIYYAH

AL-SHAYKH MUḤAMMAD IBN ṢĀLIḤ AL-ʿUTHAYMĪN

SPECIAL EDITION

DAR AL-ARQAM

978-1-9164756-9-4

British Library Cataloguing in Publishing Data
A catalogue record for this book is available from the British Library

First edition, 2016
Special edition, first printed in 2021

Prepared and published by Dar al-Arqam Publishing
Birmingham, United Kingdom

www.daralarqam.bigcartel.com
Email: daralarqam@hotmail.co.uk

Translated by Ash-Shafie Abdullah
BA in the Arabic Language from the Islamic University of Madinah, currently in the final year of an MA course in teaching Arabic to non-native speakers from the Islamic University of Madinah.
Edited by Adnan Karim
Head of translation at Dar al-Arqam. He has translated and edited a number of works for Dar al-Arqam.

If you would like to support our work, donations can be made via:

- www.daralarqam.bigcartel.com/product/donate
- www.patreon.com/daralarqam
- www.paypal.me/daralarqam

Printed in Turkey by Mega | export@mega.com

A Commentary on the Poem al-Bayqūniyyah

By al-Shaykh Muḥammad ibn Ṣāliḥ al-ʿUthaymīn

Contents

متن المنظومة البيقونية

THE TEXT OF AL-MANẒŪMAT AL-BAYQŪNIYYAH

١ : أَبْدَأُ بِالْحَمْدِ مُصَلِّياً عَلَى

مُحَمَّدٍ خَيرِ نَبِيٍّ أُرْسِلاَ

(1) I begin with praise, and prayers and salutations,
Upon Muhammad the finest prophet ever given the message.

٢ : وَذِي مِنْ أَقْسَامِ الْحَدِيثِ عِدَّه

وَكُلُّ وَاحِدٍ أَتَى وَحَدَّه

(2) And these are a number of categories of ḥadīth,
Each one having come with its definition.

٣ : أَوَّلُهَا الصَّحِيحُ وَهْوَ مَا اتَّصَلْ

إِسْنَادُهُ وَلَمْ يَشُذَّ أَوْ يُعَلّ

(3) The first of them is sahīh which is what is connected,
In its chain, and is neither contradicting nor defected.

٤ : يَرْوِيهِ عَدْلٌ ضَابِطٌ عَنْ مِثْلِهِ

مُعْتَمَدٌ فِي ضَبْطِهِ وَنَقْلِهِ

(4) Narrated by one who is just and precise from his like,
Reliable in his precision and his transmission.

٥: وَالْحَسَنُ الْمَعْرُوفُ طُرْقاً وَغَدَتْ

رِجَالُهُ لاَ كَالصَّحِيحِ اشْتَهَرَتْ

(5) Al-ḥasan is the one known in its chains but,
Whose transmitters are not as famous as the ṣaḥīḥ.

٦: وَكُلُّ مَا عَنْ رُتْبَةِ الْحُسْنِ قَصُرْ

فَهْوَ الضَّعِيفُ وَهْوَ أَقْسَاماً كَثُرْ

(6) All that falls below the rank of ḥasan,
Is thus ḍaʿīf and it has many categories.

٧: وَمَا أُضِيفَ لِلنَّبِي الْمَرْفُوعُ

وَمَا لِتَابِعٍ هُوَ الْمَقْطُوعُ

(7) What was attributed to the Prophet is known as al-marfūʿ,
While the one to a tābiʿi is known as al-maqṭūʿ.

٨: وَالْمُسْنَدُ الْمُتَّصِلُ الإِسْنَادِ مِنْ

رَاوِيهِ حَتَّى الْمُصْطَفَى وَلَمْ يَبِنْ

(8) The musnad is that with an isnād connected from,
Its narrator up to the Chosen One and not detached.

٩: وَمَا بِسَمْعِ كُلِّ رَاوٍ يَتَّصِلْ

إِسْنَادُهُ لِلْمُصْطَفَى فَالْمُتَّصِلْ

(9) And one whose chain, by every narrator's hearing,
Is connected to al-Muṣṭafā is the muttaṣil.

١٠: مُسَلْسَلٌ قُلْ مَا عَلَى وَصْفٍ أَتَى

مِثْلُ أَمَا وَاللَّهِ أَنْبَانِي الْفَتَى

(10) Say musalsal is one which comes with a trait,
Such as: "Indeed by Allāh, the youth informed me.

١١: كَذَاكَ قَدْ حَدَّثَنِيهِ قَائِماَ

أَوْ بَعْدَ أَنْ حَدَّثَنِي تَبَسَّماَ

(11) Similarly: "Indeed he narrated it to me while standing."
Or "After he narrated it to me he smiled.

١٢: عَزِيزُ مَرْوِي اثْنَينِ أَوْ ثَلاثَهْ

مَشْهُورُ مَرْوِي فَوقَ مَا ثَلاثَهْ

(12) 'Azīz is narrated by two or three,
Mash-hūr is narrated by more than three.

١٣: مُعَنْعَنٌ كَعَنْ سَعِيدٍ عَنْ كَرَمْ

وَمُبْهَمٌ مَا فِيهِ رَاوٍ لَمْ يُسَمّ

(13) Mu'an'an is like "from Sa'īd from Karam,"
Mubham is that in which a narrator hasn't been named.

١٤: وَكُلُّ مَا قَلَّتْ رِجَالُهُ عَلاَ

وَضِدُّهُ ذَاكَ الَّذِي قَدْ نَزَلاَ

(14) That which has few narrators shall arise,
And its opposite is the one which shall descend.

١٥: وَمَا أَضَفْتَهُ إِلَى الأَصْحَابِ مِنْ
قَولٍ وَفِعْلٍ فَهْوَ مَوْقُوفٌ زُكِنْ

(15) And whatever you attributed to the companions such as,
A statement or an action is known as mawqūf.

١٦: وَمُرْسَلٌ مِنْهُ الصَّحَابِيُّ سَقَطْ
وَقُلْ غَرِيبٌ مَا رَوَى رَاوٍ فَقَطْ

(16) And al-mursal, from it the companion was omitted,
And say that gharīb is that which was narrated by only one.

١٧: وَكُلُّ مَا لَمْ يَتَّصِلْ بِحَالِ
إِسْنَادُهُ مُنْقَطِعُ الأَوْصَالِ

(17) And all that is not connected in any instance,
Its chain has munqaṭiʿ (severed) ties.

١٨: وَالْمُعْضَلُ السَّاقِطُ مِنْهُ اثْنَانِ
وَمَا أَتَى مُدَلَّساً نَوْعَانِ

(18) And the muʿḍal has two omitted from it,
That which comes as mudallas is of two types:

١٩: الأَوَّلُ الإِسْقَاطُ لِلشَّيْخِ وَأَنْ

يَنْقُلَ عَمَّنْ فَوقَهُ بِعَنْ وَأَنْ

(19) The first is omission of the shaykh and to,
Transmit from the one above him by using "'an" and "anna";

٢٠: وَالثَّانِي لاَ يُسْقِطُهُ لَكِنْ يَصِفْ

أَوْصَافَهُ بِمَا بِهِ لاَ يَنْعَرِفْ

(20) And in the second he does not omit him but he describes,
His characteristics with that by which he is not known.

٢١: وَمَا يُخَالِفْ ثِقَةٌ بِهِ الْمَلاَ

فَالشَّاذُّ وَالْمَقْلُوبُ قِسمَانِ تَلاَ

(21) And when a trustworthy narrator contradicts the assembly,
It is al-shādh while al-maqlūb has two types that follow:

٢٢: إِبْدَالُ رَاوٍ مَا بِرَاوٍ قِسْمُ

وَقَلْبُ إِسْنَادٍ لِمَتْنٍ قِسْمُ

(22) Substituting a narrator for a narrator is a category,
And exchanging a chain of a text is a category.

٢٣: وَالْفَرْدُ مَا قَيَّدْتَهُ بِثِقَةِ

أَوْ جَمْعٍ أَوْ قَصْرٍ عَلَى رِوَايَةِ

(23) And al-fard is what you limit to a trustworthy narrator,
Or a group or a restriction upon a particular narration.

٢٤: وَمَا بِعِلَّةٍ غُمُوضٌ أَوْ خَفَا

مُعَلَّلٌ عِنْدَهُمُ قَدْ عُرِفَا

(24) And that which has an obscure or hidden defect,
Is known to them as mu'allal.

٢٥: وَذُو اخْتِلاَفِ سَنَدٍ أَوْ مَتْنِ
مُضْطَرِبٌ عِنْدَ أُهَيلِ الْفَنِّ

(25) And that which has a discrepancy in a chain or text is,
Muḍṭarib according to the people of the art.

٢٦: وَالْمُدْرَجَاتُ فِي الْحَدِيثِ مَا أَتَتْ
مِنْ بَعْضِ أَلْفَاظِ الرُّوَاةِ اتَّصَلَتْ

(26) Insertions in the ḥadīth are what came,
From some of the words of the narrators that were connected.

٢٧: وَمَا رَوَى كُلُّ قَرِينٍ عَنْ أَخِهْ
مُدَبَّجٌ فَاعْرِفْهُ حَقاًّ وَانْتَخِهْ

(27) And what was narrated by every qarīn from his associate,
Is mudabbaj, know it well and be proud of it.

٢٨: مُتَّفِقٌ لَفْظاً وَخَطاًّ مُتَّفِقْ
وَضِدُّهُ فِيمَا ذَكَرْنَا الْمُفْتَرِقْ

(28) Identical in pronunciation and writing is muttafiq,
While the opposite of what we mentioned is muftariq.

٢٩: مُؤْتَلِفٌ مُتَّفِقُ الْخَطِّ فَقَطْ

وَضِدُّهُ مُخْتَلِفٌ فَاخْشَ الْغَلَطْ

(29) Mu'talif is similar only in writing,
And its opposite is mukhtalif, so beware of mistakes.

٣٠: وَالْمُنْكَرُ الْفَرْدُ بِهِ رَاوٍ غَدَا
تَعْدِيلُهُ لاَ يَحْمِلُ التَّفَرُّدَا

(30) Munkar is the singular narration by a narrator,
Whose standing does not allow for a singular narration.

٣١: مَتْرُوكُهُ مَا وَاحِدٌ بِهِ انْفَرَدْ
وَأَجْمَعُواْ لِضَعْفِهِ فَهُوَ كَرَدّ

(31) Matrūk is that in which there is a solitary narrator,
And they agreed upon its weakness like the rejected.

٣٢: وَالْكَذِبُ الْمُخْتَلَقُ الْمَصْنُوعُ
عَلَى النَّبِي فَذَلِكَ الْمَوْضُوعُ

(32) And the lie which was fabricated and created,
Upon the Prophet is thus al-mawḍū'.

٣٣: وَقَدْ أَتَتْ كَالْجَوْهَرِ الْمَكْنُونِ
سَمَّيْتُهَا مَنْظُومَةَ الْبَيْقُونِي

(33) Indeed it came like a hidden gem,
Which I have entitled "The Poem of al-Bayqūnī".

٣٤: فَوْقَ الثَّلاَثِينَ بِأَرْبَعٍ أَتَتْ

أَقْسَامُهَا تَمَّتْ بِخَيْرٍ خُتِمَتْ

(34) It came with four above thirty,
Its sections, concluded and sealed with goodness.

الناظم رحمه الله تعلى

A BRIEF BIOGRAPHY OF THE COMPOSER

He - may Allāh have mercy on him - is known for the poem, *al-Manẓūmat al-Bayqūniyyah* in the science of *muṣṭalah al-ḥadīth*. The attribution of this poem to him is apparent in the thirty-third line:

وَقَدْ أَتَتْ كَالْجَوْهَرِ الْمَكْنُونِ

سَمَّيْتُهَا مَنْظُومَةَ الْبَيْقُونِي

(33) Indeed it came like a hidden gem,
Which I have entitled "The Poem of al-Bayqūnī".

His name: 'Umar[1] and it was said that he was Ṭaha[2] ibn Muḥammad ibn Futūḥ al-Bayqūnī al-Dimashqī al-Shāfi'ī.

Regarding his *laqab* (nickname) "al-Bayqūnī": It is not known if the origin of this name is an attribution to the country he came from or his father etc.

As for his year of death, may Allāh have mercy on him: It was mentioned by those who wrote about him that he was alive before the year 1080 H.[3]

1 *Mu'jam al-Mu'allifīn* (volume 2, page 18, published in 1414 H. by Mu'assasat al-Risālah, Beirut).
2 *Al-A'lām* by al-Zirqānī (volume 5, page 64).
3 *Al-A'lām* by al-Zirqānī (volume 5, page 64).

تقديم الناشر

Publisher's Note

As copies of the first print of this book began to run low in late 2020, we decided to place effort into crafting a special edition, rather than a reprint. Before you is the end result, praise be to Allah.

We would like to thank our team who worked hard in producing this work amidst the plethora of other projects. May Allah reward them.

Dar al-Arqam Publishing

مقدمة في علم مصطلح الحديث

An Introduction to the Science of Ḥadīth Terminology

بسم الله الرحمن الرحيم. إن الحمد لله نحمده ونستعينه ونستغفره، ونعوذ بالله من شرور أنفسنا ومن سيئات أعمالنا، من يهده الله فلا مضل له، ومن يضلل فلا هادي له، وأشهد أن لا إله إلا الله وحده لا شريك له، وأشهد أن محمداً عبده ورسوله صلى الله عليه وعلى آله وأصحابه ومن تبعهم بإحسان إلى يوم الدين وسلم تسليماً.

In the Name of Allāh, the Entirely Merciful, the Especially Merciful. Verily all praise is due to Allāh, we praise Him and seek His Assistance and Forgiveness, and we seek refuge in Allāh from the evils of our souls and our bad deeds. Whomsoever Allāh guides, none can mislead him, and whomsoever He leaves astray, there is none who can guide him. I bear witness that there is no god rightful of being worshipped except Allāh alone without ascribing partners to Him, and I bear witness that Muhammad is His servant and messenger, may Allāh Bestow His blessings, peace and salutations upon him, his family, companions and all those following them in goodness until the Day of Judgement.

أما بعد:

To proceed:

فهذه مقدمة في علم مصطلح الحديث:

In this opening section we will provide a brief introduction to the science of *musṭalah al-ḥadīth* (terminology of *ḥadīth*):

المصطلح: علم يعرف به أحوال الراوي والمروي من حيث القبول والرد.

The science of *muṣṭalah* is the study of the status of the narrator and the narration in terms of acceptance and rejection.

وفائدة علم المصطلح: هو تنقية الأدلة الحديثية وتخليصها مما يشوبها من: ضعيف وغيره، ليتمكن من الاستدلال بها لأن المستدل بالسنة يحتاج إلى أمرين هما:

From the benefits of this science is to purify and clarify the evidence of *ḥadīth* from that which taints it, such as *ḍaʿīf ḥadīth*s (weak narrations) etc. in order to be able to make conclusions from it. This is because the one making inferences from the Sunnah requires two conditions and they are:

١ - ثبوتها عن النبي صلى الله عليه وسلّم.

One. That it is established from the Prophet ﷺ.

٢ - ثبوت دلالتها على الحكم.

Two. That its use as a proof for the ruling is justified.

فتكون العناية بالسنة النبوية أمراً مهماً، لأنه ينبني عليها أمرٌ مهم وهو ما كلف الله به العباد من عقائد وعبادات وأخلاق وغير ذلك.

As such, giving careful analysis to the Prophetic Sunnah is something of extreme importance. This is because a grave matter is built upon it, which is Allāh's commands to His slaves pertaining to creed, worship, manners etc.

وثبوت السنة إلى النبي صلى الله عليه وسلّم يختص بالحديث، لأن القرآن نُقل إلينا نقلاً متواتراً قطعياً، لفظاً ومعنى، ونقله الأصاغر عن الأكابر فلا يحتاج إلى البحث عن ثبوته.

Establishing the Sunnah to the Prophet is specific to the *ḥadīth* corpus.

This is because the Qur'ān has been mass-transmitted by the Ummah with certainty—in its wording and meanings—transmitted from generation to generation. As such, there is no need to establish its authenticity.

ثم اعلم أن علم الحديث ينقسم إلى قسمين:

Following which, know that the science of al-ḥadith is divided into two categories:

١ - علم الحديث رواية.

1. The science of *ḥadīth* in terms of *riwāyah* (narration).

٢ - علم الحديث دراية.

2. The science of *ḥadīth* in terms of *dirāyah* (transmission).

فعلم الحديث رواية يبحث عما ينقل عن النبي صلى الله عليه وسلّم من أقواله وأفعاله وأحواله. ويبحث فيما يُنقل لا في النقل.

As for the science in terms of *riwāyah*, it is the study of what was narrated from the Prophet ﷺ from his statements, actions and circumstances. What was transmitted is the focus of the study and not the transmission itself.

مثاله: إذا جاءنا حديث عن النبي صلى الله عليه وسلّم فإننا نبحث فيه هل هو قول أو فعل أو حال؟

For example, if there is a *ḥadīth* narrated from the Prophet ﷺ, we shall investigate if it is a statement, an action or a circumstance.

وهل يدل على كذا أو لا يدل؟

And whether it implies such and such or if it does not.

فهذا هو علم الحديث رواية، وموضوعه البحث في ذات النبي صلى الله عليه وسلّم وما يصدر عن هذه الذات من أقوال وأفعال وأحوال، ومن الأفعال الإقرار،

فإنه يعتبر فعلاً، وأما الأحوال فهي صفاته كالطول والقِصَر واللون، والغضب والفرح وما أشبه ذلك.

Hence, this is the science of *ḥadīth* in terms of *riwāyah*, and it studies the Prophet ﷺ himself and what emanates from him in the form of statement, action and circumstances, and his actions include his endorsements as they are considered acts. His circumstances include his characteristics such as height, shortness, skin colour, anger, happiness etc.

أما علم الحديث دراية فهو: علم يُبحث فيه عن أحوال الراوي والمروي من حيث القبول والرد.

As for the science in terms of *dirāyah*, it is the study of the circumstances of the narrator and the narration, concerning its acceptance or rejection.

مثاله: إذا وجدنا راوياً فإنا نبحث هل هذا الراوي مقبول أم مردود؟

For example: If we find a narrator, we will investigate if this narrator is accepted or if he is to be rejected.

أما المروي فإنه يُبحث فيه ما هو المقبول منه وما هو المردود؟

As for the narration, the investigation is concerning what can be accepted from it and what has to be rejected.

وبهذا نعرف أن قبول الراوي لا يستلزم قبول المروي؛ لأن السند قد يكون رجاله ثقاةً عدولاً، لكن قد يكون المتن شاذًّا أو معللاً فحينئذ لا نقبله. كما أنه أحياناً لا يكون رجال السند يصِلون إلى حد القبول والثقة، ولكن الحديث نفسه يكون مقبولاً وذلك لأن له شواهد من الكتاب والسنة، أو قواعد الشريعة تؤيده.

Based upon this, we learn that the acceptance of a narrator does not mean that the narration is acceptable, as the chain of narration could be comprised of reliable and righteous narrators but the *matn* (text) could be *shādh* (contradictory) or having an *'illah* (hidden defect) and hence it cannot be accepted. Similarly, it could be the case that the chain of narrators may not be acceptable and reliable but the *ḥadīth* itself is acceptable due to the presence of other supporting evidences from the Qur'ān and the Sunnah, or because maxims of the *Sharīʿah* (legislation) support it.

إذن فائدة علم مصطلح الحديث هو: معرفة ما يُقبل وما يردّ من الحديث.

So the benefit of the science of *muṣṭalah al-ḥadīth* is the identification of what is acceptable and rejected from the *ḥadīth*.

وهذا مهمّ بحد ذاته؛ لأن الأحكام الشرعية مبنية على ثبوت الدليل وعدمه، وصحته وضعفه.

And this is very important in of itself, because the *Sharīʿah's* rulings are dependent upon whether the evidence is established or not, and its authenticity or weakness.

The author.

شرح المنظومة البيقونية

A Commentary on *al-Manẓūmat al-Bayqūniyyah*

قال المؤلف رحمه الله:

The author, may Allāh have mercy upon him, said:

المتن

بِسْمِ اللَّهِ الرَّحْمَنِ الرَّحِيمِ

In the Name of Allāh, the Entirely Merciful, the Especially Merciful.

الشرح

البسملة آية من كتاب الله عز وجل، فهي من كلام الله تعالى، يُبتدأ بها في كل سورة من سور القرآن الكريم؛ إلا سورة (براءة) فإنها لا تُبدأ بالبسملة، اتباعاً للصحابة رضوان الله عليهم، ولو أن البسملة كانت قد نزلت في أول هذه السورة لكانت محفوظة كما حفظت في باقي السور، ولكنها لم تنزل على النبي صلى الله عليه وسلّم، ولكن الصحابة أشكل عليهم، هل سورة (براءة) من الأنفال أم أنها سورة مستقلة؟ فوضعوا فاصلاً بينهما دون البسملة.

The *basmalah* is an *āyah* from the Book of Allāh ﷻ. Hence, it is from the Speech of Allāh. Each *sūrah* of the Holy Qur'ān begins with it except Sūrah Barā'ah (Sūrah al-Tawbah) as it does not start with the *basmalah,* following the way of the Companions. If the *basmalah* was revealed at the start of this *sūrah*, it would have been preserved just like in the rest of the *sūrahs* but it was not revealed as such to the Prophet ﷺ. However, the Companions would sometimes become confused whether Sūrah Barā'ah is part of Sūrah al-Anfāl or whether it is an independent *sūrah*. Thus they put a divider between the two other than the *basmalah*.

والبسملة فيها جار ومجرور، ومضاف إليه، وصفة.

In the *basmalah*, there is a *jār* (preposition) and a *majrūr* (noun of the preposition), *a muḍāf ilayhi* (possessor) and a *ṣifah* (adjective).

فالجار والمجرور هو (بسم).

As for the *jār* and the *majrūr*, it is "*bism*" (in the name).

والمضاف إليه هو لفظ الجلالة (الله).

The *muḍāf ilayhi* is the *lafẓ al-jalālah* (Majestic word): "Allāh".

والصفة هي (الرحمن الرحيم).

And the *ṣifah* is "*al-raḥmān al-raḥīm*" (the Entirely Merciful, the Especially Merciful).

وكل جارّ ومجرور لابد له من التعلق إما بفعل كقام، أو معناه كاسم الفاعل، أو اسم المفعول مثلاً.

And every *jār* and *majrūr* must have an attachment either to a verb such as "stood" or its meaning such as an *ism al-fā'il* (the doer) or *ism al-maf'ūl* (the direct object) for example.

فالبسملة متعلقة بمحذوف فما هو هذا المحذوف؟

As such, the *basmalah* is attached to an erased attachment, so what is this erased attachment?

اختلف النحويون في تقدير هذا المحذوف، لكن أحسن ما قيل فيه وهو الصحيح: أن المحذوف فعلٌ متأخرٌ مناسب للمقام.

The grammarians differed in the assessment of this erased attachment, but the best of what has been said and the correct opinion is that the erased attachment is a verb appropriate to the situation delayed in the order of the sentence structure.

مثاله: إذا قال رجل بسم الله، وهو يريد أن يقرأ النظم فإن التقدير يكون: بسم الله اقرأ، وإذا كان الناظم هو الذي قال: بسم الله فإن التقدير يكون: بسم الله أنظم.

For example, if a man said, "In the Name of Allāh," and he wants to read a poem (e.g. *al-Bayqūniyyah*), then the assessment of what it alludes to is, "In the Name of Allāh I read". And if the composer of a poem is the one who says, "In the Name of Allāh", then the assessment is, "In the Name of Allāh I compose".

ولماذا قدّرناه فعلاً ولم نقدّره اسم فاعلٍ مثلاً؟

Why did we assess the meaning using a verb and not an *ism fā'il* (the doer) for example?

نقول: قدّرناه فعلاً، لأن الأصل في العمل الأفعال، ولهذا يعمل الفعل بدون شرط، وما سواه من العوامل الاسمية فإنها تحتاج إلى شرط.

We say: We deciphered it as a verb because verbs are the basis of any action and hence this act works without any conditions, while actions of the other nominal factors need to have a condition.

ولماذا قدرناه متأخراً؟

And why did we analyse the verb as being delayed in the order of the sentence structure?

نقول قدّرناه متأخراً لوجهين:

We say that it is delayed for two reasons:

١ - التيمُّن بالبداءة باسم الله تعالى؛ ليكون اسم الله تعالى هو المقدّم، وحق له

أن يُقدّم.

1. To begin the sentence with the Name of Allāh ﷻ on the right such that it precedes the action, and it is rightful for Him to precede.

٢ - لإفادة الحصر؛ وذلك لأن تأخير العامل يفيد الحصر، فإن تقديم ما حقه التأخير يفيد الحصر. فإذا قلت: بسم الله اقرأ، تعيَّن أنك تقرأ باسم الله لا باسم غيره.

2. To bring about a restriction of the statement. Delaying the verb or the action achieves this goal. Stating Allāh's name first brings a connotation of singularity. As such, if you say, "In the Name of Allāh I read", it means that you read in the Name of Allāh and not in the name of other than Him.

ونحن قدرناه مناسباً للمقام لأنه أدل على المقصود، ولأنه لا يخطر في ذهن المبسمل إلا هذا التقدير.

We also assess the appropriate verb according to the situation because it is indicative of the meaning, and because nothing crosses the mind of the speaker of the *basmalah* except this meaning.

مثاله: لو أنك سألت الرجل الذي قال عند الوضوء بسم الله عن التقدير في قوله: بسم الله، لقال: بسم الله أتوضأ.

For example: a man who says, "In the Name of Allāh" when he is performing his ablution. If it was asked to him what he meant by saying, "In the Name of Allāh," he would reply, "In the Name of Allāh I make my ablution."

ولو قال قائل: أنا أُريد أن أُقدّر المتعلق بسم الله أبتدئ.

If someone were to say, "I want to assess the attachment to the *basmalah* as 'I begin.'"

فإننا نقول: لا بأس بذلك، لكن أبتدئ: فعل عام يشمل ابتداءك بالأكل والوضوء والنظم، وكما قلنا فإن هذا التقدير لا يتبادر إلى ذهن المبسمل.

We say: There is nothing wrong with that, but the verb "I begin" is a general statement that can include your other actions such as eating, making ablution and composing a poem. And as we have said, this intended meaning does not come to the mind of the speaker of the *basmalah*.

أما اسم فيقولون: إنه مشتق من السمو، وهو العلو.

As for the noun *ism* (name), it is derived from the word "*al-sumū*" which means highness.

وقيل: من السمة وهي العلامة.

It is also said that it comes from the word "*al-simah*" which means the sign of something.

والاسم مهما كان اشتقاقه فإنه يُراد به هنا كل اسم من أسماء الله الحسنى، أي أنه لا يُراد به اسم واحد بعينه مع أنه مفرد؛ لأن القاعدة: أن المفرد المضاف يفيد العموم، فبذلك يلزم من قولنا: بسم الله، أن يكون المعنى: بكل اسم من أسماء الله الحسنى. ولهذا تجد القائل: بسم الله، لا يخطر بباله اسم معين كالرحمن والرحيم والغفور والودود والشكور ونحوها، بل هو يريد العموم ويدل على ذلك، أي على أن المفرد المضاف للعموم قوله تعالى: ﴿**وَإِن تَعُدُّواْ نِعْمَةَ اللهِ لاَ تُحْصُوهَا إِنَّ الإنسان لَظَلُومٌ كَفَّارٌ**﴾ [إبراهيم: ٣٤]. ولو كان المراد نعمة واحدة لما قال ﴿**لاَ تُحْصُوهَا**﴾. إذاً فالمعنى ابتدئ بكل اسم من أسماء الله عز وجل.

Regardless of the root of *al-ism*, here it refers to all the beautiful names of Allāh, not specific to any name in particular despite its singular form. This is due to the principle that states that any singular *mudāf* (possession) connotes generality. Henceforth, it is understood from one who says, "In the Name of Allāh", that he intends all of the beautiful Names of Allāh. As such you will find that the one who says, "In the Name of Allāh", it does not occur to him a certain name such as *al-Raḥmān* (the Entirely Merciful) or *al-Raḥīm* (the Especially Merciful) or *al-Ghafūr* (the Forgiving) or *al-Wadūd* (the Affectionate) or *al-Shakūr* (the Grateful) etc. Rather, the one making the statement intends generalisation. And the evidence that shows that the singular *muḍāf* connotes generality is the ayah: **{And if you should count the favour [i.e. blessings] of Allāh, you could not enumerate them.}**[1] If what is meant in the ayah is a single favour, "you could not enumerate them" would not have been said. In light of this, the meaning of the *basmalah* is, "I start my action with every one of all the beautiful Names of Allāh ﷻ."

والباء في قوله: بسم الله أهي للاستعانة أم للمصاحبة؟

Is the preposition *bā* in the phrase "*bism*" for the sake of *al-isti'ānah* (seeking assistance) or for *al-muṣāḥabah* (accompaniment)?

هناك من قال: إنها للاستعانة.

There are those who say that it is for the sake of *al-isti'ānah.*

ومنهم من قال: إنها للمصاحبة.

And there are others who say that it is for the sake of *al-muṣāḥabah.*

وممن قال إنها للمصاحبة؛ الزمخشري صاحب الكشاف وهو معتزلي من المعتزلة، وكتابه الكشاف فيه اعتزاليات كثيرة قد لا يستطيع أن يعرفها كل إنسان، حتى قال البلقيني: أخرجت من الكشاف اعتزاليات بالمناقيش. وهذا يدل على أنها خفية.

Amongst those who said that it is for the sake of *al-muṣāḥabah* is al-Zamakhsharī—the author of *al-Kashāf*—and he is a Mu'tazilite from the Mu'tazilah sect. His book *al-Kashāf* contains a great amount of the *i'tizāl* ideologies that not many could identify within it. In fact, al-Bulqīnī said, "I extracted the *i'tizāl* ideologies from *al-Kashāf* using chisels," which shows

1 Ibrāhīm: 34

that they were hidden.

والزمخشري رجَّح أن الباء للمصاحبة، مع أن الظاهر أنها للاستعانة! لكنه رجّح المصاحبة؛ لأن المعتزلة يرون أن الإنسان مستقلٌّ بعمله فإذا كان مستقلاً بعمله فإنه لا يحتاج للاستعانة.

Al-Zamakhsharī favoured the opinion that the preposition *bā* is for *al-muṣāḥabah* even though it is obvious that it is for *al-isti'ānah*! He favoured *al-muṣāḥabah* because the Mu'tazilites view that man is independent in his actions, as such he does not require assistance to perform them.

لكن لا شك أن المراد بالباء هو: الاستعانة التي تصاحب كل الفعل، فهي في الأصل للاستعانة وهي مصاحبة للإنسان من أول الفعل إلى آخره، وقد تفيد معنى آخراً وهو التبرك إذا لم نحمل التبرك على الاستعانة، ونقول كل مستعين بشيء فإنه متبرك به.

However, it is beyond doubt that the preposition *bā* refers to *al-isti'ānah* that accompanies every action due to the fact that it is originally for seeking assistance, which accompanies the person from the start of the action until the end. It could also refer to another meaning which is *al-tabarruk* (the seeking of blessings), if we do not take *al-isti'ānah* as carrying the meaning of *al-tabarruk*, though we say that every person seeking assistance with something is seeking its blessings as well.

الله: لفظ الجلالة علمٌ على الذات العلية لا يسمى به غيره، وهو مشتق من الألوهية، وأصله إله لكن حذفت الهمزة، وعُوض عنها بـ(أل) فصارت (الله).

"Allāh": The *lafẓ al-jalālah* (word of the Majestic) is a name of the Highest Self which is not assigned to anyone other than Him. And it is derived from the word *al-ulūhiyyah* (divinity) and its origin is the word *ilāh* (god) but the letter *hamzah* was deleted and replaced with the prefix "*al*" and thus it becomes Allāh.

وقيل: أصله الإله وأنَّ (أل) موجودة في بنائه من الأصل وحُذفت الهمزة للتخفيف، كما حذفت من الناس وأصلها (الأناس) وكما حُذفت الهمزة من (خير وشر) وأصلها أخير وأشر.

And it was said that its root word is from *al-ilāh* (the god) and that the prefix *al* is present originally in its structure and the letter *hamzah* was deleted to ease pronunciation just like it was deleted from *al-nās* (the people) which was originally *al-unās*, and just like *khayr* (good) and *sharr* (evil) and the original forms are *akhayr* and *asharr* respectively.

ومعنى الله: مأخوذة من الألوهية وهي التعبد بحب وتعظيم، يقال: ألهَ إليه أي: اشتاق إليه، وأحبه، وأناب إليه، وعظمه.

The meaning of Allāh is taken from the word *al-ulūhiyyah* which is defined as worship with love and glorification. It is said that the phrase, "*Alaha ilayhi*" means that he yearns for him, loves him, turns to him and glorifies him.

فهي مشتقة من الألوهية، وهي المحبة والتعظيم.

As such, it is derived from *al-ulūhiyyah,* which is love and glorification.

وعليه فيكون إله بمعنى مألوه، أي: معبود.

Thus the word *ilāh* means *málūh,* which is the one worshipped.

وهل فِعَال تأتي بمعنى مفعول؟

And does the word structure *fi'āl* imply the meaning of *maf'ūl* (the direct object)?

نقول: نعم؛ مثل فراش بمعنى مفروش، وبناء بمعنى مبنوء. وغراس بمعنى مغروس.

We say: Yes. For example; the word *firāsh* (mattress) refers to the *mafrūsh* (the object that was slept on), *binā'* (building) refers to the *mabnū'* (the object that was built), and *ghirās* (plant) refers to the *maghrūs* (the object being planted).

وأما الرحمن: فهو نعت للفظ الجلالة، وهو أيضاً اسم من أسماء الله تعالى يدل على الرحمة، وجميع الذين حدوا الرحمة حدوها بآثارها فمثلاً: أنا أرحم الصغير فما هو معنى أرحم هل هو العطف أو هو الرفق به.

As for *al-Raḥmān*, it is an adjective to the *lafẓ al-jalālah*. It is also one of the names of Allāh ﷻ which signifies mercy. And all those who describe mercy actually describe the effects of mercy. For example, if one says, "I was merciful to the young child." What is meant by merciful; does it refer to the act of kindness towards him or being tolerant of him?

الجواب: لا؛ لأن العطف من آثار الرحمة، وكذلك الرفق به من آثار الرحمة.

The answer is no, because showing kindness is the effect of being merciful, and likewise tolerance is the effect of being merciful.

فالرحمة هي الرحمة! فلا تستطيع أن تعرِّفها أو تحددها بأوضح من لفظها.

As such, mercy is mercy! Hence we are unable to define mercy or describe its extent with any other clearer term.

فنقول إن الرحمة معلومة المعنى، ومجهولة الكيفية بالنسبة لله عز وجل، ولكنها معلومة الاثار، فالرحمن اسم من أسماء الله تعالى يدل على صفة الرحمة.

Thus we say that the meaning of mercy is clear. However, how the mercy is with regards to Allāh ﷻ is unknown but its effects are known. As such, *al-Raḥmān* is one of the Names of Allāh which implies mercy.

وأما الرحيم: فهو اسم متضمن للرحمة.

As for *al-Raḥīm*, it is a noun which encompasses mercy.

وهل الرحيم بمعنى الرحمن، أم أنه يختلف؟

Does *al-Raḥīm* mean *al-Raḥmān* or does it have a different meaning?

قال بعض العلماء: إنه بمعنى الرحمن، وعلى هذا فيكون مؤكداً لا كلاماً مستقلاً، ولكن بعض العلماء قال: إن المعنى يختلف؛ ولا يمكن أن نقول إنه بمعنى الرحمن لوجهين:

Some scholars said that it has the same meaning as *al-Raḥmān*. As such, the second word is an emphasis of the first and does not come with a separate meaning. However other scholars said that it has a different meaning and it is not possible that it has the same meaning as *al-Raḥmān* due to two reasons:

١ - أن الأصل في الكلام التأسيس لا التوكيد، يعني أنه إذا قال لنا شخص إن هذه الكلمة مؤكدة لما قبلها، فإننا نقول له إن الأصل أنها كلمة مستقلة، تفيد معنى غير الأول، وذلك لأن الأصل في التوكيد الزيادة، والأصل في الكلام عدم الزيادة.

1. The basis of speech is for *al-taʾsīs* (to establish a new meaning) and not for *al-tawkīd* (an emphasis of the previous meaning), which means that if someone told us that this word is an emphasis for the previous word, we would tell him that originally it is a separate word with a meaning other than the previous. This is because the basis of *tawkīd* is supplementation, and the basis of speech is an absence of supplementation.

٢ - اختلاف بناية الكلمة الأولى، وهي الرحمن على وزن فعلان، والرحيم على وزن فعيل، والقاعدة في اللغة العربية: أن اختلاف المبنى يدلُّ على اختلاف المعنى.

2. The difference in word structure between the two words. *Al-Raḥmān* is upon the structure of *faʿlān* while *al-Raḥīm* is upon the structure *faʿīl*. And the principle in Arabic language states that a difference in word structure implies a difference in meaning.

إذاً لابد أنه مختلف، فما وجه الخلاف؟

Therefore, the meaning should be different, so what is the difference?

قال بعض العلماء: إن الرحمن يدل على الرحمة العامة، والرحيم يدل على الرحمة الخاصة، لأن رحمة الله تعالى نوعان:

Some scholars say that *al-Raḥmān* signifies universal mercy while *al-Raḥīm* signifies specific mercy. This is because there are two categories of Allāh's Mercy:

١ - رحمة عامة؛ وهي لجميع الخلق.

(i) Raḥmat ʿāmmah (universal mercy); which is for all creation.

٢ - رحمة خاصة؛ وهي للمؤمنين كما قال تعالى: ﴿وَكَانَ بِالْمُؤْمِنِينَ رَحِيماً﴾ [الأحزاب: ٤٣].

(ii) Raḥmat khāṣah (specific mercy); which is only for the believers, as mentioned in the ayah: **{And ever is He, to the believers, Merciful.}**[2]

وبعضهم قال: الرحمن يدل على الصفة، والرحيم يدل على الفعل، فمعنى الرحمن يعني ذو الرحمة الواسعة، والمراد بالرحيم إيصال الرحمة إلى المرحوم، فيكون الرحمن ملاحظاً فيه الوصف، والرحيم ملاحظاً فيه الفعل.

And some of the scholars said that *al-Raḥmān* signifies an attribute while *al-Raḥīm* signifies an action. As such, *al-Raḥmān* means the possessor of immense mercy and *al-Raḥīm* refers to the transmission of mercy to the blessed. Thus, the attribute can be observed in *al-Raḥmān* and the action can be observed in *al-Raḥīm*.

والقول الأقرب عندي هو: القول الثاني وهو أن الرحمن يدل على الصفة، والرحيم يدل على الفعل.

And my preferred opinion is the second one, whereby *al-Raḥmān* implies

---

2 Al-Ahzāb: 43

an attribute and *al-Raḥīm* implies an action.

المتن

(١) أَبْدَأُ بِالْحَمْدِ مُصَلِّياً عَلَى مُحَمَّدٍ خَيرِ نَبِيٍّ أُرْسِلاَ

(1) I begin with praise, and prayers and salutations,
Upon Muḥammad the finest prophet ever given the message.

الشرح

قوله: أبدأ بالحمد: يوحي بأنه لم يذكر البسملة، فإنه لو بدأ بالبسملة؛ لكانت البسملة هي الأولى، ولذلك يشك الإنسان هل بدأ المؤلف بالبسملة أم لا؟ لكن الشارح ذكر أن المؤلف بدأ النظم بالبسملة، وبناء على هذا تكون البداءة هنا نسبية أي: بالنسبة للدخول في موضوع الكتاب أو صلب الكتاب.

His saying: "I begin with praise" gives the idea that he did not mention the *basmalah*. If he began with the *basmalah*, it should have been the first line. As such, one may doubt that the author began with the *basmalah*. However, the commentator mentioned that the author began the poem with the *basmalah*. Based on this, the beginning is relative i.e. in terms of the entry to the subject matter or the book.

وقوله بالحمد مصلياً: نصَبَ مصلياً على أنه حال من الضمير في أبدأ، والتقدير حال كوني مصلياً.

And his phrase: "With praise, and prayers and salutations", the word "prayers and salutations" (*muṣalliyan*) is in the accusative case as it is the *ḥāl* (state) of the *ḍamīr* (pronoun) in *abda'u* (I begin). Thus the assessment of this phrase is, "In the state of me saying the prayers and salutations".

ومعنى الحمد كما قال العلماء: هو وصف المحمود بالكمال محبة وتعظيماً،

فإن وصفَهُ بالكمال لا محبة ولا تعظيماً، ولكن خوفاً ورهبة سُمي ذلك مدحاً لا حمداً، فالحمد لابد أن يكون مقروناً بمحبة المحمود وتعظيمه.

The meaning of *al-ḥamd* (the praise), as the scholars say, is describing the perfectly praised one with love and glorification. If he described one with perfection not due to love and glorification but due to fear and dread, it is termed as *madḥ* (flattery) and not *ḥamd* (praise). This is because praise has to be coupled with the love and glorification of the praised one.

وقول المؤلف بالحمد: لم يذكر المحمود، ولكنه معلومٌ بقرينة الحال، لأن المؤلف مسلمٌ؛ فالحمد يقصد به حمد الله سبحانه وتعالى.

The author did not mention whom he praised but it is understood with the *qarīnah* (indication) of the circumstance. Due to the fact that the author is a Muslim, we assume that the praise is intended to praise Allāh ﷻ.

ومعنى الصلاة على النبي صلى الله عليه وسلّم هو: طلب الثناء عليه من الله تعالى، وهذا ما إذا وقعت الصلاة من البشر، أما إذا وقعت من الله تعالى فمعناها ثناء الله تعالى عليه في الملأ الأعلى، وهذا هو قول أبي العالية، وأما من قال إن الصلاة من الله تعالى تعني الرحمة، فإن هذا القول ضعيفٌ، يضعّفُه قوله تعالى: ﴿أُولَٰئِكَ عَلَيْهِمْ صَلَوَٰتٌ مِّن رَّبِّهِمْ وَرَحْمَةٌ﴾ [البقرة: ١٥٧]. ولو كانت الصلاة بمعنى الرحمة، لكان معنى الاية أي: أولئك عليهم رحماتٌ من ربهم ورحمة، وهذا لا يستقيم! والأصل في الكلام التأسيس؛ فإذا قلنا إن المعنى أي: رحمات من ربهم ورحمة، صار عطف مماثل على مماثل.

And the meaning of, "Prayers and salutations upon Muhammad" is the seeking of commendation upon him from Allāh ﷻ. This is if the *ṣalāt* (prayers and salutations) is from humankind. If Allāh is the One who is making the *ṣalāt*, then the meaning is that Allāh's praise is upon him in the presence of the Noble Angels (i.e. in the highest station). This is the opinion of Abu 'l-'Āliyah. As for those who say that the *ṣalāt* from Allāh refers to mercy, it is a weak opinion due to the ayah: **{Those are the ones upon whom are blessings from their Lord and mercy.}**[3] If *ṣalāt* refers to mercy, the meaning of the ayah would be, "Those are the ones upon whom are mercies from their Lord and mercy." And this does not make sense, as the basis of speech is the establishment of a new meaning. If we say, "The mercies from their Lord and mercy," it becomes a conjunction of two identical words.

فالصحيح هو: القول الأول وهو أن صلاة الله على عبده ثناؤه عليه في الملأ الأعلى.

So, the correct opinion is the first one which states that Allāh's *ṣalāt* upon his slave is His praise upon him in the presence of the Noble Angels.

وقوله محمد خير نبي أُرسلا: محمد: هو اسمٌ من أسماء النبي صلى الله عليه وسلّم، وقد ذكر الله تعالى اسمين من أسماء النبي صلى الله عليه وسلّم في القرآن الكريم وهما: أحمد ومحمد.

As for the phrase: "Upon Muḥammad the finest prophet ever given the message," Muḥammad is one of the names of the Prophet ﷺ. And Allāh has mentioned two of his names in the Holy Qur'ān and they are: Aḥmad and Muḥammad.

أما أحمد: فقد ذكره نقلاً عن عيسى عليه الصلاة والسلام، وقد اختار عيسى ذلك؛ إما لأنه لم يُوح إليه إلا بذلك، وإما لأنه يدل على التفضيل، فإن أحمد اسم تفضيل في الأصل، كما تقول: فلان أحمد الناس، فخاطب بني إسرائيل ليبين كمالَهُ.

As for the name Aḥmad, it was mentioned by 'Īsā عليه السلام. And 'Īsā mentioned this name either due to the fact it was not revealed to him except this name or because it signifies *tafḍīl* (superlative noun), as Aḥmad at its root is a superlative noun just like if you said, "*Fulān aḥmadun nās*" (so and so is the noblest of the people). Thus he addressed the Children of Israel to explain

3 Al-Baqarah: 157

his nobility.

أما محمد فهو اسم مفعول من حمده، ولكن الأقرب أن الله تعالى أوحى إليه بذلك لسببين هما:

As for the name Muḥammad, it is the direct object from the verb *ḥamidah* (he praised him). However, the correct opinion is that Allāh revealed to ʿĪsā ﷺ as such due to two reasons:

١ - لكي يبين لبني إسرائيل أن النبي صلى الله عليه وسلّم هو أحمدُ الناس وأفضلهم.

Firstly: To explain to the Children of Israel that the Prophet ﷺ is the noblest of mankind;

٢ - لكي يبتلي بني إسرائيل ويمتحنهم، وذلك لأن النصارى قالوا: إن الذي بشرنا به عيسى هو أحمد، والذي جاء للعرب هو محمد، وأحمد غير محمد، فإن أحمد لم يأتِ بعدُ، وهؤلاء قال الله فيهم: **﴿فَأَمَّا الَّذِينَ فى قُلُوبِهِمْ زَيْغٌ فَيَتَّبِعُونَ مَا تَشَبَهَ مِنْهُ﴾**. [آل عمران: ٧].

Secondly: To test the Children of Israel and to put them to trial. And this is due to the fact that the Christians said, "Indeed the one that we received glad tidings from ʿĪsā about is Aḥmad, while the one who came for the Arabs is Muḥammad, and Aḥmad is not Muḥammad, thus Aḥmad has yet to come." Those people are whom Allāh mentioned about in the ayah: **{As for those in whose hearts is deviation [from truth], they will follow that of it which is unspecific.}**[4]

ولكن نقول لهم: إن قولكم أنه لم يأتِ بعدُ؛ كذب لأن الله تعالى قال في نفس الاية **﴿فَلَمَّا جَاءَهُم بِالْبَيِّنَتِ قَالُواْ هَذَا سِحْرٌ مُّبِينٌ﴾**. [الصف: ٦].

However, we say to them that their belief that he has yet to come is false

4 Āli ʿImrān: 7

because Allāh mentioned in the same ayah: **{But when he came to them with clear evidences, they said, "This is obvious magic."}**[5]

و(جاء) فعلٌ ماضي، يعني أن أحمد جاء، ولا نعلم أن أحداً جاء بعد عيسى إلا محمد صلى الله عليه وسلّم.

The verb "came" in this ayah is in the past tense, which means that Aḥmad came and we know no one else who came after 'Isā ﷺ except Muḥammad ﷺ.

وبين محمد وأحمد فرق في الصيغة والمعنى:

There is a difference between Aḥmad and Muhammad in terms of word form and meaning.

أما في الصيغة: فمحمد: اسم مفعول، وأحمد: اسم تفضيل.

As for the word form; Muhammad is an *ism maf'ūl* (direct object) while Aḥmad is an *ism tafḍīl* (superlative noun).

أما الفرق بينهما في المعنى:

As for the difference between the two in terms of meaning:

ففي محمد: يكون الفعل واقعاً من الناس. أي: أن الناس يحمدونه.

In Muḥammad; the action takes place from the people i.e. that the people praise him.

وفي أحمد: يكون الفعل واقعاً منه، يعني أنه صلى الله عليه وسلّم أحمدُ الناس لله تعالى، يكون واقعاً عليه يعني أنه هو أحقُ الناس أن يُحمد.

Whereas in Aḥmad; the action takes place from himself, i.e. that he ﷺ is the noblest of mankind to Allāh, and the action that takes place from himself is that he is the most deserving to be praised of all mankind.

---

5 Al-Ṣaff: 6

فيكون محمدٌ حُمدَ بالفعل. وأحمد أي كان حمده على وجه يستحقه؛ لأنه أحقُّ الناس أن يُحمد، ولعل هذا هو السر في أن الله تعالى ألهم عيسى أن يقول: ﴿وَمُبَشِّراً بِرَسُولٍ يَأْتِي مِن بَعْدِي اسْمُهُ أَحْمَدُ﴾ [الصف: ٦]. حتى يبين لبني إسرائيل أنه أحمدُ الناس لله تعالى، وأنه أحقُّ الناس بأن يُحمد.

As such, Muḥammad is praised by action, and Aḥmad in terms of being praised in the manner that he deserves because he is the most worthy of all mankind to be praised. Perhaps this is the secret behind the fact that Allāh inspired ʿIsā to say: **{And bringing good tidings of a messenger to come after me, whose name is Aḥmad.}**[6] This was to elucidate to the Children of Israel that he is the noblest of mankind to Allāh ﷻ and that he is the most worthy of all mankind to be praised.

وقوله خير نبي أرسلا: جمع المؤلف هنا بين النبوة والرسالة، لأن النبي مشتق مع النبأ فهو فعيلٌ بمعنى مفعول، أو هو مشتق من النبوة أي نبا ينبوا إذا ارتفع، والنبي لا شك أنه رفيع الرتبة، ومحمد صلى الله عليه وسلّم أكمل منْ أرسل وأكمل من أنبىء، ولهذا قال محمد خير نبي أرسلاً.

In the phrase, "Finest prophet ever given the message," the author here combined between prophecy and bestowment of the message. The word *nabī* (prophet) is derived from *nab'ā* (news) and is upon the *fa'īl* structure with the meaning of the *maf'ūl* (direct object). Or it is derived from *al-nubūwah* (the prophecy) i.e. the verbs *naba yanbū* which mean he has risen in the past and present tenses respectively. There is no doubt that the prophet is high in ranking, and Muḥammad ﷺ is the best who was given the message and prophecy. For these reasons, the author said that he is the finest prophet ever given the message.

والمؤلف هنا قال نبي أُرسلا: ولم يقل خير رسول أُرسلا، وذلك لأن كل رسول نبي، ودلالة الرسالة على النبوة من باب دلالة اللزوم؛ لأن من لازم كونه رسولاً أن

6 Al-Ṣaff: 6

يكون نبيًّا، فإذا ذُكر اللفظ صريحاً كان ذلك أفصح في الدلالة على المقصود، فالجمع بين النبوة والرسالة نستفيد منه أنه نصّ على النبوة، ولو اقتُصر على الرسالة لم نستفد معنى النبوة إلا عن طريق اللزوم، وكون اللفظ دالاً على المعنى بنصه أولى من كونه دالاً باستلزامه. كما في حديث البراء بن عازب - رضي الله عنه - عند تعليم النبي صلى الله عليه وسلّم له دعاء النوم فلما أعاد البراء بن عازب - رضي الله عنه - الدعاء قال: وبرسولك الذي أرسلت. فقال له النبي صلى الله عليه وسلّم: ((لا؛ قل: وبنبيك الذي أرسلت)). لأجل أن تكون الدلالة على النبوة دلالة نصيَّة، هذا من جهة.

The author here mentioned, "Prophet ever given the message," instead of, "The finest messenger ever given the message." This is because all messengers were prophets and the indication of the message upon the prophecy is inevitable, as it is certain that a messenger would be a prophet as well. As such, the explicit mention of the word is more eloquent in the implication of the intended meaning. Thus the combination of the prophecy and message tells us that the author mentioned the prophecy in the text, and if he just mentioned the message alone, the meaning of prophecy would not be obvious except through deduction. And the fact that a word is indicative of the meaning in its own text is better than the deduction of its indication, as in the narration of Barā' ibn 'Āzib ﷺ when the Prophet ﷺ taught him the supplication before going to sleep. When Barā' ibn 'Āzib ﷺ repeated the supplication, he said, "I believe in the Messenger who You Sent." The Prophet ﷺ said to him, "No but say, 'And in the Prophet who You Sent,'" in order to ensure that the indication of the prophecy is clear. This is one perspective.

ومن جهة أخرى: أنه إذا قال: خير رسول: فإن لفظ الرسول يشمل الرسول الملكي وهو جبريل عليه السلام، ويشمل الرسول البشري وهو محمد صلى الله عليه وسلّم، لكن! على كل حال في كلام المؤلف كلمة: محمد تخرج منه جبريل

عليه السلام.

And the other perspective is that if the author had said "finest messenger", the word messenger could imply the Angelic Messenger, i.e. Jibrīl ﷤ and the human Messenger, i.e. Muḥammad ﷺ! In any case, the author did mention the name Muhammad, which excludes Jibrīl.

والألف في قوله: أُرسلا يُسميها العلماء ألف الإطلاق، أي: إطلاق الروي.

The scholars named the vowel *alif* in *ursilā* (given the message) as *alif al-iṭlāq* i.e. for the releasing of the *rawiyy* (the last consonant and vowel of the rhyme).

أقسام الحديث

THE CATEGORIES OF ḤADĪTH

قال المؤلف رحمه الله:

The author, may Allāh have mercy upon him, said:

المتن

(٢) وَذِي مِنْ أَقْسَامِ الْحَدِيثِ عِدَّه   وَكُلُّ وَاحِدٍ أَتَى وَحَدَّه

(2) And these are a number of categories of ḥadīth,
Each one having come with its definition.

الشرح

قوله (ذي) اسم إشارة.

The word *"dhī"* (this) is an *ism ishārah* (demonstrative noun).

والمشار إليه: ما ترتب في ذهن المؤلف. إن كانت الإشارة قبل التصنيف وإن كانت الإشارة بعد التصنيف، فالمشار إليه هو الشيء الحاضر الموجود في الخارج.

And it refers to what resulted in the mind of the author. It is a reference made to something that was present and existent in reality, be it if the reference was made before or after the compilation of the poem.

فما المراد بالحديث هنا، أعلمُ الدراية أم علم الرواية؟

As such, what was the author referring to here; is it the science of *al-dirāyah* (transmission) or *al-riwāyah* (narration)?

نقول المراد بقوله (أقسام الحديث) هنا علم الدراية.

We say that what he meant here is the science of *al-dirāyah,* as he mentioned *ḥadīth* categorisation.

وقوله (عدَّه) أي عدد ليس بكثير.

And when he mentions "a number", he means a number which is not many.

وقوله (وكل واحد أتى وحدَّه) أي أن كل واحد من هذه الأقسام جاء به المؤلف.

The author's statement: "Each one having come with its definition", i.e. the author brings every single one of these categories.

وقوله (أتى وحدَّه) الواو هنا واو المعيَّة، و(حدَّه) مفعول معه، وهنا قاعدة وهي: إذا عُطف على الضمير المستتر فالأفصح أن تكون الواو للمعية ويُنصب ما بعدها.

And when he said: "come with its definition", the particle *wāw* (and/with) here is called *wāw al-ma'iyyah* (particle of concomitance), and "definition" is the *maf'ūlun ma'ah* (the concomitant object). Here there is a principle: If something is conjoined to a hidden pronoun, it is more eloquent to utilise the *wāw* of *ma'iyyah* and to make that which follows it accusative.

فإذا قلت: محمدٌ جاء وعليًّا، فإنه أفصح من قولك: محمدٌ جاء وعلي. لأن واو المعية تدل على المصاحبة، فالمصحوب هو الضمير.

As such, if you say, *"Muḥammadun jā'a wa 'Aliyyan"* (Muḥammad came with 'Alī), it is more eloquent than saying, *"Muḥammadun jā'a wa 'Aliyyun"* because the letter *wāw* indicates accompaniment. And the pronoun is the accompanied one.

ومعنى (حدَّه) أي تعريفه، والحدُّ: هو التعريف بالشيء. ويشترط في الحد أن

يكون مطرد وأن يكون منعكساً، يعني أن الحدّ يُشترط ألا يخرج عنه شيء من المحدود، وألا يدخل فيه شيء من غير المحدود.

And the meaning of *"ḥaddahu"* (definition) in the poem is "defined it". *Al-ḥadd* is the definition of something. The condition of *al-ḥadd* is that the definition must be consistent and indicative, which means that it is conditioned not to exclude anything from the defined and not to include anything other than the defined.

فمثلاً: إذا حددنا الإنسان كما يقولون: أنه حيوانٌ ناطق، وهذا الحدُّ يقولون: إنه مطرد، ومنعكس.

For example: If we defined "human" in the manner that many have done so, "The living thing that speaks", this is a definition that is said to be consistent and indicative.

فقولنا: (حيوانٌ) خرج به ما ليس بحيوان كالجماد.

So when we state, "living thing", we exclude everything other than living things, such as the inanimate.

وقولنا: (ناطق) خرج به ما ليس بناطق كالبهيم، فهذا الحد الآن تام لا يدخل فيه شيء من غير المحدود ولا يخرج منه شيء من المحدود.

And when we state, "that speaks", we exclude all that does not speak, such as animals. As such, the definition is now complete and it does not include anything other than the defined and it does not exclude anything that is part of the defined.

ولو قلنا: إن الإنسان حيوان فقط؛ فهذا لا يصح! لماذا؟

Contrarily, if we say that the human is a "living thing" alone, this is not true. Why?

لأنه يدخل فيه ما ليس منه، فإننا إذا قلنا إن الإنسان حيوانٌ لدخل فيه البهيم

والناطق.

This is because it includes what is not from it. If we state that the human is a living thing then the definition shall include animals.

وإذا قلنا: إن الإنسان حيوانٌ ناطق عاقل، فهذا لا يصح أيضاً؛ لأنه يخرج منه بعض أفراد المحدود وهو المجنون.

And if we say that the human is, "The living thing that speaks and thinks", this is also not true because it excludes some individuals amongst the defined, such as the mentally unsound.

إذاً فلابد في الحد أن يكون مطرداً منعكساً.

Therefore, the definition has to be consistent and indicative.

وإذا قلنا في الوضوء: إنه غسل الأعضاء الأربعة فقط، فهذا لا يصح، فلابد أن تقول: على صفة مخصوصة، لأنك لو غسلت هذه الأعضاء غير مرتبة لم يكن هذا وضوءاً شرعيًّا.

Thus, if we say that ablution is "The washing of the four body parts" only, then this is incorrect. We will have to add, "In a specific manner." The reason for this is due to the fact that if one were to wash these body parts in a disorderly manner, the ablution would not be legitimate according to the religion.

ولو قلت: الوضوء هو غسل الأعضاء الأربعة ثلاثاً على صفة مخصوصة، فإن هذا أيضاً لا يصح، لأنه يخرج منه بعض المحدود، فإنه يخرج منه الوضوء، إذا كان غسل الأعضاء فيه مرة واحدة.

And if it is said that the definition of the ablution is, "The washing of the four body parts thrice in a specific manner", this is also incorrect because some matters that fit into the definition were excluded, one of which is the ablution whereby the body parts are washed only once.

وعلى كل حال فالحد هو التعريف، وهو: (الوصف المحيط بموصوفه، المميز له عن غيره).

In any case, we conclude that *al-ḥadd* is the definition, and it is, "The description that encompasses the described, and distinguishes it from all the others."

وشرطه: أن يكون مطرداً منعكساً، أي لا يخرج شيء من أفراده عنه، ولا يدخل فيه شيء من غير أفراده.

And its condition is that it is constant and indicative, i.e. it does not exclude any of its components from it and it does not include anything besides its components.

المتن

(٣) أَوَّلُهَا الصَّحِيحُ وَهْوَ مَا اتَّصَلْ   إِسْنَادُهُ وَلَمْ يَشُذَّ أَوْ يُعَلّ

(3) The first of them is ṣaḥīḥ which is what is connected,
In its chain, and is neither contradicting nor defected.

الشرح

قوله: (أولها الصحيح) بدأ المؤلف بذكر أقسام الحديث وقدَّم الصحيح لأنه أشرف أقسام الحديث، ثم عرَّفه فقال: (وهو ما اتصل إسناده) يعني ما رُوي بإسناد متصل بحيث يأخذه كل راوي عمن فوقه، فيقول مثلاً: حدثني رقم واحد (ولنجعلها بالأرقام) قال حدثني رقم اثنين، قال حدثني رقم ثلاثة، قال حدثني رقم أربعة، فهذا النوع يكون متصلاً، لأنه يقول حدثني فكل واحد أخذ عمن روى عنه.

In the phrase: "The first of them is *ṣaḥīḥ*", the author begins listing the categories of *ḥadīth* and commences with *al-ṣaḥīḥ* (the sound narration) as it is the most superior among all the types of *ḥadīth*. Then he defined it by saying, "Which is what is connected in its chain," i.e. that which is narrated with a connected chain of narration, whereby every narrator transmits from the one above him. So if we say, for example: Number one (and we identify the narrators with numbers) told me, and said, "Number two told me", and he said, "Number three told me," and he said, "Number four told me." This type of narration is connected because every single narrator said that the one he narrates from told him as such.

أما إن قال حدثني رقم واحد عن رقم ثلاثة لم يكن متصلاً، لأنه سقط منه رقم اثنين فيكون منقطعاً.

And if he said: Number one told me that he narrated from number three, then the narration is not connected, because number two is dropped from the chain and thus it becomes disconnected.

وقوله: (ولم يُشذَّ أو يُعَل) يعني يشترط أن لا يكون شاذًّا ولا معللاً.

And the author's statement: "neither contradicting nor defected" refers to the condition that the narration does not contradict other narrations and has no [hidden] defects in itself.

والشاذُّ هو: الذي يرويه الثقة مخالفاً لمن هو أرجح منه، إما في العدد، أو في الصدق، أو في العدالة.

The term *shādh* (contradicting) refers to what the reliable narrator narrates which is contradictory to the narration of someone else who is more reliable in terms of number, truthfulness or integrity.

فإذا جاء الحديث بسندٍ متصلٍ لكنه شاذٌّ، بحيث يكون مخالفاً لرواية أُخرى، هي أرجح منه، إما في العدد، وإما في الصدق، وإما في العدالة؛ فإنه لا يقبل ولو كان الذي رواه عدلاً، ولو كان السند متصلاً، وذلك من أجل شذوذه.

As such, if a *ḥadīth* has a connected chain of narration but is *shādh,* wherein it contradicts another narration which is more acceptable due to the numbers, truthfulness or integrity of the narrators, we are still unable to accept the *ḥadīth* even though the narrator is upright and the chain is connected, and this is due to the *shudhūdh* (contradiction) of the narration.

والشذوذ: قد يكون في حديث واحد، وقد يكون في حديثين منفصلين، يعني أنه لا يشترط في الشذوذ أن يكون الرواة قد اختلفوا في حديث واحد، بل قد يكون الشاذ أتى في حديث آخر، مثاله: ما ورد في السنن أن النبي صلى الله عليه وسلّم نهى عن الصيام إذا انتصف شعبان، والحديث لا بأس به من حيث السند، لكن ثبت عن النبي صلى الله عليه وسلّم في الصحيحين أنه قال: ((لا تقدموا رمضان بصوم يوم ولا يومين إلا رجل كان يصوم صوماً فليصمه)).

Shudhūdh may come in a *ḥadīth* or in two separate *ḥadīth*. This means that it is not conditional for *shudhūdh* to occur when the narrators differ in one *ḥadīth*. In fact, the contradiction may come in another *ḥadīth*. For example, the narration in the *Sunan* that the Prophet ﷺ prohibits fasting when half of the month of Shaʿbān has passed.[7] The *ḥadīth* has no problems in terms of its chain of narration. However, it is confirmed from the Prophet ﷺ, as reported in the *Ṣaḥīḥayn,* that he said, "Do not precede Ramaḍān by fasting a day or two except for someone who has been fasting voluntarily and so he fasted."[8]

فإذا أخذنا بالحديث الثاني الوارد في الصحيحين قلنا إن فيه دلالة على أن الصيام بعد منتصف شعبان جائز، وليس فيه شيء، لأن النهي حُدد بما قبل رمضان

7 Reported by al-Imām Aḥmad 2/325, Abū Dawūd; The Book of Fasting; Chapter: Disapproval of fasting the half of *Shaʿbān* (1990), al-Tirmidhī; The Book of Fasting; Chapter: Disapproved fasting (669) and Ibn Mājah; The Book of Fasting; Chapter: What comes in the prohibition of preceding (1641).

8 Reported by al-Bukhārī; The Book of Fasting; Chapter: Do not precede Ramaḍān with fasting a day or two (1914), and Muslim; The Book of Fasting; Chapter: Do not precede Ramaḍān (21) (1082).

بيوم أو يومين، وإذا أخذنا بالأول فنقول إن النهي يبدأ من منتصف شعبان، فأخذ الإمام أحمد بالحديث الوارد في الصحيحين وهو النهي عن تقدم رمضان بصوم يوم أو يومين، وقال إن هذا شاذ، يعني به حديث السنن، لأنه مخالف لمن هو أرجح منه إذ أن هذا في الصحيحين وذاك في السنن.

If we take the second *ḥadīth* which is narrated in the *Ṣaḥīḥayn* into consideration, we say that it implies the permissibility of fasting after half of Shaʿbān has passed and that there is no problem with it. This is because the prohibition is confined to preceding Ramaḍān by a day or two. And if we consider the first *ḥadīth*, we say that the prohibition starts from mid-Shaʿbān. As such, al-Imām Aḥmad gave due consideration to the *ḥadīth* which was narrated in the *Ṣaḥīḥayn* whereby fasting before Ramaḍān by a day or two is prohibited, and he considered the other *ḥadīth* which is narrated in the *Sunan* as *shādh* due to the fact that it contradicts the narration which is more acceptable, i.e. one is reported in the *Sunan* and the other in the *Ṣaḥīḥayn*.

ومن ذلك ما ورد في سنن أبي داود أن النبي صلى الله عليه وسلّم نهى عن صوم يوم السبت قال: ((لا تصوموا يوم السبت إلا فيما افترض عليكم)) فقد حكم بعض العلماء على هذا الحديث بالشذوذ، لأنه مخالف لقول النبي صلى الله عليه وسلّم لإحدى نسائه حين وجدها صائمة يوم الجمعة، فقال: ((هل صمت أمس))؟ فقالت: لا، قال: ((أتصومين غداً))؟ قالت: لا، قال: ((فأفطري))

Another example is the narration in *Sunan Abī Dāwūd* which states that the Prophet ﷺ forbade fasting on Saturdays, "Do not fast on Saturdays except those fasts that are obligatory upon you."[9] Some scholars regard this narration as having *shudhūdh* due to it contradicting the Prophet's ﷺ statement to one of his wives when he found her fasting on a Friday, "Did you

9 Reported by al-Imām Aḥmad (17026), Abū Dawūd; The Book of Fasting; Chapter: Prohibition of fasting on a Saturday by itself (2421), al-Tirmidhī; in the Chapters of Fasting; Chapter: What comes with regards to fasting on Saturdays (744) and he said: *ḥadīth ḥasan*.

fast yesterday?" She replied, "No." Then he asked, "Will you be fasting tomorrow?" She answered, "No." He said, "Break your fast then."[10]

وهذا الحديث ثابت في الصحيح، وفيه دليل على أن صيام يوم السبت جائز ليس فيه بأس، وهنا قال بعض العلماء: إن حديث النهي عن صيام يوم السبت شاذ؛ لأنه مخالف لما هو أرجح منه، ومن العلماء من قال: لا مخالفة هنا، وذلك لإمكان الجمع، وإذا أمكن الجمع فلا مخالفة، والجمع بين الحديثين أن يقال: إن النهي كان عن إفراده، أي أنه نُهي عن صوم يوم السبت مستقلاً بمفرده، أما إذا صامه مع يوم الجمعة، أو مع يوم الأحد فلا بأس به حينئذ، ومن المعلوم أنه إذا أمكن الجمع فلا مخالفة ولا شذوذ.

This *ḥadīth* is confirmed in *Ṣaḥīḥ al-Bukhārī* and there is evidence in it to show that fasting on a Saturday is permissible and without any problems. Some scholars say here that the *ḥadīth* that prohibits fasting on Saturdays is *shādh* because it contradicts a more acceptable narration. And there are other scholars who said that there is no contradiction here due to the fact that combining the two is possible, and if combination is possible, then there is no contradiction. As such the combination is that the prohibition is due to singling out the fast, i.e. fasting on a Saturday on its own is prohibited. As such, if the person fasts on the Friday or Sunday together with it, then there is no problem with this. And it is a known fact that if the combination of narrations is possible, then there is neither contradiction nor *shudhūth*.

ومن الشذوذ: أن يخالف ما عُلم بالضرورة من الدين.

Among the *shudhūth* is the contradiction of a narration with a fact known in the religion by necessity.

مثاله: في صحيح البخاري رواية ((أنه يبقى في النار فضلٌ عمن دخلها من أهل الدنيا، فيُنشيء الله لها أقواماً فيدخلهم النار)).

---

10 Reported by al-Bukhārī; The Book of Fasting; Chapter: Fasting on a Friday.

An example is the narration in *Ṣaḥīḥ al-Bukhārī* which states that, "There is space left in the Hellfire after the people of the Earth have been sent into it, thus Allāh created for it people and sent them into the Hellfire."[11]

فهذا الحديث وإن كان متصل السند فهو شاذ؛ لأنه مخالف لما عُلم بالضرورة من الدين، وهو أن الله تعالى لا يظلم أحداً، وهذه الرواية - في الحقيقة - قد انقلبت على الراوي، والصواب أنه يبقي في الجنة فضلٌ عمن دخلها من أهل الدنيا، فيُنشيء الله أقواماً فيدخلهم الجنة، وهذا فضل ليس فيه ظلم، أما الأول ففيه ظلم.

Even though the chain of narration for this *ḥadīth* is connected, it is regarded as *shādh* because it contradicts a known fact in the religion by necessity i.e. that Allāh shall not oppress anyone. This narration in actual fact was inverted by the narrator, and the correct narration is that there will be space left in Paradise after the people of the Earth have been sent into it, thus Allāh created people and sent them into Paradise. This narration demonstrates Allāh's Grace and there is no oppression in it, unlike the former which has an element of oppression.

على كل حال فلابد لصحة الحديث ألا يكون شاذًّا.

Whatever the case, in order for a *ḥadīth* to be sound, it must not be *shādh*.

ولو أن رجلاً ثقة عدلاً روى حديثاً على وجه، ثم رواه رجلان مثله في العدالة على وجه مخالف للأول، فماذا نقول للأول؟

If a trustworthy and righteous narrator narrated a *ḥadīth*, and two other narrators similar to him in terms of integrity and righteousness narrated in a way that contradicts the first, what do we say about the first *ḥadīth*?

نقول: الحديث الأول شاذ، فلا يكون صحيحاً وإن رواه العدل الثقة.

11 Reported by al-Bukhārī; The Book of *Tawḥīd*; Chapter: The verse: **{And He is the Exalted in Might, the Wise}** (7384).

We say that the first *ḥadīth* is *shādh* and thus it is not a *ṣaḥīḥ* narration even though it was narrated by a trustworthy and righteous narrator.

ولو روى إنسان حديثاً على وجه، ورواه إنسانٌ آخر على وجه يخالف الأول، وهذا الثاني أقوى في العدالة أو في الضبط، فيكون الأول شاذًّا.

And if someone narrated a *ḥadīth*, and another person narrated it in a way that contradicts the first, if the second narrator is better than the first in terms of righteousness or accuracy, then the first narration is *shādh*.

وهذه قاعدة مفيدة تفيد الإنسان فيما لو عرض له حديث، فإذا نظر في سنده وجده متصلاً، ووجد أن رجاله ثقات، ولكن إذا نظر إلى المتن وجده مخالفاً كما سبق فحينئذ نقول له احكم بأن هذا ليس بصحيح، وليس في ذمتك شيء.

This principle is very beneficial for someone who has been presented with a *ḥadīth*. If he looks at the chain and finds that it is connected, and finds that all the narrators are trustworthy, but when he looks at the text of the *ḥadīth* and finds that it is contradictory as previously mentioned, we tell him to regard the *ḥadīth* as not being *ṣaḥīḥ*, and that he shall not be held responsible.

فإذا قال كيف أحكم عليه بأنه غير صحيح! وسنده متصل ورجاله ثقات عدول؟

The individual may ask regarding how he can regard it as not being *ṣaḥīḥ* when the chain is connected and the narrators are trustworthy and righteous.

فنقول له: لأن فيه علة توجب ضعفه وهي الشذوذ.

We shall answer him that the *ḥadīth* has a reason that causes its weakness and the reason is the *shudhūth*.

قوله: (أو يُعَلَّ) معناه أي يُقدح فيه بعلة تمنع قبوله، فإذا وجدت في الحديث علة تمنع قبوله فليس الحديث بصحيح.

The author's phrase, "Nor defected" means that the *ṣaḥīḥ* narration does not possess a dispraise worthy *ʿillah* (hidden defect) that prevents it from being acceptable. Hence, if we found an *ʿillah* in the *ḥadīth* that prevented it from being acceptable, it is regarded as not being *ṣaḥīḥ*.

ومعنى العلة في الأصل هي: وصفٌ يوجب خروج البدن عن الاعتدال الطبيعي.

The root meaning of *ʿillah* is an attribute that causes the body to be out of its natural balance.

ولهذا يقال: فلانٌ فيه علة، يعني أنه عليل أي مريض، فالعلة مرض تمنع من سلامة البدن.

For this reason it is said that someone who has an *ʿillah*, it means that he is handicapped or sick, as the defect prevents the body's well-being.

والعلة في الحديث معناها قريبة من هذا وهي:

And the term *ʿillah* in the science of *ḥadīth* carries a meaning close to this and it is:

وصفٌ يوجب خروج الحديث عن القبول.

A characteristic that causes the *ḥadīth* to be prevented from being acceptable.

لكن هذا الشرط، يشترط فيه شرط زائد على ما قال المؤلف وهو: أن لا يُعلّ الحديث بعلةٍ قادحة، لأن الحديث قد يُعلُّ بعلةٍ لا تقدح فيه، وهذا سيأتي الكلام عليه إن شاء الله.

However, this requirement has an additional condition to what was mentioned by the author, and it is that the *ḥadīth* has no *ʿillah* that is dispraise worthy. This is because the *ḥadīth* may have a defect that is not dispraise worthy and we shall mention this in detail later, Allah willing.

إذاً فيشترط للحديث الصحيح شروط أخذنا منها ثلاثة وهي:

Therefore, the authentic *ḥadīth* has three requirements that we have studied so far and they are:

١ - اتصال السند.

1. The *sanad* must be connected.

٢ - أن يكون سالماً من الشذوذ.

2. It must be free from *shudhūth*.

٣ - أن يكون سالماً من العلة القادحة.

3. It must be free from the dispraise worthy defect.

والعلة القادحة اختلف فيها العلماء اختلافاً كثيراً!؛ وذلك لأن بعض العلماء، قد يرى أن في الحديث علة توجب القدح فيه، وبعضهم قد لا يراها علة قادحة.

As for the *'illah qādihah*, the scholars have many differing opinions. This is because some may see that the defect in the *ḥadīth* is dispraise worthy and others may not see it as being so.

ومثاله: لو أن شخصاً ظن أن هذا الحديث مخالفٌ لما هو أرجح منه لقال: إن الحديث شاذ، ثم لا يقبله، فإذا جاء آخر وتأمل الحديث وجد أنه لا يخالفه، فبالتالي يحكم بصحة الحديث! لأن أمر العلة أمر خفي، فقد يخفى على الإنسان وجه ارتفاع العلة فيعلله بهذه العلة، ويأتي آخر ويتبين له وجه ارتفاع العلة فلا يعلله.

An example we can use to understand this is: An individual may conclude that a particular *ḥadīth* contradicts another narration which is more acceptable and thus it is said to be *shādh*, then someone else analyses the *ḥadīth* and finds that it is not contradictory and thus regards the narration as *ṣaḥīḥ*. This can occur due to the obscure nature of the *'illah* subject; the lifting of the defect may be ambiguous to someone and hence he will regard the narration defective whereas another individual may detect the way to lift such an *ʿillah* and thus disregard the defect.

لذلك قلنا لابد من إضافة قيد وهو: أن تكون العلة قادحة، والعلة القادحة هي التي تكون في صميم موضوع الحديث، أما التي تكون خارجاً عن موضوعه فهذه لا تكون علة قادحة.

For this reason, we say that the definition must have a condition that the defect must be dispraise worthy, and it must be within the subject matter of the *ḥadīth*. If it is outside the subject matter of the *ḥadīth* then it is not considered as an *ʿillah qādihah*.

ولنضرب على ذلك مثلاً بحديث فضالة بن عبيد - رضي الله عنه - في قصة القلادة الذهبية التي بيعت باثني عشر ديناراً، والدينار نقد ذهبي، ففُصلت فوجد فيها أكثر من اثني عشر ديناراً.

To illustrate this, we give the example of the *ḥadīth* of Fuḍālah ibn ʿUbayd ﷺ regarding the story of the golden necklace that was sold for twelve dinars (the dinar is a currency made of gold). Then it was fragmented and found to be more than twelve dinars.[12]

واختلف الرواة في مقدار الثمن.

The narrators differ in opinion with regards to the price of the necklace.

فمنهم من قال: اثني عشر ديناراً.

There are those who said: twelve dinars.

ومنهم من قال: تسعة دنانير.

And there are those who said: nine dinars.

12 Reported by Muslim; The Book of Crop Sharing; Chapter: The sale of the necklace in which there are beads and gold (90) (1591).

ومنهم من قال: عشرة دنانير.

And also there are those who said: ten dinars.

ومنهم من قال غير ذلك، وهذه العلة - لا شك - أنها علة تهزُّ الحديث، لكنها علة غير قادحة في الحديث، وذلك لأن اختلافهم في الثمن لا يؤثر في صميم موضوع الحديث وهو: أن بيع الذهب بالذهب، إذا كان معه غيره، لا يجوز ولا يصح.

And there are those who mentioned other than these. It is evident that this is a defect that affects the *ḥadīth*. However the *'illah* here is not *qādihah* because the differing opinions with regards to the price do not affect the subject matter of the *ḥadīth,* which is: trading of gold with gold; if it comes with other than it then the transaction is not permissible and invalid.

وكذلك قصة بعير جابر - رضي الله عنه - الذي اشتراه منه النبي صلى الله عليه وسلّم، حيث اختلف الرواة في ثمن هذا البعير، هل هو أوقية، أو أكثر، أو أقل، فهذا الخلاف لا يعتبر علّة قادحة في الحديث، لأن موضوع الحديث هو: شراء النبي صلى الله عليه وسلّم الجمل من جابر بثمن معين، واشتراط جابر أن يحمله الجمل إلى المدينة، وهذا الموضوع لم يتأثر ولم يُصب بأي علة تقدح فيه، وغاية ما فيه أنهم اختلفوا في مقدار الثمن، وهذه ليست بعلة قادحة في الحديث.

Likewise in the story of the camel of Jābir [13] ﵁ where the Prophet ﷺ bought it from him. The narrators differ in the price of this camel, differing on whether it was one ounce of silver or more or less. This difference of opinion is not taken as a dispraising defect in the *ḥadīth* because the subject matter is that the Prophet ﷺ brought the camel from Jābir at a certain price and that Jābir put the condition that the camel shall carry him to Madīnah. The

13 Reported by al-Bukhārī; The Book of Transactions; Chapter: Purchase of the livestock (2097), and Muslim; The Book of Crop Sharing; Chapter: The sale of the camel and the exception of riding it (109) (715).

subject of the *ḥadīth* is not affected and not damaged by any *ʿillah* that dispraises it. This is because the extent of difference was that they differed on the price of the camel and this is not an *ʿillah qādihah* in the *ḥadīth*.

ومن العلل القادحة: أن يروي الحديث إثنان، أحدهما يرويه بصفة النفي، والآخر يرويه بصفة الإثبات، وهذا لا شك أنها علة قادحة، وسيأتي الكلام عليه إن شاء الله في الحديث المضطرب الذي اضطرب الرواة فيه على وجهٍ يتأثر به المعنى.

Amongst the dispraise worthy defects is where two narrators narrate a *ḥadīth*, one narrates in the negative and the other narrates in the positive. Definitely this is an *ʿillah qādihah* and we shall speak about it later in the chapter of *ḥadīth muḍṭarib* (inconsistent *ḥadīth*) where the narrators are inconsistent in their narrations in a manner that affects the meaning.

المتن

(٤) يَرْوِيهِ عَدْلٌ ضَابِطٌ عَنْ مِثْلِهِ مُعْتَمَدٌ فِي ضَبْطِهِ وَنَقْلِهِ

(4) Narrated by one who is just and precise from his like,
Reliable in his precision and his transmission.

الشرح

قوله: (يرويه عدل) يعني أنه لابد أن يكون الراوي عدلاً، وهذا هو الشرط الرابع من شروط صحة الحديث.

The author said, "Narrated by one who is just", which means that the narrator must be just and this is the fourth criteria for the *ḥadīth* to be *ṣaḥīḥ*.

والعدل في الأصل هو: الاستقامة، إذا كان الطريق مستقيماً ليس فيه اعوجاج، يقال: هذا طريق عدل، أي: مستقيم، ومثله العصا المستقيمة يقال لها عدلة،

هذا هو الأصل.

The root of the word *al-ʿadl* (just) is *al-istiqāmah* (straightness). When the path is straight without any curves, it is called a path of *ʿadl,* which means straight path. Its example would be a straight cane which is called *ʿadlah.* This is the root of the word.

لكنه عند أهل العلم هو: وصف في الشخص يقتضي الاستقامة، في الدين، والمروءة.

However, according to the people of knowledge it is the description of a person who displays integrity in the *dīn* (religion) as well as dignity.

فاستقامة الرجل في دينه ومروءته تسمى عدالة.

Thus the straightness of a person in his religion and his dignity is called *ʿadālah.*

وعلى هذا فالفاسق ليس بعدل؛ لأنه ليس مستقيماً في دينه. فلو رأينا رجلاً قاطعاً لرحمه فليس بعدل، ولو كان من أصدق الناس في نقله، لأنه غير مستقيم في دينه، وكذلك لو وجدنا شخصاً لا يصلي مع الجماعة، وهو من أصدق الناس، فإنه ليس بعدل، فما رواه لا يقبل منه.

Upon this, the open sinner (*fāsiq*) is not considered as *ʿadl*, because he is not *mustaqīm* (straight or correct) in his *dīn*. And if we saw someone who severs his relations, he is not considered as *ʿadl,* even if he is from the most truthful in his transmission because he is not *mustaqīm* in his religion. Likewise if we found a man who does not perform his prayers in congregation, and he may be the most truthful in speech of all the people, but he is not considered as *ʿadl*, hence his narrations shall not be accepted.

والدليل على هذا قول الله تعالى: ﴿يَٰٓأَيُّهَا ٱلَّذِينَ ءَامَنُوٓاْ إِن جَآءَكُمْ فَاسِقُۢ بِنَبَإٖ فَتَبَيَّنُوٓاْ أَن تُصِيبُواْ قَوْمَۢا بِجَهَٰلَةٖ﴾ [الحجرات: ٦]. فلما أمر الله تعالى بالتبين في خبر

الفاسق عُلم أن خبره غير مقبول، لا يقبلُ ولا يُرد حتى نتبين.

The evidence for this fact is the verse: **{O you who have believed, if there comes to you a disobedient one with information, investigate, lest you harm a people out of ignorance.}**[14] As such, when Allāh ﷻ commanded to investigate the information from the disobedient, it is understood that his information is not acceptable; it is neither accepted nor rejected until we have investigated.

ونحن نشترط في رواية الحديث: أن يكون الراوي عدلاً يمكن قبول خبره، والفاسق لا يقبل خبره.

We placed the criteria in the narration of *ḥadīth* that the narrator has to be a just individual whose narration can be accepted, and the narration from the disobedient is not to be accepted.

أما العدل فيقبلُ خبره، بدليل قوله تعالى: ﴿وَأَشْهِدُواْ ذَوَى عَدْلٍ مِّنكُمْ﴾. [الطلاق: ٢]. ولم يأمرنا بإشهادهم إلا لنقبل شهادتهم، إذ أن الأمر بقبول شهادة من لا تقبل شهادته لا فائدة منه وهو لغوٌ من القول.

As for the *ʿadl*, his narration is acceptable due to the ayah, **{And bring to witness two just men from among you.}**[15] We were not commanded regarding their testimony except to accept it, as it would be meaningless and futile if we were ordered to accept the testimony of one whose statements were rejected.

أما المروءة فقال أهل العلم في تعريفها هو: أن يفعل ما يُجمّلُهُ ويزيُنهُ، ويدع ما يُدنّسه ويشينه.

As for *murū'ah* (dignity), it is defined by the scholars as: Doing that which beautifies and adorns the person in the eyes of the people and brings forth praise from them. It is also leaving that which would stain and tarnish his

14 Al-Ḥujarāt: 6
15 Al-Ṭalāq: 2

image.

أي أن المروءة هي أن يستعمل ما يجمله أمام الناس، ويزينه ويمدحوه عليه، وأن يترك ما يدنسه ويشينه عند الناس، كما لو فعل الإنسان شيئاً أمام المجتمع وهذا الفعل مخالف لما عليه الناس، فإذا رأوا ذلك الفعل عدوه فعلاً قبيحاً، لا يفعله إلا أراذل الناس والمنحطون من السفلة، فنقول: إن هذا ليس بعدل، وذلك لأنه مروءته لم تستقم، وبفعله هذا خالف ما عليه الناس فسقطت مروءته.

This means that dignity is to perform that which beautifies one in front of the people and which emits praise for him, whilst avoiding that which sullies him in front of the people. An example is if a person was to perform an act in public which would be seen as inappropriate to the masses and they would deem it as a hideous act that only the despicable and lowly would perform, we will say that such a person is not *'adl*. This is due to the fact that his character is undignified and his action that is inappropriate to the people diminished his dignity.

ومثاله الآن: لو أن رجلاً خرج في بلدنا هذا بعد الظهر، ومعه الغداء على صحن له، وصار يمشي في الأسواق، ويأكل أمام الناس في السوق، لسقطت مروءته من أعين الناس، ولصار محلاً للسخرية والانتقاد من الجميع.

For instance, if a man in our country was to come out during noontime carrying a plate of food and eating while walking in the markets in front of the people, his dignity would lessen in their eyes and he would be the subject of mockery and criticism.

أما إذا خرج رجلٌ عند بابه ومعه إبريق الشاي والقهوة لكي يشربه عند الباب فهل يُعد هذا من خوارم المروءة أم لا؟

And if someone were to come out of his residence with a pot of tea and coffee to drink outside his house, would it be considered as undignified or not?

نقول: إن هذا فيه تفصيل:

We say that this requires further elaboration:

١ - فإن كانت العادة جرت بمثل ذلك؛ فلا يُعد من خوارم المروءة؛ لأن هذا هو عُرف الناس وهو شيء مألوف عندهم، كما يفعله بعض كبار السن عندنا الآن، وذلك إذا كان أول النهار أخرج بساطاً له عند بابه، ومعه الشاي والقهوة، وجعل يشرب أمام الناس ومن مرّ بهم قالوا له: تفضل، فهذا لا بأس به؛ لأن من عادة الناس فعله.

Firstly: If the culture of the people is as such, then it is not deemed as undignified because it is a common practice among the people and they are familiar with it. Just like our older generation do at present, placing a mat in their front yard during early daytime with coffee and tea to drink in front of the people and offering to passersby by saying, "[Help yourself]". There is no problem with this as it is the common practice of the people to do it.

٢ - أما إن أتى بهذا الفعل على غير هذا الوجه، وكان الناس ينتقدونه على فعله هذا، وصار من معائب الرجل واستهجن الناس هذا الفعل، صار هذا الفعل من خوارم المروءة.

Secondly: And if someone was to do this practice in a different way in which the people would criticise him for doing it, the practice becomes a flaw to the person as the people disapprove of this conduct, thus the action is considered as undignified.

وقد يختلف العلماء في تعديل رجل معين - وهذه تقع كثيراً - أنظر مثلاً التهذيب، أو تهذيب التهذيب لابن حجر، أو غيره تجد أن الشخص الواحد يختلف فيه الحفاظ، فيقول أحد الحفاظ: هذا رجل لا بأس به.

The scholars differed in opinion with regards to the *taʿdīl* (validation) of a certain narrator and this occurs commonly. For example, take a look in the book *Tahdhīb* or *Tahdhīb al-Tahdhīb* by Ibn Ḥajar or other books and you will find that the *ḥuffāẓ* (custodians of *ḥadīth*) differ in the validation of a particular person; one of them may say that nothing is wrong with him.

ويقول غيره: هو ثقة.

And another may say that he is trustworthy.

ويقول آخر: اضرب على حديثه، ليس بشيء.

While another may say, "Throw away his narration, he is nothing."

فإذا اختلفوا فماذا نعمل؟

As such, when they differed in opinions, what should we do?

نقول: إذا اختلف العلماء في مثل هذه المسألة وغيرها، فإننا نأخذ بما هو أرجح، فإذا كان الذي وثقه أعلم بحال الشخص من غيره، فإننا نأخذ بقوله؛ لأنه أعلمُ بحاله من غيره.

We say that if the scholars differ in this issue or others, we shall take the most justified opinion. If the one who validated the narrator is more informed than the others regarding his personality, then we shall take his opinion because he is the most knowledgeable of the status of the narrator.

ولهذا لا نرى أحداً يعلم حال الشخص إلا من كان بينه وبينه ملازمة، فإذا علمنا أنّ هذا الرجل ملازم له، ووصفه بالعدالة، قلنا هو أعلم من غيره فنأخذ بقوله.

Due to this reason, we do not see anyone as being [more] informed of a narrator's status other than the one who made acquaintance with him. Thus, if we know that the scholar frequented the narrator and described him as a person of integrity, we shall say that he is more knowledgeable than the others and thus we shall accept his opinion.

وكذا ما إذا ضعّف أحدهم رجلاً وكان ملازماً له، وهو أعرف بحاله من غيره،

فإننا نأخذ بقوله.

Likewise if one of them regarded a narrator as weak, and he used to frequent him, we shall accept his opinion because he is the most acquainted with the person when compared to the others.

فالمهم أنه إذا اختلف حفاظ الحديث في تعديل رجل، أو تجريحه، وكان أحدهما أقرب إلى معرفة الموصوف من الآخر، فإننا نأخذ بقول من هو أقرب إليه، وأعلم بحاله من غيره.

Most importantly, if the *ḥuffāẓ* of *ḥadīth* differ in praising or criticising a narrator, and one of them is superior to the others in knowledge about the specified person, then we shall take the opinion of the one who is closest to the narrator and most familiar of his status.

أما إن تساوى الأمران بأن كان كل واحد منهما بعيداً عن ذلك الشخص، أو جهلنا الأمر في ذلك.

And if in these two matters, the scholars are equal, whereby every single one of them is distant from the narrator or if we are uncertain of their knowledge of the individual:

فقد اختلف العلماء: هل نأخذ بالتعديل، أو نأخذ بالتجريح، بناء على أنه هل الأصل في الإنسان العدالة، أو الأصل فيه عدم العدالة؟

In such a scenario, the scholars differed if they should take the praise or the criticism, based on whether the origin of an individual is to regard him as someone of integrity or not.

فمن قال: إن الأصل العدالة، أخذ بالعدالة.

Those who said that the origin is integrity, will consider the person as someone of integrity.

ومن قال: إن الأصل عدم العدالة، أخذ بالجرح، وردَّ روايته.

And those who said that the origin is an absence of integrity, will give consideration to the *jarḥ* (depreciation) and reject his narration.

وفصَّل بعضهم فقال: يقبل منهما ما كان مفسراً، والمفسَّر مثل أن يقول: المعدل الذي وصفه بالعدالة: هو عدلٌ، وما ذكر فيه من الجرح فقد تاب منه، مثل: أن يُجرح بأنه يشرب الخمر.

Some of them elaborated and said that the detailed of the two shall be accepted. An example of a detailed analysis is when the one giving the praise says that he is just, and he made repentance from whatever that was discredited of him, e.g. the depreciation of his standing due to drinking alcohol.

فيقول الذي وصفه بالعدالة: هو عدل وما ذُكَرَ عنه من شْرب الخمر فقد تاب منه. إذاً نُقدِّم المفسَّر، لأنه معه زيادة علم، فقد علم أنه مجروح بالأول، ثم زال عنه ما يقتضي الجرح.

As such, the one describing him as having integrity would say, "He is just, and whatever that was mentioned of him such as drinking alcohol, he has made repentance from it". Hence, we give preference to the detailed description because it comes with additional knowledge; that is he knew the narrator was discredited at first, and then the depreciation was withdrawn from him.

وإن كان الأمر بالعكس بأن قال الجارح: هذا الرجل ليس بعدل، لأنه مدمن على شرب الخمر، ففي هذه الحالة نقدِّم الجارح.

If the issue was the opposite, whereby the one dispraising said, "This narrator is not just because he is addicted to drinking alcohol," we give preference to the one dispraising in this case.

وإن لم يكن أحدهما مفسِّراً، أو فَسَّرا جميعاً شيئاً عن الراوي، فهنا نقول: إن كان

الجرح أو التعديل غير مفسر، فينبغي أن نتوقف إذا لم نجد مرجحاً، فالواجب التوقف في حال هذا الرجل.

And if neither of the two are detailed, or both elaborated something about the narrator, here we say that if the *jarḥ* or the *taʿdīl* is not elaborated, then we should put a halt if we do not find something to give preponderance. Thus it is obligatory to hold back from determining the status of this narrator.

وليُعلم أن بعض علماء الحديث عندهم تشدد في التعديل، وبعضهم عندهم تساهل في التعديل.

It is known that some scholars of *ḥadīth* were strict in their validations, and some were lenient.

يعني أن بعضهم من تشدده يجرح بما لا يكون جارحاً.

This means that there are some who made *jarḥ* with a matter that is not considered as discrediting due to their rigor.

ومنهم من يكون على العكس فيتساهل فيعدِّل من لا يستحق التعيدل، وهذا معروف عند أهل العلم، فمن كان شديداً في الرواة فإن تعديله يكون أقرب للقبول ممن كان متساهلاً، وإن كان الحق أن يكون الإنسان قائماً بالعدل لا يشدد ولا يتساهل، لأننا إذا تشددنا فربما نرد حديثاً صحَّ عن النبي صلى الله عليه وسلّم، بناء على هذا التشدد، وكذا ما إذا تساهل الإنسان، فربما ينسب حديثاً إلى النبي صلى الله عليه وسلّم، وهو لم يصحّ ثبوته إليه بسبب هذا التساهل.

And amongst them are the opposite, who are lenient and thus regarded someone undeserving as just. This fact is well known to the people of knowledge. As such, the accreditation of the one who is strict upon the narrators is closer to acceptance than that of the one who is overly-lenient. Nevertheless, it is rightful for one to be fair, being neither strict nor lax. This is because, should we be strict, perhaps we may reject a *ḥadīth* which is confirmed from the Prophet ﷺ based on this rigor. Likewise if one were to be lax, perhaps he may attribute a *ḥadīth* which is not authentically established to the Prophet ﷺ due to this leniency.

وقوله (ضابط).

The author's statement, "[One who is] precise."

هو الذي يحفظ ما روى تحمّلاً وأداءً.

He is the one who preserves what he narrates in terms of receiving and transmission.

مثل: أن يكون نبيهاً يقظاً عند تحديث الشيخ للحديث، فلا تكاد تخرج كلمة من فم الشيخ إلا وقد ضبطها وحفظها وهذا هو التحمل.

For example, an intelligent and attentive student listens to his teacher narrating the *ḥadīth*. There is hardly any word that comes out from the mouth of his teacher except that he has preserved it with precision and this is called *al-taḥammul* (reception).

أما الأداء: فأن يكون قليل النسيان، بحيث أنه إذا أراد أن يحدث بما سمعه من الشيخ، أداه كما سمعه تماماً، فلابد من الضبط في الحالين في حال التحمل، وحال الأداء.

As for *al-adā'* (transmission), it is the state of being retentive such that if he was to report what he heard from the teacher, he would be able to transmit it exactly how he heard it. Thus precision is required in both situations, during the process of *taḥammul* and *adā'*.

وضد الضبط هو: أن يكون الإنسان لديه غفلة عند التحمل، أو أن يكون كثير النسيان عند الأداء.

The opposite of *al-ḍabṭ* (precision) is someone who displays negligence during the process of *taḥammul* or excess forgetfulness during the process of *adā'*.

ولا نقول أن لا ينسى؛ لأننا إذا قلنا: إنه يشترط أن لا ينسى، لم نأخذ عُشر ما صح عن النبي صلى الله عليه وسلّم، ولكن المراد ألا يكون كثير النسيان، فإن كان كثير النسيان فإن حديثه لا يكون صحيحاً، لماذا؟

And we do not say that he does not forget at all. If we were to set the criteria that he is one who does not forget, we would have abandoned a tenth of what is confirmed from the Prophet ﷺ. However, what we mean by retentiveness is to not be excessively forgetful. If the person is very forgetful, his narration would not be authentic. Why?

لاحتمال أن يكون قد نسي، والناس يختلفون في هذا اختلافاً كبيراً، لا[16] عند التحمل ولا عند الأداء، فبعض الناس يرزقه الله فهماً وحفظاً جيداً، فبمجرد ما أن يسمع الكلمة، إلا وقد تصورها، وقد حفظها وضبطها تماماً وأودعها الحافظة عنده، على ما هي عليه تماماً، وبعض الناس يفهم الشيء خطأ ثم يُودع ما فهمه إلى الحافظة.

Due to the possibility that he could have forgotten [the particular narration.] And each individual's memory strength differs with so much variation during the process of *taḥammul* or *adā'*. For some people, Allāh Bestowed upon them good understanding and memorisation. As such, when he hears a word, he would have conceptualized, memorised with precision and kept it in his memory at once exactly the way it is. And some people would misunderstand something and retain these mistakes in their memory.

وكذلك النسيان فإن الناس يختلفون فيه اختلافاً عظيماً، فمن الناس من إذا حفظ الحديث استودعه تماماً كما حفظه، لا ينسى منه شيئاً، وإن نسي فهو نادر،

16 [T] The *lā* here appears to return back to (لا يكون صحيحا) in the previous paragraph. However, I have amended the sentence structure to fit into the context dictated by the separation in paragraphing, and to allow more fluidity in the translation.

ومن الناس من يكون بالعكس.

Likewise people differ with great variation with regards to forgetfulness. There are amongst the people those that whenever they memorise a *ḥadīth*, they would have stored it exactly the way they memorised it and would not forget a thing from it. Even if they were to forget, it would be on rare occasions. Likewise, there are the opposite in relation to this.

أما الأول: فمعروفٌ أنه ضابط.

As for the first example, it is a known fact that he is precise.

أما الثاني: وهو كثير النسيان فليس بضابط، ولكن يجب عليه تعاهد ما تحمله أكثر مما يجب على الأول، لأنه إذا لم يتعاهده فسوف يُنسى ويضيع.

As for the second, i.e. the excessively forgetful, he is not considered as being precise. However, it is obligatory upon him to safeguard the narrations he hears more than the aforementioned type [of narrator]. This is because, if he does not safeguard them (e.g. by writing them etc), the [knowledge] will be forgotten and lost in the long run.

فإن قال قائل هل للنسيان من علاج أو دواء؟

If someone were to ask if there is a cure or treatment for forgetfulness?

قلنا: نعم له دواء - بفضل الله - وهي الكتابة، ولهذا امتن الله عز وجل على عباده بها فقال: ﴿اقْرَأْ بِاسْمِ رَبِّكَ الَّذِى خَلَقَ ۝١ خَلَقَ الْإِنْسَانَ مِنْ عَلَقٍ ۝٢ اقْرَأْ وَرَبُّكَ الْأَكْرَمُ ۝٣ الَّذِى عَلَّمَ بِالْقَلَمِ﴾ [العلق: ١ - ٤]. فقال (اقرأ) ثم قال: ﴿الَّذِى عَلَّمَ بِالْقَلَمِ﴾ يعني اقرأ من حفظك، فإن لم يكن فمن قلمك، فالله تبارك وتعالى بين لنا كيف نداوي هذه العلة، وهي علة النسيان وذلك بأن نداويها بالكتابة، والآن أصبحت الكتابة أدقُّ من الأول، لأنه وجد - بحمد الله - الآن المسجِّل.

We would reply: Yes. There is a cure for it with Allāh's Grace and it is writing. Due to this, Allāh ﷻ favoured His slaves with it and He said in the ayah: **{Recite in the name of your Lord who created. [Who] created man from a clinging substance. Recite, and your Lord is the most Generous. Who taught by the pen.}**[17] Indeed He said "Recite", and later He said, "Who taught by the pen" i.e. recite from your memory or otherwise from your writing. As such, Allāh ﷻ taught us how to cure this ailment, which is the ailment of forgetfulness, by treating it with writing. And now, penning knowledge down has become a more precise means of retention than before because we have audio recordings,[18] all praise to Allāh.

وقوله: (عن مثله).

The author's phrase, "From his like":

أي أنه لابد أن يكون الراوي متصفاً بالعدالة والضبط، ويرويه عمن اتصف بالعدالة والضبط.

This means that the narrator, who is described as having integrity and precision, has to narrate from someone who is also described as having *'adālah* and *ḍabṭ*.

فلو روى عدل عن فاسق، فلا يكون حديثه صحيحاً، وكذا إذا روى إنسان عدل جيد الحفظ، عن رجل سيء الحفظ، كثير النسيان، فإن حديثه لا يقبل، ولا يكون صحيحاً، لأنه لم يروه عن رجل ضابط مثله.

If the just narrator narrated from a sinner, his narration is not considered as *ṣaḥīḥ*. Likewise, if a person who is just and strong in memorisation were to narrate from another narrator who has poor memorisation and is very forgetful, his narration would not be accepted or considered as *ṣaḥīḥ,* as he did not narrate from someone precise like him.

17 Al-'Alaq: 1-4

18 [T] An example of this is the *shaykh* himself; his lectures were recorded and they continue to be transcribed into books to the current day.

مباحث الحديث

RESEARCH TOPICS OF ḤADĪTH

المبحث الأول:

First topic:

تنقسم الأخبار المنقولة إلينا إلى ثلاثة أقسم:

The *akhbār* (statements) that were transmitted to us are categorised into three types:

١ - الحديث: وهو يختص بما أُضيف إلى النبي صلى الله عليه وسلّم.

One. *Al-Ḥadīth*: It is specific to what was attributed to the Prophet ﷺ.

٢ - الأثر: وهو يختص بما أضيف إلى من دونه، من الصحابة، أو التابعين، أو من بعدهم.

Two. *Al-Athar*: It is specific to what was attributed to other than him, such as the companions, the *tābiʿīn* or those who came after them.

٣ - الخبر: وهو يعم الحديث والأثر.

Three. *Al-Khabar*: It includes the *ḥadīth* and *athar*.

ولا يطلق الأثر على المرفوع للنبي صلى الله عليه وسلّم إلا مقيَّداً، مثل أن يقال: وفي الأثر عن النبي صلى الله عليه وسلّم، أما عند الإطلاق فهو ما أُضيف إلى الصحابي فمن دونه.

And the *athar* is not taken as *marfūʿ* (raised) to the Prophet ﷺ unless it is specifically attributed to him (lit. it is qualified [as so]) e.g. by saying that the *athar* is from the Prophet ﷺ. However when unqualified, the *athar* is something attributed to a companion or someone from the later generations.

المبحث الثاني:

Second topic:

أحوال التلقي ثلاثة:

The three states of *talaqqī* (reception):

١ - أن يصِّرح بالسماع منه.

One. Proclamation that the narrator heard from the teacher.

٢ - أن يثبت لُقيّهُ به دون السماع منه.

Two. Confirmation of the meeting between the two without one hearing from the other.

٣ - أن يكون معاصراً له ولكن لم يثبت أنه لقيه.

Three. Both were contemporaries, but it is not confirmed that one met the other.

فأما إذا ثبت السماع منه فقال: سمعت فلاناً أو حدثني فلان، فالاتصال واضح.

As for the confirmation of hearing directly from the teacher, it is to say, "I heard from so-and-so" or, "So-and-so told me." Hence the connection is clear.

أما إذا ثبت اللقي دون السماع فقال الراوي: قال فلان كذا وكذا، أو عن فلان كذا وكذا، ولم يقل سمعتُ أو حدثني، لكن قد ثبتت الملاقاة بينهما فهنا يكون متصلاً، أيضاً؛ لأنه مادام أن الراوي عدلٌ، فإنه لا ينسب إلى أحدٍ كلاماً إلا ما قد سمعه منه، هذا هو الأصل.

As for the confirmation of the meeting without the hearing, where the narrator said, "So-and-so said such-and-such" or "On the authority of so-and-so." He does not say "I heard" or "He told me" but the meeting between the two is confirmed. Hence, the narration is considered to be connected as long as the narrator has integrity, for he would not have attributed a saying to anyone except that he would have heard it from him and this is the root principle.

وإذا كان معاصراً له، لكنه لم يثبت أنه لقيه فهل يُحمل الحديث على الاتصال؟

And if he lived in the same era but it is not confirmed that he met the narrator above him in the chain, is the *ḥadīth* taken as connected?

قال البخاري - رحمه الله -: لا يحمل على الاتصال، حتى يثبت أنه لاقاه.

Al-Bukhārī said, "It is not considered as connected until it is confirmed that he met him."

وقال مسلم - رحمه الله -: بل يحمل على الاتصال؛ لأنه مادام أنه معاصٌر له ونسب الحديث إليه فالأصل أنه سمعه منه.

And Muslim said, "It is regarded as being connected, for so long as he lived in the same era as him and attributed the narration to him, then the root rule is that he heard it from him."

ولكن قول البخاري أصحُّ، وهو أنه لابد أن يثبت أن الراوي قد لقي من روى عنه.

However, al-Bukhārī's opinion that it is a must to confirm that the narrator met whom he narrated from is the stronger of the two.

ولهذا كان صحيح البخاري أصح من صحيح مسلم، لأن البخاري يشترط الملاقاة، أما مسلم فلا يشترطها.

Due to this reason, *Ṣaḥīḥ al-Bukhārī* is taken to be sounder than *Ṣaḥīḥ Muslim,* as al-Bukhārī made the meeting between narrators as a requirement whereas Muslim did not take it into account.

وذهب بعض العلماء الذين يتشددون في نقل الحديث، إلى أنه لابد من ثبوت السماع، لأنه ربما يلاقيه ولا يسمع منه، وهذا لا شك أنه أقوى، لكننا لو اشترطنا السماع لفات علينا الكثير من السنة الصحيحة.

And some of the scholars who were strict in the transmission of *ḥadīth* said that it is a necessity to confirm the hearing because the narrator may have met the one he narrated from but did not hear from him. Definitely this requirement is even stronger. However, if we take the hearing as a prerequisite, we would have missed out on a significant amount of the authentic Sunnah.

وما هو أصحُّ كتب السنة؟

Which is the most authentic of all the books of the Sunnah?

وما هو أصحُّ الصحيح؟

And which is the most authentic of the *ṣaḥīḥ*?

نقول: الأحاديث التي اتفق عليها البخاري ومسلم، تعتبر أصح الأحاديث، فمثلاً في بلوغ المرام يقول الحافظ عقب الحديث: متفق عليه، يعني رواه البخاري ومسلم.

We say that the *aḥadīth* (plural of *ḥadīth*) that al-Bukhārī and Muslim agreed upon are considered as the most authentic *aḥadīth*. For example, al-Ḥāfiẓ [Ibn Ḥajar] said after a *ḥadīth* in *Bulūgh al-Marām*, "*Muttafaqun 'alayhi* (agreed upon)" i.e. it was reported by al-Bukhārī and Muslim.

ثم ما انفرد به البخاري، لأن شرط البخاري أقوى من شرط مسلم، وهو ثبوت اللقاء بين الراوي ومن روى عنه، بخلاف مسلم الذي اشترط المعاصرة دون الملاقاة، فكان شرط البخاري أشد وأقوى، فلذلك قالوا: إن صحيح البخاري أصحُّ من صحيح مسلم.

This is followed by what al-Bukhārī reported, as his stipulation was stronger than that of Muslim, which is the confirmation of the meeting between the narrator and the one he narrated from. This is contrary to Muslim, who regarded the existence of the two in the same era as sufficient, without having to confirm the meeting. As such, al-Bukhārī's criterion is stronger and more rigorous. Therefore the scholars say that *Ṣaḥīḥ al-Bukhārī* is more authentic than *Ṣaḥīḥ Muslim*.

قال الناظم:

The composer of the poem said:

تَشاجَرَ قومٌ في البُخاريِّ ومُسلِمٍ   لَدَيَّ وَقالوا: أَيّ ذَينِ تَقَدَّمُ

فَقُلتُ لَقَدْ فاقَ البُخاريُّ صِحَّةً   كَما فاقَ في حُسْنِ الصِناعَةِ مُسْلِمُ

The people quarrel regarding al-Bukhārī and Muslim,
In my presence, and they said: Which of the two precedes?

So I answered: Indeed al-Bukhārī outshines in terms of soundness,
Just like Muslim excelled in terms of crafting excellence.[19]

يعني أن مسلماً في الترتيب، وسياق طرق الحديث، أحسن من البخاري، لكن من حيث الصحة فالبخاري يفوق مسلماً.

He meant that Muslim's arrangement and sequence of the routes of *ḥadīth* is better than that of al-Bukhārī, but in terms of soundness, al-Bukhārī outshines Muslim.

ونحن في بحث الحديث يهمنا الصحة أكثر مما يهمنا التنسيق وحسن الصناعة.

And in the science of *ḥadīth*, we are more concerned with soundness than the arrangement and quality craftsmanship.

19 [T] Reported by 'Abd al-Qādir ibn 'Abdullāh al-Aydarūs in his book *al-Nūr al-Sāfir 'An Akhbār al-Qarn al-'Āshir* Volume 1, page 143 and he attributed the lines to al-Ḥāfiẓ 'Abd al-Raḥmān ibn 'Alī al-Daybaʿī.

فمراتب الأحاديث سبعة وهي:

Thus, there are seven ranks of *aḥadīth*:

١ - ما اتفق عليه البخاري ومسلم.

One. What al-Bukhārī and Muslim agreed upon.

٢ - ما انفرد به البخاري.

Two. What is reported by al-Bukhārī alone.

٣ - ما انفرد به مسلم.

Three. What is reported by Muslim alone.

٤ - ما كان على شرطهما. وأحياناً يعبرون بقولهم: على شرط الصحيحين، أو على شرط البخاري ومسلم.

Four. What is upon the conditions of both scholars. Sometimes it is also referred to as being upon the conditions of the *Ṣaḥīḥayn* or the conditions of al-Bukhārī and Muslim.

٥ - ما كان على شرط البخاري.

Five. What is upon al-Bukhārī's conditions.

٦ - ما كان على شرط مسلم.

Six. What is upon Muslim's conditions.

٧ - ما كان على شرط غيرهما.

Seven. What is upon the conditions of other than the two.

المبحث الثالث:

Third topic:

هل جميع ما اتفق عليه البخاري ومسلم صحيح؟

Are all that were agreed upon by al-Bukhārī and Muslim considered as *ṣaḥīḥ*?

بمعنى أننا لا نبحث عن رواته ولا نسأل عن متونه أم لا؟

Does this mean that we need not scrutinise the narrators and ask about the text or not?

نقول: أكثر العلماء يقولون: إن ما فيهما صحيح، مفيدٌ للعلم، لأن الأمة تلقتهما بالقبول، والأمة معصومة من الخطأ، وهذا رأي ابن الصلاح، وأظنه رأي شيخ الإسلام ابن تيمية وتلميذه ابن القيم رحمه الله.

We say: Most scholars are in agreement that the narrations found in both compilations are considered as *ṣaḥīḥ* and provide knowledge, as the Ummah (Muslim nation) acknowledged them with acceptance and our Ummah is safeguarded from making mistakes. This is the opinion of Ibn al-Ṣalāḥ and I believe it is the opinion of Shaykh al-Islām Ibn Taymiyyah and his student Ibn al-Qayyim.

وأما ما انفرد به أحدهما: فإنه صحيح، لكنه ليس كما اتفقا عليه، ولهذا انُتقدَ على البخاري بعض الأحاديث، وانتقد على مسلم أكثر، وأجاب الحفاظ عن هذا الانتقاد بوجهين:

As for the narration that is reported by either one, it is taken as authentic; however it is lesser in degree than the ones that are agreed upon. As such, some of al-Bukhārī's narrations were criticised, and a greater number of Muslim's narrations were scrutinised likewise. Al-Ḥāfiẓ [Ibn Ḥajar] replied to such criticisms from two perspectives:

الوجه الأول: أن هذا الانتقاد يعارضه قول البخاري، أي أن المنتقد على البخاري، يعارضه قول البخاري، والبخاري إمامٌ حافظ، فيكون مقدَّماً على من بعده ممن

انتقده، وكما هي العادة أنه إذا تعارض قولان لأهل العلم، فإننا نأخذ بالأرجح.

The first perspective: The criticisms contradict the view of al-Bukhārī i.e. the critics of al-Bukhārī went against al-Bukhārī's opinion while al-Bukhārī is an *imām* amongst the *ḥadīth* masters. Thus his view is given precedence over the rest who came after him, including his critics. Moreover, if there are two contradicting opinions from the people of knowledge, normally we take the preponderant opinion.

فيقولون: البخاري إمام حافظ في الحديث، فإذا جاء من بعده، وقال هذا الحديث ليس بصحيح، والبخاري قد صححه، ووضعه في صحيحه، والبخاري أحفظ من هذا المنتقد، وأعلمُ منه، فقوله هذا يتعارض مع قول البخاري، وهذا الجواب مجمل.

Therefore it is said that al-Bukhārī is a leading custodian of *ḥadīth*, and if someone were to come and say that a particular *ḥadīth* is not *ṣaḥīḥ* whereas al-Bukhārī already regarded it as such and reported it in his collection, if al-Bukhārī is more proficient and more knowledgeable in the science of *ḥadīth* than the critic, then we view the criticism as contradictory to al-Bukhārī's opinion. This is the answer in general.

أما الجواب المفصل فهو في:

As for the elaborated answer, it is:

الوجه الثاني: أن أهل العلم تصدوا لمن انتقد على البخاري ومسلم، وردوا عليه حديثاً حديثاً، وبهذا يزول الانتقاد على البخاري ومسلم، لكنه لا شك أنه قد يقع الوهم من بعض الرواة، في البخاري ومسلم، لكن هذا لا يقدح في نقل البخاري ومسلم له، لأن الوهم لا يكاد يسلم منه أحد، وليس من شرط عدالة الراوي أن لا يخطئ أبداً، لأن هذا غير موجود.

The second perspective: The scholars refuted those who criticised al-Bukhārī and Muslim, and they refuted the criticism of each and every *ḥadīth*. With this, the objections upon al-Bukhārī and Muslim were removed. However, there is no doubt that misconceptions may arise from the narrators of al-Bukhārī and Muslim, but this does not depreciate the transmissions from al-Bukhārī and Muslim. The reason is that no one can free himself from misconceptions and it is never a criterion of the narrator's integrity that he be completely free of mistakes as such a person never existed in the first place.

المتن

٥ - وَالْحَسَنُ الْمَعْرُوفُ طُرْقاً وَغَدَتْ   رِجَالُهُ لاَ كَالصَّحِيحِ اشْتَهَرَتْ

(5) Al-ḥasan is the one known in its chains but,
Whose transmitters are not as famous as the ṣaḥīḥ.

الشرح

انتقل المؤلف إلى تعريف الحسن، والحسن في المنظومة هو: القسم الثاني من أقسام الحديث.

The author has now moved on to the definition of *al-ḥasan* (the fair *ḥadīth*). And *al-ḥasan* in the poem refers to the second category of *ḥadīth*.

ويقول في تعريفه (المعروف طرقاً) يعني المعروفة طرقه، بحيث يكون معلوماً أن هذا الراوي يروي عن أهل البصرة، وهذا عن أهل الكوفة، وهذا عن أهل الشام، وهذا عن أهل مصر، وهذا عن أهل الحجاز، وما أشبه ذلك.

He says in his definition, "the one known in its chains," which means that the routes of the *ḥadīth* are known in such a way that it is known that a narrator reports from the people of Basra, another narrates from the people of Kufa, while another reports from the people of Greater Syria, and another from the people of Egypt, and another from the people of the Hejaz (the western strip of the Arabian Peninsula) etc.

قوله: (وغدت رجاله لا كالصحيح) يعني أن رجاله أخف من رجال الصحيح، ولهذا قال (لا كالصحيح اشتهرت) إذاً يختلف الحسن عن الصحيح، بأن رجاله ليسوا كرجال الحديث الصحيح، والمراد أنهم ليسوا كرجال الحديث الصحيح في الضبط.

The phrase, "But whose transmitters are not as famous as the *ṣaḥīḥ*" means that the narrators of the *ḥasan ḥadīth* are lesser [in standing] than those of the *ṣaḥīḥ ḥadīth*. Thus the *ḥasan* differs from the *ṣaḥīḥ* in such a way that the narrators of the *ḥasan* do not match the narrators of the *ṣaḥīḥ*. And what is meant by them not matching the narrators of the *ṣaḥīḥ ḥadīth* is in terms of precision.

ولهذا قال العلماء المتأخرون الذين بسطوا هذا الفن، كالحافظ ابن حجر رحمه الله: إن الفرق بين الحديث الصحيح والحديث الحسن، فرق واحد وهو بدل أن تقول في الصحيح تامُّ الضبط، قل في الحسن: خفيف الضبط، وإلا فبقية الشروط الموجودة في الصحيح موجودة في الحسن.

Due to this, the scholars of later generations who expanded this science such as al-Ḥāfiẓ Ibn Ḥajar said that the difference between the *ṣaḥīḥ ḥadīth* and the *ḥasan ḥadīth* is only one: Which is to say that we find "light in precision" in the *ḥasan* contrary to "complete in precision" in the *ṣaḥīḥ*. Other than this, the conditions in the *ṣaḥīḥ* are present in the *ḥasan* narrations.

وعلى هذا فتعريف الحسن هو: ما رواه عدلٌ، خفيف الضبط، بسند متصل، وخلا من الشذوذ، والعلة القادحة.

Upon this, we can say that the definition of the *ḥasan ḥadīth* is: What is narrated by one who has integrity and lesser precision in a connected chain whilst being free from contradiction and dispraise worthy defects.

المتن

٦ - وَكُلُّ مَا عَنْ رُتْبَةِ الْحُسْنِ قَصُرْ فَهْوَ الضَّعِيفُ وَهْوَ أَقْسَاماً كَثُرْ

(6) All that falls below the rank of ḥasan,
Is thus ḍaʿīf and it has many categories.

الشرح

الحديث الضعيف هو القسم الثالث في النظم، وهو: ما خلا عن رتبة الحديث الحسن.

The *ḍaʿīf* (weak) narration is the third category mentioned in the poem. It is the narration that falls short of the rank of *al-ḥasan*.

ومعلوم أنه إذا خلا عن رتبة الحديث الحسن، فقد خلا عن رتبة الصحة، وحينئذ نقول: الحديث الضعيف: ما لم تتوافر فيه شروط الصحة والُحسن، أي ما لم يكن صحيحاً ولا حسناً، فلو رواه شخص عدل لكن ضبطه ضعيف، وليس بخفيف الضبط، فإن هذا الحديث يكون ضعيفاً، وإذا رواه بسند منقطع يكون ضعيفاً أيضاً؛ وهلمَّ جرّا.

It is also understood that anything lower than the rank of *ḥasan* will also fall short of *ṣaḥīḥ* narrations. As such, we say that *ḍaʿīf* narrations are those that do not meet the requirements of the *ṣaḥīḥ* and *ḥasan* i.e. they are neither *ṣaḥīḥ* nor *ḥasan*. If a person narrated a *ḥadīth* and he is of integrity but his level of precision is weak and not "light", then the *ḥadīth* is regarded as *ḍaʿīf*. And if the chain of narration is disconnected, the narration is also considered as weak and so forth.

وقد ذكر المؤلف الآن ثلاثة أقسام من أقسام الحديث وهي: (١) الصحيح. (٢) الحسن. (٣) الضعيف.

At this point, the author has mentioned three categories of *ḥadīth* and they are: (i) *Al-ṣaḥīḥ* (authentic), (ii) *al-ḥasan* (fair), (iii) *al-ḍaʿīf* (weak).

لكن الواقع أن الأقسام خمسة على ما حرره ابن حجر وغيره: (١) الصحيح لذاته.
(٢) الصحيح لغيره. (٣) الحسن لذاته. (٤) الحسن لغيره. (٥) الضعيف.

However, in reality, there are five categories, as stated by Ibn Ḥajar and others: (i) *Al-ṣaḥīḥ li dhātihi* (authentic in of itself), (ii) *al-ṣaḥīḥ li ghayrihi* (authentic due to others), (iii) *al-ḥasan li dhātihi* (fair in of itself), (iv) *al-ḥasan li ghayrihi* (fair due to others), and (v) *al-ḍaʿīf* (weak).

فالصحيح لذاته: هو ما تقدم تعريفه.

As for *al-ṣaḥīḥ li dhātihi*, its definition is as we mentioned earlier.

والصحيح لغيره: هو الحسن إذا تعددت طرقه، وسُمي صحيحاً لغيره؛ لأنه إنما وصل إلى درجة الصحة من أجل تعدد الطرق.

As for *al-ṣaḥīḥ li ghayrihi*, it is a *ḥasan ḥadīth* which has numerous routes of transmission. It is termed as *ṣaḥīḥ* due to others because it only reached the level of *ṣaḥīḥ* due to its numerous routes.

فمثلاً: إذا جاءنا حديث له أربعة أسانيد، وكل إسناد منه فيه راوي خفيف الضبط، فنقول: الآن يصل إلى درجة الصحة، وصار صحيحاً لغيره.

For example, if we have a *ḥadīth* with four *asānīd* (plural of *sanad*), and each route has a narrator who is fair (lit. light) in terms of precision, then we say that now the *ḥadīth* reaches the level of *ṣaḥīḥ*, and becomes *ṣaḥīḥ li ghayrihi.*

أما الحسن لذاته: فقد تقدم تعريفه وهو ما رواه عدل خفيف الضبط، بسند متصل، وخلا من الشذوذ، والعلة القادحة.

As for *al-ḥasan li dhātihi*, its definition is as mentioned earlier, i.e. what is narrated by a just narrator with fair precision in a connected chain, and free from contradiction and dispraise worthy defects.

وأما الحسن لغيره: فهو الضعيف إذا تعددت طرقه، على وجه يجبر بعضها بعضاً، فإنه يكون حسناً لغيره، لماذا؟

Regarding *al-ḥasan li ghayrihi*, it is the weak *ḥadīth* of which its routes are numerous in such a way that each one patches up the other, hence it becomes fair due to others. Why?

لأننا لو نظرنا إلى كل إسناد على انفراده لم يصل إلى درجة الحسن، لكن باجتماع بعضها إلى بعض صار حسناً.

This is because, if we look at every *isnad* individually, it does not reach the rank of *al-ḥasan*, but collectively taken together, it becomes *ḥasan*.

أما الضعيف فهو: ما ليس بصحيح ولا حسن.

As for *al-ḍaʿīf*; it refers to that which is neither *ṣaḥīḥ* nor *ḥasan*.

وجميع هذه الأقسام مقبولة ما عدا الضعيف، وكلها حُجة ما عدا الضعيف.

All the types of *ḥadīth* are acceptable except the *ḍaʿīf* narrations, and all are valid evidences except the *ḍaʿīf*.

وجميع هذه الأقسام يجوز نقله للناس والتحديث بها؛ لأنها كلها مقبولة، وحجة، ما عدا الضعيف، فلا يجوز نقله، أو التحدث به، إلا مبيناً ضعفه، لأن الذي ينقل الحديث الضعيف، بدون أن يبين ضعفه للناس، فهو أحد الكاذبين على النبي صلى الله عليه وسلّم، لما روى مسلم في صحيحه أن النبي صلى الله عليه وسلّم قال: ((من حدث عني بحديث، يرى أنه كذب، فهو أحد الكاذبين)). وفي حديث آخر: ((من كذب عليّ متعمداً فليتبوأ مقعده من النار)).

And it is permissible for people to transmit and report all these categories of the *ḥadīth* as they are acceptable and taken as valid evidences except the *ḍaʿīf*, which is not allowed to be transmitted or reported unless it is mentioned clearly that it is weak. This is due to the fact that when one narrates a weak *ḥadīth* and does not declare its weakness to the people, he is considered as one of the liars who lied about the Prophet ﷺ, as reported by Muslim in his *Ṣaḥīḥ* that the Prophet ﷺ said, "If someone narrated from me a *ḥadīth* and he knew it was a lie, then he is one of the liars,"[20] and in another narration, "Whoever deliberately lied upon me, let him take his place in the Hellfire."[21]

إذاً فلا تجوز رواية الحديث الضعيف إلا بشرط واحد وهو أن يبين ضعفه للناس، فمثلاً إذا روى حديثاً ضعيفاً قال: رُوي عن النبي صلى الله عليه وسلّم هذا الحديث وهو ضعيف.

Therefore, the narration of weak *ḥadīth* is not permissible except with one condition, which is that its weakness is announced to the people. For example, if someone narrates a *ḍaʿīf* narration, he is to say, "This *ḥadīth* was narrated from the Prophet ﷺ and it is *ḍaʿīf*."

واستثنى بعض العلماء الأحاديث التي تُروى في الترغيب والترهيب، فأجازوا رواية الضعيف منها لكن بأربعة شروط:

Some scholars made exceptions to the *aḥādīth* that were narrated for the sake of *al-targhīb* (enticements) and *al-tarhīb* (warning). So they allowed the narration of weak *ḥadīth* but with four conditions:

١ - أن يكون الحديث في الترغيب والترهيب.

(i) The *ḥadīth* has to be for *al-targhīb* or *al-tarhīb*.

٢ - ألا يكون الضعيف شديداً، فإن كان شديداً فلا تجوز روايته، ولو كان في

20 Recorded by Muslim in the introduction; Chapter: The obligation of narrating from the reliable and leaving the liars (1).

21 Recorded by al-Bukhārī; The book of funerals; Chapter: What was disliked of mourning (1291) (105), and Muslim in the introduction; Chapter; The harsh warning against lying upon the Messenger of Allāh (3-3).

الترغيب والترهيب.

(ii) The narration must not be extremely weak. If it is extremely weak, then it is not permissible to narrate it, even for the sake of enticing or warning.

٣ - أن يكون الحديث له أصل صحيح ثابت في الكتاب أو السنة، مثاله: لو جاءنا حديث يرغِّب في بر الوالدين، وحديث آخر يرغب في صلاة الجماعة، وآخر يُرغب في قراءة القرآن وكلها أحاديث ضعيفة، ولكن قد ورد في بر الوالدين، وفي صلاة الجماعة، وفي قراءة القرآن أحاديث صحيحة ثابتة في الكتاب والسنة.

(iii) The *ḥadīth* must have a correct origin that is confirmed from the Qur'ān or the Sunnah. For example, if we come across a weak *ḥadīth* that encourages dutifulness to parents, another weak *ḥadīth* that encourages congregational prayers, and another that encourages reciting the Qur'ān. They are all weak, but there are authentic narrations confirmed in the Qur'ān and the *Sunnah* which convey the same meaning regarding these subjects.

٤ - ألا يعتقد أن النبي صلى الله عليه وسلّم قاله، لأنه لا يجوز أن يعتقد أن النبي صلى الله عليه وسلّم قال حديثاً إلا إذا كان قد صح عنه ذلك.

(iv) One should not believe that the Prophet ﷺ said it because it is not permissible to believe that he ﷺ said a *ḥadīth* except that it is confirmed to have been narrated from him.

ولكن الذي يظهر لي: أن الحديث الضعيف لا تجوز روايته، إلا مبيناً ضعفه مطلقاً، لاسيما بين العامة، لأن العامة متى ما قلت لهم حديثاً، فإنهم سوف يعتقدون أنه حديث صحيح، وأن النبي صلى الله عليه وسلّم قاله.

However, it seems to me that it is not permissible to narrate a weak *ḥadīth* except to make clear of its weakness in all circumstances, especially to the public. This is because whenever you narrate to the common people a *ḥadīth*, they will believe that the *ḥadīth* is *ṣaḥīḥ* and that the Prophet ﷺ said it.

ولهذا من القواعد المقررة عندهم هو: أن ما قيل في المحراب فهو صواب وهذه القاعدة مقررة عند العامة، فلو تأتي لهم بأكذب حديث على وجه الأرض لصدقوك، ولهذا فالعامة سيصدقونك حتى لو بينت لهم ضعفه، لاسيما في الترغيب والترهيب، فإن العامي لو سمع أي حديث لَحفِظَهُ دون الانتباه لدرجته وصحته.

As such, one of the principles that is established amongst them is that whatever is said at the pulpit is taken to be correct. And this principle is affirmed among the members of the public. As such, they would believe in you even if you were to present to them the most fabricated narration on the surface of the earth. Due to this, the commoner would believe in you even if you told them that the *ḥadīth* is *ḍaʿīf*, especially in the subject of *al-targhīb* and *al-tarhīb,* as he would memorise any *ḥadīth* that he heard without paying attention to its ranking or soundness.

والحمد لله فإن في القرآن الكريم والسنة النبوية المطهرة الصحيحة، ما يغني عن هذه الأحاديث.

Furthermore, there are sufficient evidences from the Noble Qurʾān and the pure and authentic prophetic traditions that can be used instead of these narrations.

والغريب أن بعض الوضّاعين الذين يكذبون على رسول الله صلى الله عليه وسلّم وضعوا أحاديث النبي صلى الله عليه وسلّم في حثِّ الناس على التمسك بالسنة، وقالوا: إننا لم نكذب على الرسول صلى الله عليه وسلّم، وإنما كذبنا له، والرسول صلى الله عليه وسلّم يقول: ((من كذب عليّ فليتبوأ مقعده من النار)) أما نحن فقد كذبنا له، وهذا تحريف للكلم عن مواضعه، لأنك نسبت إلى الرسول صلى الله عليه وسلّم ما لم يقله، وهذا هو الكذب عليه صراحة، وفي السنة الصحيحة غنى عما كذبت عليه.

And it is strange that some of the fabricators of *ḥadīth* who lied upon the Messenger of Allāh ﷺ fabricated Prophet narrations to encourage the people to hold firmly onto the Sunnah and said, "We did not lie upon the Messenger ﷺ. Rather we fabricated for him. The Messenger ﷺ said, 'Whoever deliberately lies upon me, let him take his place in the Hellfire.'[22] As for us, we fabricated for him and not upon him." This is a distortion of words from their proper usage, because they attribute to the Messenger ﷺ what he did not say, and this is clear falsification against him, despite there being other evidences from the authentic Sunnah that could take the place of what they lied upon him.

المتن

٧ - وَمَا أُضِيفَ لِلنَّبِي (الْمَرْفُوع)　　وَمَا لِتَابِعٍ هُوَ (الْمَقْطُوعُ)

(7) What was attributed to the Prophet is known as al-marfū',
While the one to a tābi'i is known as al-maqṭū'.

الشرح

ذكر المؤلف رحمه الله نوعين من أنواع الحديث وهما (المرفوع - والمقطوع) وهما القسم الرابع والخامس مما ذكر في النظم.

The author mentions another two types of *ḥadīth,* and they are *al-marfū'* (raised) and *al-maqṭū'* (disconnected). These two are the fourth and fifth categories mentioned in the poem.

ونقول: إن الحديث باعتبار من أسند إليه ينقسم إلى ثلاثة أقسام:

We say that the *ḥadīth* are categorised into three types with regards to whom they are attributed to:

١ - المرفوع.

22 Mentioned previously.

1. *Al-marfū‘* (raised).

٢ - الموقوف، ولم يذكره الناظم هنا وسيذكره فيما بعد.

2. *Al-mawqūf* (stopped), and the author does not make mention about it here, but it shall be discussed later.[23]

٣ - المقطوع.

3. *Al-maqṭū‘* (severed).

وتختلف هذه الثلاثة باختلاف منتهى السند.

And these three categories differ from one another via differences in the end point of the chain:

فما انتهى سنده إلى النبي صلى الله عليه وسلّم فهو المرفوع.

When the chain ends at the Prophet ﷺ, it is *marfū‘*.

وما انتهى إلى الصحابي فهو الموقوف.

When the chain ends at a companion, it is *al-mawqūf*.

وما انتهى إلى من بعده فهو المقطوع. والمقطوع غير المنقطع كما سيأتي.

Anything else that ends after the companions is regarded as *al-maqṭū‘*. It is important to note that *al-maqṭū‘* is different to *al-munqaṭi‘*, which will be discussed later.

فالمرفوع هو: ما أضيف إلى النبي صلى الله عليه وسلّم من قول، أو فعل، أو تقرير.

The definition of *al-marfū‘* is the speech, action or tacit approval attributed to the Prophet ﷺ.

23 Mentioned previously.

مثال القول: قوله صلى الله عليه وسلّم: ((إنما الأعمال بالنيات وإنما لكل امرئ ما نوى)). فهذا مرفوعٌ من القول.

For example; the Prophet ﷺ said, "Verily actions are according to intentions, and everyone will receive what was intended."[24] This is an example of speech which is *marfū'*.

ومثال الفعل: توضأ النبي صلى الله عليه وسلّم فمسح على خفيه. وهذا مرفوع من الفعل.

As for the example of an action, the Prophet ﷺ used to make ablution and he wiped over his leather socks. This is an example of an action which is *marfū'*.

ومثال التقرير: قوله صلى الله عليه وسلّم للجارية: ((أين الله؟)) قالت: في السماء. فأقرّها على ذلك، وهذا مرفوع من التقرير.

And an example of an approval is when he ﷺ asked a slave girl, "Where is Allāh?" She replied, "In the sky" and he approved of this.[25] This is an example of a tacit approval which is *marfū'*.

وهل ما فُعل في وقته، أو قيل في وقته، يكون مرفوعاً؟

Is everything that was done or said in the Prophet's time considered as *marfū'*?

نقول: إن علم به فهو مرفوع؛ لأنه يكون قد أقر ذلك، وإن لم يعلم به فليس بمرفوع؛ لأنه لم يُضف إليه، ولكنه حُجة على القول الصحيح، ووجه كونه حُجة إقرار الله إيَّاه.

---

24 Recorded by al-Bukhārī; The Book of Revelations; Chapter: How revelations started (1) and Muslim; The Book of Leadership; Chapter: Verily actions are according to intentions (1907).

25 Recorded by Muslim; The Book of Mosques; Chapter: The forbidding of talking during prayer 33 (537).

We say: If the Prophet knew about it, then it is taken to be *marfūʿ*, because he approved it. If it is not known to be as such, then it is not considered as *marfūʿ* because it is not attributed to him. However, the correct opinion is that this is taken to be valid evidence due to the fact that Allāh approved it.

والدليل على هذا: أن الصحابة - رضوان الله عليهم - احتجوا بإقرار الله لهم في بعض ما يفعلونه، ولم ينكر عليهم ذلك، كما قال جابر - رضي الله عنه -: (كنا نعزل والقرآن ينزل)، وكان القرآن ينزل في عهد النبي صلى الله عليه وسلّم وكأنهم يقولون: لو كان هذا الفعل حراماً، لنهى الله عنه في كتابه، أو أوحى إلى رسوله صلى الله عليه وسلّم بذلك، لأن الله لا يقرّ الحرام.

The proof for this is that the companions took Allāh's consent upon some of their actions as evidence, as the actions were not objected to. For example, Jābir ﷺ said, "We practised coitus interruptus while the Qur'ān was being revealed."[26] The Qur'ān was revealed during the lifetime of the Prophet ﷺ and it is as though they said, "If this practice was forbidden, Allāh would have prohibited it in His Book or revealed to the Prophet ﷺ about its prohibition because Allāh would not approve of the forbidden."

والدليل على ذلك قوله تعالى: ﴿يَسْتَخْفُونَ مِنَ النَّاسِ وَلاَ يَسْتَخْفُونَ مِنَ اللهِ وَهُوَ مَعَهُمْ إِذْ يُبَيِّتُونَ مَا لاَ يَرْضَى مِنَ الْقَوْلِ﴾ [النساء: ١٠٨] . فهؤلاء الذين بيّتوا ما لا يرضاه الله تعالى، من القول، قد استخفوا عن أعين الناس، ولم يعلم بهم الناس، ولكن لما كان فعلهم غير مرضي عند الله تعالى أنكر الله عليهم ذلك.

And the evidence for this is the ayah: **{They try to hide (their deception) from people, but they can never hide it from Allah—in Whose presence they plot by night what is displeasing to Him.}**[27] As such, those who spent the night in a manner that caused Allāh ﷻ to be displeased with

26 Recorded by al-Bukhārī; The Book of Marriage; Chapter: Coitus interruptus (5208) and Muslim; The Book of Marriage; Chapter: The ruling of coitus interruptus 136 (1440).
27 Al-Nisā': 108

their speech, they had concealed themselves from the eyes of the people and the public did not know about them. But when Allāh was not pleased with their actions, He disapproved of them.

فدلَّ هذا على أن ما فُعل في عهدِ النبي صلى الله عليه وسلَّم ولم ينكره الله تعالى فإنه حُجة، لكننا لا نسمّيه مرفوعاً، وذلك لأنه لا تصحُّ نسبته إلى النبي صلى الله عليه وسلَّم.

Thus, this shows that whatever was done during the time of the Prophet ﷺ and Allāh did not object to it, then it is taken as valid evidence. However, we do not consider it as *marfūʿ* because it is not correct to attribute it to the Prophet ﷺ.

وإنما سُمي المرفوع مرفوعاً لارتفاع مرتبته لأن السند غايته النبي صلى الله عليه وسلَّم فإن هذا أرفع ما يكون مرتبة.

The *marfūʿ* is termed as "raised" due to its high ranking, as at the utmost end of the *sanad* is the Prophet ﷺ. Thus, this is the highest of rankings.

وأما ما أضيف إلى الله تعالى من الحديث فإنه يسمى: الحديث القدسي، أو الحديث الإلهي، أو الحديث الرباني؛ لأنَّ منتهاه إلى رب العالمين عز وجل، والمرفوع منتهاه إلى النبي صلى الله عليه وسلَّم.

As for any narration attributed to Allāh, it is called *al-ḥadīth al-qudsī* (sacred narration), or *al-ḥadīth al-ilāhī* (Divine speech) or *al-ḥadīth al-rabbānī* (Lordly speech). This is due to the fact that the chain of narration ends with the Lord of the worlds, whereas the *marfūʿ* ends with the Prophet ﷺ.

وقوله: (وما لتابعٍ هو المقطوعُ).

The author said: "While the one to a *tābiʿī* is known as *al-maqṭūʿ*."

وهذا هو القسم السابع. والمقطوع هو: ما أضيف إلى التابعي ومن بعده، هكذا

سماه أهل العلم بالحديث.

This is the seventh category. The definition of *al-maqṭūʿ* (severed) is a narration that is attributed to a *tābiʿī* (successor of the companions) or anyone after, and this is how the scholars of *ḥadīth* termed it.

سمي بذلك لأنه: منقطع في الرتبة عن المرفوع، وعن الموقوف.

It is named as such because it is severed below the levels of the *marfūʿ* and the *mawqūf*.

مثل: ما لو نُقل كلام عن الحسن البصري رحمه الله فنقول عنه هذا أثرٌ مقطوع.

An example would be: If a statement was transmitted from al-Ḥasan al-Baṣrī, then we say that this is an *athar maqṭūʿ*.

وما أضيف إلى الصحابي نوعان:

Meanwhile, the narration that is attributed to a companion is classified into two categories.

١ - ما ثبت له حكم الرفع، فإنه يسمى عندهم المرفوع حكماً.

1. The narration that is established as being *marfūʿ*. This is termed *al-marfūʿ ḥukman*.

٢ - وما لم يثبت له حكم الرفع، فإنه يسمى موقوفاً.

2. The narration that is not *marfūʿ*. This is called *al-mawqūf*.

فالآثار التي تروى عن أبي بكر وعمر - رضي الله عنهما - أو عن أي واحد من الصحابة، نسميها موقوفة، وهذا هو الاصطلاح، ولا مشاحة في الاصطلاح، وإلا فإنه من المعلوم أنه يصح أن نقول حتى في المرفوع أنه موقوف، لأنه وقف عند النبي صلى الله عليه وسلّم، لكن هذا اصطلاح ولا مشاحة في الاصطلاح.

As such, the *āthār* (plural of *athar*) that were narrated from Abū Bakr and

'Umar ﵁ or any of the other companions are called *mawqūf*. And this is the terminology and there is no argument in terminology, though it is known that we may call the *marfūʿ* narration *al-mawqūf* due to it stopping at the Prophet ﷺ. However, the aforementioned is the terminology, and there is no argument in *muṣṭalah*.

والعلماء قالوا في الضابط في المرفوع حكماً، هو الذي ليس للاجتهاد، والرأي فيه مجال، وإنما يؤخذ هذا عن الشرع.

The scholars mentioned that the criteria for a narration to be termed *al-marfūʿ ḥukman* is the absence of the possibility for *ijtihād* (independent reasoning) and opinion in the subject matter, and it can only be taken from the Islamic law.

مثل: ما إذا حدَّث الصحابي عن أخبار يوم القيامة، أو الأخبار الغيبية، فإننا نقول فيه: هذا مرفوع حكماً؛ لأنه ليس للاجتهاد فيه مجال، وكذلك لو أن الصحابي فعل عبادة لم ترد بها السنة، لقلنا هذا أيضاً مرفوع حكماً.

For example: If a companion described the events of the Day of Judgement, or tidings of the unseen, then we say that these narrations are *marfūʿ ḥukman*. This is because there is no room for *ijtihād* in it. Likewise if a companion performed an act of worship which was not mentioned in the Sunnah, then we say that this is also *marfūʿ ḥukman*.

ومثَّلوا لذلك بأن علي بن أبي طالب - رضي الله عنه - صلى في صلاة الكسوف، في كل ركعة ثلاث ركوعات، مع أن السنة جاءت بركوعين في كل ركعة، وقالوا: هذا لا مجال للرأي فيه، ولا يمكن فيه اجتهادٌ، لأن عدد الركعات أمرٌ توقيفي يحتاج إلى دليل من الكتاب أو السنة، فلولا أن عند علي بن أبي طالب - رضي الله عنه - علماً بهذا ما صلى ثلاث ركوعات في ركعة واحدة، فهذا مرفوعٌ حكماً؛ لأنه لا مجال للاجتهاد فيه.

The scholars gave an example of when 'Alī ibn Abī Ṭālib ﵁ prayed the *kusūf* (eclipse) prayer and made three *rukū'* (bows) in every unit of prayer,[28] whereas the *Sunnah* came with two *rukū'* in every unit.[29] They said that there is neither room for opinion nor the possibility of *ijtihād* here because the number of bows is *tawqīfī* (restricted by religious text) and requires evidence from the Qur'ān or the Sunnah. As such, if 'Alī ibn Abī Ṭālib ﷺ did not possess this knowledge he would not have made three *rukū'* in one unit. Therefore, this is an example of *al-marfū' ḥukman* as there is no room for *ijtihād* in it.

وكذلك إذا قال الصحابي: من السنة كذا، فإنه مرفوع حكماً؛ لأن الصحابي إذا قال: من السنة، فإنما يعني به سنة الرسول صلى الله عليه وسلّم، كقول ابن عباس - رضي الله عنهما - حين قرأ الفاتحة في صلاة الجنازة وجهر بها، قال: لتعلموا أنها سنة، أو ليعلموا أنها سنة.

And likewise if a companion mentioned that a particular practice is from the Sunnah, then this is also classified as *marfū' ḥukman*. This is because if a companion said that it is from the Sunnah, he meant that it is the practice of the Prophet ﷺ. An example would be the speech of Ibn 'Abbās ﷺ when he recited al-Fātihah loudly during the *janāzah* prayer. He said, "I did this so that you learn that it is from the Sunnah."[30]

وكما قال أنس بن مالك - رضي الله عنه -: من السنة إذا تزوج البكر على الثيب، أقام عندها سبعاً، فهذا وأمثاله يكون من المرفوع حكماً؛ لأن الصحابي لا يُضيف السنة إلا إلى سنة الرسول صلى الله عليه وسلّم.

Similarly, the incident where Anas ibn Mālik ﷺ said that it is from the Sunnah for one to spend seven days with a virgin newlywed if he already has a

28 *Al-Mughnī* 3/328.

29 Recorded by al-Bukhārī; The Book of the Solar Eclipse Prayer; Chapter: The *imām*'s sermon during the solar eclipse (1046), and Muslim; The Book of the Solar Eclipse Prayer; Chapter: The mention of the punishments of the grave during the solar eclipse prayer (8-903).

30 Recorded by al-Bukhārī; The Book of the Deceased; Chapter: Recitation of al-Fātihah (1335).

matron wife.[31] Thus this narration and its likes are considered as *al-marfū' ḥukman* because the companions would not attribute a practice to the Sunnah except if it was truly from the Messenger ﷺ.

وأيضاً لو أخبر أحدٌ من الصحابة عن الجنة والنار لقلنا: هذا مرفوعٌ حكماً، إلا أنه يُشترط في هذا النوع: ألا يكون الصحابي ممن عُرف بكثرة الأخذ عن بني إسرائيل، فإن كان ممن عُرفوا بذلك، فإنه لا يُعتبر له حكم الرفع؛ لاحتمال أن يكون ما نقله عن بني إسرائيل، وهؤلاء كثيرون أمثال: عبد الله بن عمرو بن العاص - رضي الله عنه - فإنه أخذ جملة كبيرة عن كتب أهل الكتاب، في غزوة اليرموك، مما خلَّفه الروم أو غيرهم، لأن في هذا رخصة، فإذا عُرف الصحابي بأنه ينقل عن بني إسرائيل، فإنه لا يكون قوله مرفوعاً حكماً.

And if one of the companions were to describe Paradise and the Hellfire, then we would classify it as *al-marfū' ḥukman*. However, there is one requirement for this type of narration which is that the companion should not be amongst those who were known to take from the narrations of the Children of Israel. If the companion is known to be as such, then his statement is not taken to be *al-marfū' ḥukman*. This is because there is the possibility that the narration came from the Children of Israel. There are a number of such companions, for example 'Abdullāh ibn 'Amr ibn al-'Āṣ ﷺ who acquired a large number of the books of the *Ahl al-Kitāb* (the People of the Scripture) which were left behind by the Romans or others during the battle of Yarmūk because there was *ruksah* (permission) to do this. Thus, if the companion is known to quote from the Children of Israel, then his statement is not considered as *al-marfū' ḥukman*.

وهل ما أضيف إلى الصحابي ولم يثبت له حكم الرفع، هل هو حجة أم لا؟

Is the narration that is attributed to a companion but does not have the sta-

---

31 Recorded by al-Bukhārī; The Book of Wedlock; Chapter: If one were to marry a virgin and he already had a matron wife (5213), and Muslim; The Book of Breastfeeding; Chapter: The number of days that the virgin deserves (1461).

tus of *al-marfūʿ ḥukman* considered as valid evidence or not?

نقول: في هذا خلاف بين أهل العلم.

We say that the scholars have different opinions on the matter.

فمنهم من قال: بأنه حجة، بشرط ألا يُخالف نصاً، ولا صحابياً آخر، فإن خالف نصًّا أُخذ بالنص، وإن خالف صحابياً آخر أُخذ بالراجح.

Amongst them are those who said that it is considered as valid evidence with the condition that it does not contradict any religious text or other companion. If the narration contradicts a text, then the text is given precedence, and if it contradicts another companion, then the correct opinion is taken.

ومنهم من قال: إن قول الصحابي ليس بحجة، لأن الصحابي بشر يجتهد، ويصيب ويخطئ.

And there are those who said that the opinion of a companion is not a valid evidence because he is a human being and when he makes an *ijtihād*, he may be correct or wrong in his judgement.

ومنهم من قال: الحجة من أقوال الصحابة قول أبي بكر وعمر - رضي الله عنهما - لأن النبي صلى الله عليه وسلّم قال: ((اقتدوا بالذين من بعدي أبو بكر وعمر)) وقال أيضاً: ((إن يطيعوا أبا بكر وعمر يرشدوا)).

There are also those who said that the valid evidences are those that come from the statements of Abū Bakr and ʿUmar ﵄ because the Prophet ﷺ said, "Follow the way of those after me; Abū Bakr and ʿUmar,"[32] and he also said, "If they were to abide by Abū Bakr and ʿUmar, they would be guided."[33]

32 Recorded by al-Imām Aḥmad (382), al-Tirmidhī; The Book of Virtues; Chapter: *Ḥadīth* of Ḥudhayfah (3662), and Ibn Mājah in the Introduction (97).
33 Recorded by Muslim; The Book of Mosques; Chapter: The fulfillment of missed prayers (311-681).

وأما من سواهما فليس قوله بحجة.

As for the rest of the companions other than the two, their statements are not considered as valid evidence.

والذي يظهر لي أن قول الصحابي حجة إن كان من أهل الفقه والعلم، وإلا فليس بحجة، لأن بعض الصحابة كان يفدُ على النبي صلى الله عليه وسلّم، ويتلقى منه بعض الأحكام الشرعية، وهو ليس من الفقهاء، وليس من علماء الصحابة، فهذا لا يكون قوله حجة.

The opinion which is most manifest to me is that the statement of the companion is considered as valid evidence if he is amongst the people of knowledge and understanding. If he is not, then it is not a valid evidence because some of the companions came to the Prophet ﷺ and heard from him some of the laws of the *Sharīʿah* but they were not from the jurists or scholars amongst the companions, thus their speech would not be regarded as valid evidence.

وهذا القول وسط بين الأقوال، وهو القول الراجح في هذه المسألة.

And this is the moderate opinion amongst them all, and it is the correct opinion in this matter.

وما الحكم فيما إذا قال التابعي: من السنة كذا، هل له حكم الرفع أم لا؟

What would be the ruling of a statement of a *tābiʿī*, if he were to say that such-and-such is from the Sunnah; is it ruled as *marfūʿ* or not?

نقول: قد اختلف المحدثون في ذلك.

We say that the scholars of *ḥadīth* have differing opinions on this matter.

فمنهم من قال: إنه موقوف، وليس من قسم المرفوع؛ لأن التابعي لم يدرك عهد النبي صلى الله عليه وسلّم، فلذلك لا نستطيع أن نقول أن ما سماه سنة، فيعني

به سنة النبي صلى الله عليه وسلّم، بل يحتمل أن يريد سنة الصحابة.

There are those who said that it is regarded as *mawqūf* and not from the classification of *marfū'* because the *tābi'ī* did not live during the era of the Prophet ﷺ. Due to this reason we are unable to say that when he states *"Sunnah"* he is referring to the Sunnah of the Prophet ﷺ. In fact, there is the possibility that he meant the Sunnah of the companions.

وقال بعض العلماء: بل هو مرفوع؛ لكنه مرسل منقطع؛ لأنه سقط منه الصحابي، ويكون المراد بالسنة عنده هي: سنة النبي صلى الله عليه وسلّم.

And some scholars stated that it is in fact *marfū'*, but disconnected *mursal*[34] in chain because the companion was abandoned. Therefore the Sunnah here refers to the Sunnah of the Prophet ﷺ.

وعموماً فعلى كلا القولين: إن كان مرسلاً: فهو ضعيف، وذلك لعدم اتصال السند.

In general, upon both opinions, if the *ḥadīth* is considered as *mursal* then it is a *ḍa'īf* narration because the *sanad* is disconnected.

وإذا كان موقوفاً: فهو من باب قول الصحابي، أو فعله.

And if it is considered as *mawqūf*, then it is considered as a statement of the companion or his action.

وقد تقدم الخلاف في حجية قول الصحابي، وبيان الخلاف فيه وأن القول الصحيح هو أنه حجة بثلاثة شروط:

We have mentioned previously regarding the different opinions concerning whether the speech of a companion is taken to be a valid evidence, as well as

34 [T] Definition of *mursal*: Khaṭīb al-Baghdādī said, "*Mursal* refers to a report whose *isnād* is interrupted, meaning that among its narrators is one who did not hear it from the one whose name comes before his. But in most cases, what is described as *mursal* is that which was narrated by the *tābi'ī* from the Prophet ﷺ." (*Al-Kifāyah*)

its explanation and that the correct opinion is that it is considered as valid evidence if it meets three requirements:

١ - أن يكون الصحابي من فقهاء الصحابة.

One. The companion has to be amongst the scholars.

٢ - ألا يخالف نصاً.

Two. The narration does not contradict a religious text.

٣ - ألا يخالف قول صحابي آخر.

Three. The narration does not contradict another companion's opinion.

فإن كان ليس من فقهاء الصحابة، فقوله ليس بحجة، وإن كان من فقهائهم، ولكن خالف نصاً، فالعبرة بالنص، ولا عبرة بقوله، وإن كان من فقهاء الصحابة، ولم يخالف نصاً ولكن خالفه صحابي آخر، فإننا نطلب المرجح.

If the companion is not one of the scholars amongst them, then his opinion is not taken to be a valid evidence. Likewise if he is among their scholars but his opinion contradicts a religious text, then the text is given precedence over his opinion, even if he is one of the scholars of the companions. And if he is among their scholars and his opinion does not contradict a religious text but conflicts with the opinion of another companion, then we seek out the correct opinion.

كذلك من المرفوع حكماً، إذا نسب الشيء إلى عهد النبي صلى الله عليه وسلّم فقيل: كانوا يفعلون كذا في عهد النبي صلى الله عليه وسلّم، فهذا من المرفوع حكماً.

Amongst that which is considered as *marfūʿ ḥukman* is when something is attributed to the era of the Prophet ﷺ. If it was said that the people did such an action during the time of the Prophet ﷺ, then this is considered as *marfūʿ ḥukman*.

وأمثلته كثيرة: مثل قول أسماء بنت أبي بكر - رضي الله عنهما - (نحرنا في عهد النبي صلى الله عليه وسلّم فرساً في المدينة وأكلناه).

There are many examples of this, one of which is the narration of Asmā' bint Abī Bakr ﷺ where she said, "We slaughtered a horse during the time of the Prophet ﷺ in al-Madīnah and we ate it."[35]

فهنا لم تصرح بأن النبي صلى الله عليه وسلّم علم به، لأنها لو صرحت به لكان مرفوعاً صريحاً، فإذاً هو مرفوع حكماً.

It was not made explicit here that the Prophet ﷺ knew about this incident. If it was made explicit then this narration would be considered as explicitly *marfū'*. Thus this narration is considered to be *marfū' ḥukman*.

ووجه ذلك: أنه لو كان حراماً ما أقره الله تعالى، فإقرار الله عز وجل له يقتضي أن يكون حجة - وقد علمت فيما سبق - أن من العلماء من يقول: هذا ليس مرفوعاً حكماً، ولكنه حجة، وقال: إنه ليس مرفوعاً لأن النبي صلى الله عليه وسلّم لم يعلم به، لكنه حجة لأن الله تعالى علم به فأقره.

And the reason for this is that if it was forbidden, then Allāh ﷻ would not have permitted it. Thus, the approval from Allāh means that it is a valid evidence. As we have mentioned previously, there are scholars that say that this narration is not *marfū' ḥukman* but it is a valid evidence. They state that it is not considered to be *marfū'* because the Prophet ﷺ did not know about it, but it is still considered to be valid evidence because Allāh knew about it and hence approved it.

كذلك من المرفوع حكماً ما إذا قال الصحابي: روايةً.

Likewise, if a companion said "it is narrated", this is considered as *marfū' ḥukman* as well.

---

35 Recorded by al-Bukhārī; The Book of Slaughter; Chapter: The meat of horses (5519).

مثاله: اتصل السند إلى الصحابي فقال: عن أبي هريرة رواية: من فعل كذا وكذا، أو من قال كذا وكذا، فإن هذا من المرفوع حكماً، لأن قول الصحابي رواية، لم يصرح أنها رواية عن النبي صلى الله عليه وسلّم، لكن لما كان الغالب أن الصحابة يتلقون عن الرسول صلى الله عليه وسلّم، جعله العلماء من المرفوع حكماً.

An example would be the connection of a *sanad* to a companion and he said, "On the authority of Abī Hurayrah, it is narrated that whoever did such-and-such or whoever said such-and-such," then this is taken as being *marfū' ḥukman*. This is because it is a statement comprising of a companion's narration, and it is not explicit that it was narrated from the Prophet ﷺ. However, as it is most often the case that the companions took from the Messenger ﷺ, the scholars considered this as *marfū' ḥukman*.

كذلك من المرفوع حكماً: إذا قال التابعي عن الصحابي: رفعه إلى النبي صلى الله عليه وسلّم، مثل ما يقوله بعض التابعين: عن أبي هريرة يرفعه، أو عن أبي هريرة رفعه، أو عن أبي هريرة يبلغ به، كل هذا من المرفوع حكماً وذلك لأنه لم يصرح فيه بنسبته إلى النبي صلى الله عليه وسلّم.

Likewise, if a *tābi'ī* were to say on the authority of a companion, "He raised it to the Prophet ﷺ," it is also considered as *marfū' ḥukman*. For instance, what some of the *tābi'īn* (plural of *tābi'ī*) said, "On the authority of Abī Hurayrah, he raised it," or "On the authority of Abī Hurayrah its raising," or "On the authority of Abī Hurayrah, he attained it." All of these are considered as *marfū' ḥukman* as the attribution to the Prophet ﷺ was not clearly stated.

۞۞۞

المتن

٨ - وَالْمُسْنَدُ الْمُتَّصِلُ الإِسْنَادِ مِنْ   رَاوِيهِ حَتَّى الْمُصْطَفَى وَلَمْ يَبِنْ

(8) The musnad is that with an isnād connected from,
Its narrator up to the Chosen One and not detached.

الشرح

هذا هو القسم السادس من أقسام الحديث المذكورة في النظم، وعندنا فيما يتعلق بالسند خمسة أشياء:

This is the sixth classification of the categories of *ḥadīth* mentioned in the poem, and we have five things that are related to the *sanad*:

١ - مُسْنَد.

1. *Musnad* (the attributed narration).

٢ - مُسْنِد.

2. *Musnid* (the one who attributes).

٣ - مُسْنَد إليه.

3. *Musnad ilayhi* (the one attributed to).

٤ - إسناد.

4. *Isnād* (the attribution).

٥ - سَنَد.

5. *Sanad* (the chain).

يقول المؤلف في تعريف المسنَد: هو المتصل الإسناد، من راويه حتى المصطفى محمد صلى الله عليه وسلّم.

The author defined the *musnad* as one whose *isnād* is connected from its narrator up to Muhammad the Chosen One ﷺ.

وقوله: (ولم يَبِنْ) هذا تفسير للاتصال، يعني لم ينقطع، فالمسند عنده إذاً هو المرفوع المتصل إسناده.

His statement, "Not detached": this is explaining the connection of the chain i.e. not disconnected. Thus, the *musnad* according to the author is the *marfū'* narration of which its *isnād* is connected.

أما كونه مرفوعاً فيؤخذ من قوله: (حتى المصطفى).

As for it being defined as *al-marfū'*, it is deduced from the phrase, "Up to the Chosen One".

أما كونه متصل الإسناد فمن قوله (المتصل الإسناد - ولم يبن) هذا هو المسند.

And as for the continuity of the chain, it is deduced from the phrase, "Is that with an *isnād* connected... not detached." This is the definition of *al-musnad*.

وعلى هذا فالموقوف ليس بمسند، لأنه غير مرفوع أي لم يتصل إلى النبي صلى الله عليه وسلّم.

Based on this definition, the *mawqūf* is not classified as *musnad* because it is not taken to be *marfū'* i.e. it is not connected to the Prophet ﷺ.

وكذلك المنقطع الذي سقط منه بعض الرواة ليس بمسند، لأننا اشترطنا أن يكون متصلاً، وهذا هو ما ذهب إليه المؤلف وهو رأي جمهور علماء الحديث.

Likewise the *munqaṭi'* where some of its narrators are omitted is not considered as *musnad* because we have laid the requirement that it has to be connected. This is the opinion of the author and the majority of the scholars of *ḥadīth*.

وبعضهم يقول: إن المسند أعم من ذلك، فكل ما أسند إليه راويه، فهو مسند، فيشمل المرفوع، والموقوف، والمقطوع، والمتصل، والمنقطع.

And some of them said that the *musnad* is more general than this definition. As such, everything that was attributed by its narrator is termed as *musnad*. Hence, it includes the *marfūʿ*, *mawqūf*, *maqṭūʿ*, *muttaṣil* and *munqaṭiʿ*.

ولا شك أن هذا القول هو الذي يوافق اللغة، فإن اللغة تدل على أن المسند هو الذي أُسند إلى راويه، سواء كان مرفوعاً، أم غير مرفوع، أو كان متصلاً، أو منقطعاً، لكن الذي عليه أكثر المحدثين أن المسند هو الذي اتصل إسناده إلى رسول الله صلى الله عليه وسلّم.

There is no doubt that this opinion is in line with the linguistic meaning of the word, because *al-musnad* refers to anything that is attributed to its narrator, whether it is *marfūʿ* or not and whether it is *muttaṣil* or *munqaṭiʿ*. However, most scholars of *ḥadīth* define *musnad* as the narration whose *isnād* is continuous to the Messenger of Allāh ﷺ.

أما (المُسنِد) فهو الراوي الذي أسند الحديث إلى راويه، فإذا قال: حدثني فلان.

As for *al-musnid*, it refers to the narrator who attributed the *ḥadīth* to its narrator. As such, if one said, "So-and-so told me":

فالأول مسنِد.

The speaker here is the *musnid*.

والثاني مسنَد إليه.

And the person he mentioned is the *musnad ilayhi*.

يعني أن كل من نسب الحديث فهو مسنِد، ومن نُسب إليه الحديثُ فهو مسند إليه.

Which means that all those who attributed a narration are called the *musnid*, and all those whom the *ḥadīth* was attributed to are the *musnad ilayhi*.

أما (السند) فهم رجال الحديث أي رواته، فإذا قال: حدثني فلانٌ عن فلان عن

فلان، فهؤلاء هم سند الحديث؛ لأن الحديث اعتمد عليهم، وصاروا سنداً له.

As for the *sanad*, they are the *rijāl* (men) of the *ḥadīth* i.e. its narrators. If someone were to say, "So-and-so told me from so-and-so from so-and-so", all of them are the *sanad* of the *ḥadīth.* This is because the narration is dependent on them, thus they become the *sanad* (support) for it.

أما (الإسنادُ): فقال بعض المحدثين: الإسناد هو السند، وهذا التعبير يقع كثيراً عندهم فيقولون: إسناده صحيح، ويعنون بذلك سنده أي الرواة.

As for *al-isnād*; some scholars of *ḥadīth* say that the *isnād* is the *sanad* itself. This expression is commonly used amongst them, hence they say, "Its *isnād* is *ṣaḥīḥ,*" in reference to its *sanad* i.e. the narrators.

وقال بعضهم: الإسناد هو نسبة الحديث إلى راويه.

And some of them say that the *isnād* is the attribution of the *ḥadīth* to its narrator.

يقالُ: أسند الحديث إلى فلان أي نسبه إليه.

It is said, "He made *isnād* of the *ḥadīth* to so-and-so," i.e. he attributed it to him.

والصحيح فيه: أنه يُطلق على هذا وعلى هذا.

And the correct opinion is that it can be used for both.

فيطلق الإسناد أحياناً: على السند الذين هم الرواة.

As such, sometimes the *isnād* refers to the *sanad,* which is the narrators.

ويطلق أحياناً: على نسبة الحديث إلى راويه، فيقال أسند الحديث إلى فلان، أسنده إلى أبي هريرة، أسنده إلى ابن عباس، أسنده إلى ابن عمر وهكذا.

And sometimes it refers to the attribution of the narration to its narrator, hence it is said, "He made *isnād* of the *ḥadīth* to so-and-so", "He made *isnād* of it to Abī Hurayrah", "He made *isnād* of it to Ibn 'Abbās", "He made *isnād* of it to Ibn 'Umar", etc.

وهل يلزم من الإسناد أن يكون الحديث صحيحاً؟

Does an *isnād* confirm that the *ḥadīth* is *ṣaḥīḥ*?

نقول: لا؛ لأنه قد يتصل السند من الراوي إلى النبي صلى الله عليه وسلّم، ويكون في الرواة ضعفاء، ومجهولون ونحوهم.

We say no, because the *sanad* may be connected from the narrator to the Prophet ﷺ, but there may be narrators who are weak or unknown etc.

إذاً فليس كل مسندٍ صحيحاً، فقد يكون الحديثُ صحيحاً، وهو غير مسند، كما لو أُضيف إلى الصحابي بسند صحيح، فإنه موقوف وصحيح، لكن ليس بمسند، لأنه غير مرفوع إلى النبي صلى الله عليه وسلّم، وقد يكون مسنداً متصل الإسناد، لكن الرواة ضعفاء، فهذا يكون مسنداً، ولا يكون صحيحاً.

As such, not all *musnad* narrations are considered to be *ṣaḥīḥ*, and sometimes a *ḥadīth* may be authentic but not *musnad*. For instance, if it was attributed to a companion with an authentic *sanad*, it would be considered *mawqūf* and *ṣaḥīḥ* but not *musnad*. This is because it is not attributed to the Prophet ﷺ. It could also be *musnad* with a continuous *isnād* but the narrators are weak thus the narration is *musnad* but not *ṣaḥīḥ*.

وبين المسند لغةً، وبين المسند اصطلاحاً فرق، والنسبة بينهما العموم والخصوص.

Therefore, there is a difference between the definition of *musnad* in terms of language and terminology, and the relation between the two is that one is generic and the other is specific.

فالمسند في اللغة هو: ما أسند إلى قائله، سواء كان مرفوعاً، أو موقوفاً أو مقطوعاً.

As for *al-musnad* in terms of language; it is the speech that was attributed to its speaker, whether it is *marfū'*, *mawqūf* or *maqṭū'*.

فإذا قلت: قال فلان كذا، فهذا مسند، حتى ولو أضفته إلى واحد موجود تخاطبه الآن.

Thus, if you were to say: "So-and-so said this," this sentence is considered as *musnad* even if you were to attribute it to someone who is present with you and you are speaking to him right now.

فلو قلتُ: قال فلان كذا، فهذا مسند؛ لأني أسندتُ الحديث إلى قائله.

And if I were to say, "So-and-so said this", this is considered as *musnad* because I attributed the speech to its speaker.

لكن في الاصطلاح: المسندُ هو المرفوع المتصل السند.

However, in terms of terminology, the *musnad* is one that is *marfūʿ* with a *sanad* that is *muttaṣil*.

فالمسند اصطلاحاً، أخصُّ من المسند لغة، فكل مسندٍ اصطلاحاً، فهو مسندٌ لغة، ولا عكس، فبينهما العموم والخصوص.

Thus the *musnad* in terminology is more specific than its linguistic meaning. Hence, all that is considered as *musnad* in terminology is *musnad* linguistically, but the opposite is incorrect. Therefore the relationship between the two is *ʿumūm* and *khuṣūṣ* [i.e. the linguistic definition is generic and the terminological definition is specific.]

المتن

٩ - وَمَا بِسَمْعِ كُلِّ رَاوٍ يَتَّصِلْ إِسْنَادُهُ لِلْمُصْطَفَى فَالْمُتَّصِلْ

(9) And one whose chain, by every narrator's hearing,
Is connected to al-Muṣṭafā is al-muttaṣil.

الشرح

قوله: (المصطفى) مأخوذة من الصفوة، وهي خيار الشيء، وأصلها في اللغة (المصتفى) بالتاء.

The word *al-Muṣṭafā* (the chosen one) is derived from the word *al-ṣafwah,* which means the best of something. Its linguistic origin is *al-muṣtafā* with the letter *tā*.

والقاعدة: أنه إذا اجتمعت الصاد والتاء، وسبقت إحداهما بالسكون فإنها تُقلب طاءً فتصير (المصطفى).

And the principle states that if the letters *tā* and *sād* were to meet, and one of the two precedes the other with a *sukūn* (absence of a vowel), then the letter ت shall change into the letter ط and thus it becomes *al-muṣṭafā* [with a ط].

واللام في قوله (للمصطفى) بمعنى (إلى) أي إلى المصطفى. والمتصل هو القسم السابع من أقسام الحديث المذكور في النظم.

And the preposition *lām* in the author's words, *"lilmuṣṭafā"* has the meaning of "to" i.e. to the chosen one. And *al-muttaṣil* is the seventh category of the classifications of *ḥadīth* mentioned in the poem.

وفي تعريفه قولان لأهل العلم:

There are two opinions on its definition:

فالمتصلُ على كلام المؤلف هو: المرفوع الذي أخذه كل راوي عمن فوقه سماعاً.

Al-muttaṣil according to the author is the *marfū'* narration that was taken by each of its narrators from the one above him through hearing.

فاشترط المؤلف للمتصل شرطين:

As such, the author laid down two requirements for a narration to be considered as *muttaṣil*:

١ - السماع بأن يسمع كل راوٍ ممن روى عنه.

1. Hearing i.e. where every single narrator heard the narration from the one before him.

٢ - أن يكون مرفوعاً إلى النبي صلى الله عليه وسلّم.

2. The narration must be *marfū‘* to the Prophet ﷺ.

لقوله (للمصطفى) يعني إلى المصطفى، وبناء على ذلك، فالموقوف، والمقطوع، لا يسمى متصلاً؛ لأن المؤلف اشترط أن يكون متصلاً إلى النبي صلى الله عليه وسلّم، وفي المقطوع، والموقوف لم يتصل السند إلى النبي صلى الله عليه وسلّم.

This is due to the author's speech, *"lilmuṣṭafā"* i.e. to the chosen one. Hence, based on this, the *mawqūf* and the *maqṭū‘* are not considered as *muttaṣil.* This is because the author laid the condition that the narration must be connected to the Prophet ﷺ. As for the *maqṭū‘* and the *mawqūf*, the *sanad* is not connected to the Prophet ﷺ.

وكذلك المرفوع، إذا كان فيه سقط في الرواة، فإنه لا يسمى متصلاً، لأنه منقطع.

Likewise for the *marfū‘*, if one of the narrators were to be omitted, it would also not be considered *muttaṣil* because it is disconnected.

وعلى ظاهر كلام المؤلف إذا لم يُصّرح الراوي بالسماع، أو ما يقوم مقامه، فليس بمتصل، فلابد أن يكون سماعاً، والسماع من الراوي هو أقوى أنواع التحمل وهذا هو ما ذهب إليه المؤلف في تعريف المتصل.

Upon the apparent meaning of the author's definition, if the hearing or anything else in its place is not clearly stated by the narrator, then it is not considered as *muttaṣil.* Therefore, the hearing is a must, and the hearing from the narrator is the strongest form of *al-tahammul* (reception) and this is the opinion of the author in defining the *muttaṣil.*

وقيل بل المتصل هو: ما اتصل إسناده، بأخذ كل راوي عمن فوقه إلى منتهاه.

And it is said that the *muttaṣil* is the one whose *isnād* is connected whereby each and every narrator takes from the one above him until its end.

وعلى هذا فيشمل الموقوف، والمقطوع، ويشمل ما روي بالسماع وما روي بغير السماع، لكن لابد من الاتصال.

Upon this definition, it includes the *mawqūf*, *maqṭū*ʿ as well as the narration through hearing and other than hearing. The crucial matter is that it must be connected.

وهذا أصح من قول المؤلف وهو أن المتصل هو: ما اتصل إسناده بأن يروي كل راوي عمن فوقه، سواء كان مرفوعاً، أو موقوفاً، أو مقطوعاً، وسواء كانت الصيغة هي السماع، أو غير السماع، فكل ما اتصل إسناده يكون متصلاً.

And this opinion is more correct than the author's, and it is that the *muttaṣil* is one whose *isnād* is connected whereby each and every narrator narrates from the one above him, regardless whether the narration is *marfū*ʿ or *mawqūf* or *maqṭū*ʿ, and regardless whether the transmission is through hearing or other than hearing. Thus everything that has a connected chain is considered as *muttaṣil*.

وقد سبق لنا خلاف المحدثين حول مسألة: (هل تُشترط الملاقاة أو تكفي المعاصرة) وتقدم الجواب عليه.

With regards to the differing opinions regarding whether the meeting of narrators is a criterion or if it is acceptable if they lived in the same era, we have already discussed it earlier with the answer regarding it.[36]

ولا يشترط في الاتصال أن يثبت سماع هذا الحديث بعينه منه، بل إذا ثبت سماعه منه فيكفي ذلك، إلا إذا قيل إنه لم يسمع منه إلا حديثاً واحداً وهو

36 Previously mentioned on page 40 in the Arabic text.

حديث كذا وكذا مثلاً، فإن ما سوى هذا الحديث لا يعدّ متصلاً.

And it is not a requirement that the hearing from an individual be established for this *ḥadīth* specifically. Rather, it is sufficient to establish the hearing in general unless if it is said that the narrator did not actually hear from the other except for one narration and it is the *ḥadīth* of such-and-such for example, then all the other narrations are not considered as *muttaṣil.*

كما قيل: إن الحسن البصري لم يسمع من سمرة بن جندب رضي الله عنه إلا حديثاً واحداً وهو حديث العقيقة.

For instance, it was said that al-Ḥasan al-Baṣrī did not hear from Samurah ibn Jundub ﷺ except one *ḥadīth,* which is the one regarding *al-ʿaqīqah* (the sacrifice for the newborn).

وبناء على هذا القول: إذا روى الحسن البصري عن سمرة بن جندب حديثاً، سوى حديث العقيقة فهو غير متصل.

Based on this, if al-Ḥasan al-Baṣrī were to narrate from Samurah ibn Jundub ﷺ another *ḥadīth* besides the *ḥadīth* of *al-ʿaqīqah*, then the narration would not be considered as *muttaṣil*.

والمسألة فيها خلاف بين العلماء، ولكن نقول: إن الحصر صعب، فكوننا نقول إن الحسن لم يسمع من سمرة إلا حديث العقيقة فيه نوع صعوبة جداً، حتى لو فُرض أن الحسن قال: لم أسمع سوى هذا الحديث، فإننا نقول: إن كان قد قال هذه الكلمة بعد موت سمرة، حَكَمنا بأنه لم يسمع من سمرة سواه، لأنه لا يمكن أن يسمع من سمرة بعد موته، وأما إذا كان قد قاله في حال حياة سمرة، فيحتمل أنه قال لم أسمع من سمرة سوى هذا الحديث، ثم يكون قد سمع بعد ذلك حديثاً آخر. والله أعلم.

And the scholars have different opinions on the issue. But we say that it is difficult to limit the narrations, thus there is difficulty in confirming our statement that al-Ḥasan did not hear from Samurah except the *ḥadīth* of *al-'aqīqah*. Even if we were to assume that al-Ḥasan said, "I did not hear from him except this *ḥadīth*", we say that if he were to declare this statement after the death of Samurah, then we conclude that he did not hear from Samurah except this one narration because it was not possible for him to hear from Samurah after he died. As for the case whereby he proclaimed this during Samurah's lifetime, then there is the possibility that when he said, "I did not hear from him except this *ḥadīth*", he may have heard another narration after that point of time. And Allāh Knows best.

المتن

١٠ - مُسَلْسَلٌ قُلْ مَا عَلَى وَصْفٍ أَتَى   مِثلُ أَمَـا وَاللهِ أَنْبَانِي الْفَتَى

(10) Say musalsal is one which comes with a trait,
Such as: "Indeed by Allāh, the youth informed me."

الشرح

ومن أقسام الحديث أيضاً (المسلسل) وهذا هو القسم الثامن في النظم وهو اسم مفعول من (سَلسله) إذا ربطه في سلسلة، هذا في اللغة.

Al-musalsal is also one of the classifications of *ḥadīth*. It is the eighth category in the poem and it is the direct object from the word *salsalahu* which means: he tied him in a *silsilah* (chain). This is the linguistic meaning of the word.

وفي الاصطلاح: هو الذي اتفق فيه الرواة، فنقلوه بصيغة معينة، أو حال معينة.

As for its definition in terminology, it is the narration where the narrators concurred in the narration and transmitted it in a particular way or in a particular state.

يعني أن الرواة اتفقوا فيه على وصفٍ معيَّن، إما وصف الأداء، أو وصف حال

الراوي أو غير ذلك.

It means that the narrators concurred upon a certain trait in it, either it could be a trait of the delivery or state of the narrators etc.

والمسلسل من مباحث السند والمتن جميعاً؛ لأن التسلسل قد يكون فيهما، أو في أحدهما دون الآخر.

The *musalsal* entails study of the *sanad* and the *matn* together because it can occur in both or in either one of the two without the other.

وفائدة المسلسل هو: التنبيه على أن الراوي قد ضبط الرواية، ولذلك أمثلة كثيرة منها: حديث معاذ بن جبل - رضي الله عنه - أن النبي صلى الله عليه وسلّم قال له: ((إني أحبُّك فلا تدعنَّ أن تقول دبر كل صلاة: اللهم أعني على ذكرك وشكرك وحُسن عبادتك)).

The benefit of *al-musalsal* is the observation that the narrator was precise in the narration. There are many examples of this, one of which is the *ḥadīth* of Muʿādh ibn Jabal ﷺ that the Prophet ﷺ said to him,"Indeed I love you dearly, so never forget to recite after every prayer, 'O Allāh help me in remembering You, in offering thanks to You, and in worshipping You properly.'"[37]

فقد تسلسل هذا الحديث وصار كل راوٍ إذا أراد أن يحدّث به غيره، قال لمن يحدثه هذه الجملة ((إني أحبُّك فلا تدعنَّ أن تقول ...)) الحديث.

This *ḥadīth* was repeated sequentially such that every narrator that wished to narrate it to another person, he would state to him the sentence, "Indeed I love you dearly, so never forget to recite [to the end of the *ḥadīth*]."

فهذا مسلسل لأن الرواة اتفقوا فيه على هذه الجملة.

Thus this narration is considered as *musalsal* because the narrators con-

37 Recorded by al-Imām Aḥmad 5/ 244.

curred in it with this sentence.

وكذلك لو قال: حدثني على الغداء، ثم إن هذا الراوي حدث الذي تحته وهو على الغداء فقال: حدثني فلان على الغداء، قال حدثني فلانٌ على الغداء، قال حدثني فلان على الغداء، فنُسمي هذا مسلسلاً، لأن الرواة اتفقوا فيه على حال واحدة فأدّوا وهم على الغداء.

Likewise if one were to say, "So-and-so told me while he was having lunch," and then this narrator told the one after him and he was having his lunch and said, "So-and-so told me while he was having lunch," and the next narrator in the chain said,"So-and-so told me while he was having lunch," and this was repeated by those following in the chain. Thus we term this narration as *musalsal* as the narrators concurred upon one state in it and thus transmitted the *ḥadīth* during lunch.

وكذلك إذا اتفق الرواة على صيغة معينة من الأداء بحيث أنهم كلهم قالوا: أنبأني فلانٌ، قال أنبأني فلان، قال: أنبأني فلان، إلى نهاية السند، فإننا نسمي هذا أيضاً مسلسلاً، لاتفاق الرواة على صيغة معين وهي (أنبأني).

Similarly if the narrators were to concur upon a certain format of transmission whereby they all said, "So-and-so reported to me and he said, 'So-and-so reported to me and he said, 'So-and-so reported to me,'" until the end of the *sanad*, then we term this narration as *musalsal* as well. This is due to the fact that the narrators concurred upon a certain format which is "he reported to me".

قوله: (مسلسل قل ما على وصفٍ أتى).

The author's phrase,"Say *musalsal* is one which comes with a trait".

يعني أن ما أتى على وصف واحد من الرواة، سواء كان هذا الوصف في صيغة الأداء، أو في حال الراوي، فإذا اتفق الرواة على شيء، إما في صيغة الأداء، أو

حال الراوي فإن ذلك يسمى مسلسلاً.

I.e. it is that which comes with one trait from the narrators, regardless whether the trait was in the format of transmission or the state of the narrator. If the narrators concurred upon something, whether it is in the format of transmission or state of the narrator, then the narration is called *musalsal*.

قوله: (مثل أما والله أنبأني الفتى).

As for the phrase, "Such as, 'Indeed by Allāh, the youth informed me.'"

وقد تقدم هذا المثال، وذلك بأن يقول كل واحد منهم: أنبأني فلان، قال: أنبأني فلان إلى نهاية السند، فإننا نسمي هذا مسلسلاً؛ لأن الرواة اتفقوا فيه على صيغة واحدة في الأداء، ومثله ما لو اتفقوا على صيغة سمعت، أو قال، أو نحو ذلك فإن كل هذا يسمى مسلسلاً.

Its example is as mentioned earlier which is that every single one of them said, "So-and-so reported to me and he said, 'So-and-so reported to me,'" until the end of the *sanad*. We call this narration *musalsal* because the narrators concurred upon a particular format for transmission. Likewise if they were to concur upon the formats "I heard" or "He said" and its likes, all of these are called *musalsal*.

المتن

(١١) كَـذَاكَ قَدْ حَدَّثَنِيـهِ قَائِـماَ   أَوْ بَـعْدَ أَنْ حَدَّثَنِـي تَبَسَّماَ

(11) Similarly: "Indeed he narrated it to me while standing."
Or "After he narrated it to me he smiled."

الشرح

يعني أن من صور المسلسل، أن يقول الراوي: حدثني فلان قائماً، قال: حدثني

فلان قائماً، قال: حدثني فلان قائماً، قال: حدثني فلان قائماً وهكذا إلى نهاية السند.

He meant that these are illustrations of *musalsal,* e.g. where the narrators say, "So-and-so narrated to me while standing and he said, 'So-and-so narrated to me while standing and he said, 'So-and-so narrated to me while standing,''" in this manner to the end of the *sanad*.

ومثله ما لو قال: حدثني فلان وهو مضطجع على فراشه، ثم اتفق الرواة على مثل ذلك فإنه يكون مسلسلاً. ومن صوره أن يقول: حدثني، ثم تبسم، ويستمر ذلك في جميع السند.

Similarly if one was to say, "So-and-so narrated to me while lying on his mattress," or "He narrated to me and then he smiled," and then the narrators concurred upon this wording, thus the narration is considered as *musalsal*.

ولو أن الرواة اتفقوا في رواية حديث أبي هريرة رضي الله عنه، في قصة الرجل المجامع في نهار رمضان، الذي قال بعد أن أتته الصدقة: يا رسول الله، أعلى أفقر مني؟ فوالله ما بين لابتيها أهل بيت أفقر مني، فضحك النبي صلى الله عليه وسلّم حتى بدت نواجذه، فصار كل محدث يضحك إذا وصل إلى هذه الجملة، حتى تبدوا نواجذه، فنُسمِّي هذا أيضاً مسلسلاً، لأن الرواة اتفقوا فيه على حال واحدة وهي الضحك.

And if the narrators concurred in the narration of the *ḥadīth* of Abu Hurayrah ﵁ regarding the story of the man who had intercourse during the daytime of Ramaḍān. The man said after alms were brought to him, "O Messenger of Allāh, do I give it away to anyone poorer than me? Indeed by Allāh there is no family between its (Madīnah) two lava fields who is poorer than me", then the Prophet ﷺ laughed until his molars were seen.[38] If all of

38 Recorded by al-Bukhārī; The Book of Fasting; Chapter: When one had intercourse during the daytime in Ramaḍān (1936) and Muslim; The Book of Fasting; Chapter:

the narrators of this *ḥadīth* laughed when they arrived at this sentence until their molars were seen, then this narration is also considered as *musalsal* because the narrators concurred in it upon one situation which is the laughter.

ما هي الفائدة من معرفة المسلسل؟

What is the benefit of identifying the *musalsal*?

نقول: إن معرفة المسلسل لها فوائد هي:

We say that there are benefits from knowing the *musalsal* and they are:

أولاً: هو في الحقيقة فن طريف، حيث إن الرواة يتفقون فيه على حال معينة لاسيما إذا قال: حدثني وهو على فراشه نائمٌ، حدثني وهو يتوضأ، حدثني وهو يأكل، حدثني ثم تبسم، حدثني ثم بكى، فهذه الحالة طريفة، وهي أن يتفق الرواة كلهم على حال واحدة.

Firstly: It is actually an interesting art whereby the narrators concurred in it upon a specific state, especially if one said, "He told me as he was lying on his mattress", "He told me as he was making ablution", "He told me as he was eating", "He told me then he smiled", "He told me and then he cried", thus the scenarios are interesting, as all of the narrators concurred upon one state.

ثانياً: أن في نقله مسلسلاً هكذا؛ حتى لدرجة وصف حال الراوي، فيه دليل على تمام ضبط الرواة، وأن بعضهم قد ضبط حتى حال الراوي حين رواه، فهو يزيد الحديث قوة.

Secondly: The transmission of the *musalsal* in such a manner, to the level that the state of the narrator was described, is an evidence of the full precision of the narrators and that some of them had accuracy even in the description of the state the narrator was in when he narrated from him, and hence this strengthens the *ḥadīth*.

The penalty for the prohibition of intercourse during the daytime in Ramaḍān (1111).

ثالثاً: أنه كان التسلسل مما يقرب إلى الله، صار فيه زيادة قربة وعبادة، مثل ما في حديث معاذ - رضي الله عنه - ((إني أحبك فلا تدعنَّ ...)) فكون كل واحد من الرواة يقول للثاني إني أحبُّك، كان هذا مما يزيد في الإيمان، ويزيد الإنسان قربة إلى الله تعالى، لأن من أوثق عرى الإيمان الحب في الله، والبغض في الله.

Thirdly: If the state of the *musalsal* is one of the acts of getting closer to Allāh, then there is additional worship and means of getting closer to Allāh in the *ḥadīth*. An example would be in the previously mentioned *ḥadīth* of Muʿādh ﷺ, "Indeed I love you dearly, so never forget..." whereby every single one of the narrators told the other, "Indeed I love you dearly." This is something that increases *imān*, and it gets the person closer to Allāh ﷻ because love and hatred for the sake of Allāh is one of the strongest manifestations of true faith.

المتن

(١٢) عَزِيزُ مَرْوِي اثْنَينِ أَوْ ثَلاَثَهْ مَشْهُورُ مَرْوِي فَوقَ مَا ثَلاَثَهْ

(12) ʿAzīz is narrated by two or three,
Mash-hūr is narrated by more than three.

الشرح

ذكر المؤلف في هذا البيت قسمين من أقسام الحديث وهما: العزيز والمشهور، وبهما يتم التاسع والعاشر من أقسام الحديث التي في النظم.

The author mentioned two types of the classifications of *ḥadīth* in this line and they are: *al-ʿazīz* and *al-mash-hūr*. With these two, the ninth and tenth of the classifications of *ḥadīth* have been completed in the poem.

العزيز في اللغة: مأخوذ من عزَّ إذا قوي، وله معاني أُخرى، منها القوة، والغلبة،

والامتناع، لكن الذي يهمنا في باب المصطلح هو المعنى الأول وهو القوة.

The word *'azīz* linguistically is taken from the verb *'azza* which means "he became powerful". It also has other meanings; amongst them are strength, overcoming and invulnerability. However, the one that we are concerned with in terms of terminology is the first meaning, which is strength.

أما في الاصطلاح فهو: ما رواه اثنان عن اثنين عن اثنين إلى أن يصل إلى منتهى السند.

As for its definition in *ḥadīth* terminology, it is what was narrated by two narrators from two narrators from another two until the end of the chain.

والمؤلف هنا لم يشترط أن يكون مرفوعاً، فيشمل المرفوع، والموقوف، والمقطوع، لأنه قال (مروي اثنين) ولم يقل (مروي اثنين مرفوعاً)، ولهذا فإنه لا يشترط في العزيز أن يكون مرفوعاً.

The author here did not state the condition that the narration has to be *marfū'*. Thus it includes the *marfū'*, *mawqūf* and *maqṭū'* because he said, "Narrated by two," and he did not specify the *marfū'* which was narrated by two. Due to this reason, it is not a requirement for the *'azīz* to be *marfū'*.

ووجه تسميته عزيزاً: لأنه قوي برواية الثاني، وكلما كثُرَ المخبرون ازداد الحديث أو الخبر قوة، فإنه لو أخبرك ثقة بخبر، ثم جاء ثقة آخر فأخبرك بنفس الخبر، ثم جاءك ثالث، ثم رابع، فأخبروك بالخبر، لكان هذا الخبر يزداد قوة بازدياد المخبر به.

The logic behind naming this type of narration as *'azīz* is that it becomes stronger with the support of the second narration. And the more the narrators, the stronger the *ḥadīth* or *khabar*. As such, if a trustworthy person reported to you about an incident, and another trustworthy person came and told you the same thing, followed by a third person and a fourth who told you the same, then this piece of news shall increase in strength due to the increase in numbers of reporters.

وقوله (أو ثلاثة).

And his statement, "or three":

(أو) للتنويع، ومن حيث الصيغة يحتمل أن تكون للخلاف لكنه لما قال فيما بعد (مشهور مروي فوق ما ثلاثة) عرفنا أن (أو) هنا للتنويع يعني أن العزيز هو ما رواه اثنان عن اثنين إلى آخره، أو ما رواه ثلاثة عن ثلاثة إلى آخره. فما رواه ثلاثة عن ثلاثة إلى منتهى السند يعتبر - في رأي المؤلف - عزيزاً لأنه قوي بالطريقين الآخرين.

The preposition *aw* (or) denotes variety. It is possible that it can denote change due to the context, but as the author said after it that the *mash-hūr* is narrated by more than three, we know that the preposition here is for variety i.e. that the *'azīz* is what was narrated by two from two until its end, or what was narrated by three from three until its end. Thus, what was narrated by three narrators from another three until the end of the *sanad* is taken to be *'azīz* according to the author, because it is strengthened by the two other routes.

ولكن المشهور عند المتأخرين: أن العزيز هو: ما رواه اثنان فقط.

However, it is commonly accepted amongst the later generations of scholars that the *'azīz* is what was narrated by only two narrators.

وأن المشهور هو: ما رواه ثلاثة فأكثر، وعلى هذا فيكون قول المؤلف (أو ثلاثة) مرجوحاً، والصواب أن العزيز هو: ما رواه اثنان فقط من أول السند إلى آخره.

As such, *al-mash-hūr* is known as what was narrated by three or more. Based on this fact, the opinion of the author that it could also be narrated by three is incorrect. Thus, the correct opinion is that the *'azīz* is one that is narrated by only two from the start of the *sanad* until its end.

أما لو رواه اثنان عن واحد عن اثنين عن اثنين إلى منتهاه فإنه لا يسمى عزيزاً، لأنه اختل شرط، في طبقة من الطبقات، وإذا اختل شرط ولو في طبقة من الطبقات اختل المشروط.

If the narration was narrated by two narrators from one narrator and then from two, then another two until its end, then it is not called *ʿazīz* because the criterion is not met at one of the levels. And even if the criterion is not met at only one of the levels, the term still does not apply.

وهل العزيز شرطٌ للصحيح؟

Is being *ʿazīz* a condition for *ṣaḥīḥ* narrations?

نقول: إن العزيز ليس شرطاً للصحيح.

We say that *ʿazīz* is not a condition for the *ṣaḥīḥ* status.

وقال بعض العلماء: بل إنه شرط للصحيح.

However some scholars said that it is in fact a condition for *ṣaḥīḥ* narrations.

قالوا: لأن الشهادة لا تقبل إلا من اثنين، ولا شك أن الحديث عن النبي صلى الله عليه وسلّم أعظم مشهود به، ولهذا فإن من كذب على النبي صلى الله عليه وسلّم متعمداً فليتبوأ مقعده من النار.

They reasoned by saying that the testimony is not acceptable except from two witnesses, and definitely the narration from the Prophet ﷺ is the greatest thing ever witnessed. As such, [it was said:] whoever deliberately lies upon the Prophet ﷺ, let him take his place in Hellfire.

ولكن قد سبق لنا في كلام المؤلف أن هذا ليس بشرط وهو في قوله (... ما اتصل إسناده ولم يُشذ أو يُعل) ولم يذكر اشتراط أن يكون عزيزاً.

However, the author stated earlier that this is not a condition for the *ṣaḥīḥ* status by saying, "What is connected in its chain, and is neither contradicting nor defected," and he did not mention the requirement of being *'azīz*.

ويُجاب عن قول من قال: بأن الشهادة لا تُقبل إلا باثنين.

And the rebuttal to those who hold the opinion that the testimony cannot be accepted except from two witnesses:

بأن هذا خبّر، وليس بشهادة، والخبر يكفي فيه الواحد، بدليل أن المؤذن يؤذن، ويفطر الناس على أذانه، مع أنه واحد، لأن هذا خبر ديني يكفي فيه الواحد، ويدلُّ لهذا: أن العلماء اتفقوا على قبول حديث أمير المؤمنين عمر بن الخطاب - رضي الله عنه - وأرضاه أنه سمع النبي صلى الله عليه وسلّم يقول: ((إنما الأعمال بالنيات وإنما لكل امرئ ما نوى ...)). وهذا الحديث في ثلاث طبقات لم يُرو إلا عن واحد واحد، فدل ذلك على أنه ليس من شرط الصحيح أن يكون مروي اثنين فأكثر.

This is a form of report (*khabr*) and not a testimony, and one source suffices for the report. Evidence of this is the case of the *mu'adhin* who makes the *adhān* and the people break their fast upon hearing his call despite the fact that he is only one person. This is because it is a form of religious report and one source is sufficient. And it is evident from the fact that the scholars agreed upon accepting the *ḥadīth* of the Commander of the Faithful 'Umar ibn al-Khaṭṭāb ﵁ where he heard the Prophet ﷺ say, "Indeed actions are according to intentions, and indeed for every man is what he intended."[39] The scholars do so despite the fact that it is narrated by only one narrator in three levels in the chain of this *ḥadīth*. Thus this shows that it is not a criterion of the *ṣaḥīḥ* status for the narrators to be two or more.

قوله: (مشهور مروي فوق ما ثلاثة).

The author's phrase: "*Mash-hūr* is narrated by more than three":

39 Reported by al-Bukhāri (1) and Muslim (1957)

هذا رأي المؤلف، وعلى القول الراجح نقول: مشهور مروي فوق ما اثنين، فالمشهور على كلام المؤلف هو ما رواه أربعة فصاعداً، وعلى القول الصحيح هو: ما رواه ثلاثة فصاعداً، ولم يصل إلى حد التواتر.

This is according to the author, while we say that the correct opinion is that the *mash-hūr* is what was narrated by more than two. As such, according to the author, the *mash-hūr* is that which was narrated by four narrators and above whereas based on the correct opinion, it is what was narrated by three or more narrators but is still below the level of mass transmission.

والمشهور يُطلق على معنيين هما:

The word *mash-hūr* has two meanings:

١ - ما اشتهر بين الناس.

1. What is widespread amongst the people.

٢ - ما اصطلح على تسميته مشهوراً.

2. What has been termed by the scholars as *mash-hūr*.

أما ما اشتهر بين الناس فإنه أيضاً على نوعين:

As for that which is widespread amongst the people, it is of two types:

(أ) ما اشتهر عند العامة.

(i) What is widespread amongst the laity.

(ب) ما اشتهر عند أهل العلم.

(ii) What is widespread amongst the people of knowledge.

فأما ما اشتهر عند العامة: فلا حكم له؛ لأنه قد يشتهر عند العامة بعض الأحاديث الموضوعة فهذا لا عبرة به، ولا أثر لاشتهاره عند العامة، لأن العامة

ليسوا أهلاً للقبول أو الرد، حتى نقول إن ما اشتهر عندهم مقبول، ولهذا نجد كثيراً من الأحاديث المشتهرة عند العامة قد ألَّف العلماء فيها مؤلفات مثل كتاب (تمييز الطيب من الخبيث فيما يدور على ألسنة الناس من الحديث).

As for what is widespread among the laity, there is no ruling for it because some fabricated narrations may be widespread among the commoners and thus it is not taken into account, and the fact that it is widespread among the people is given no consideration. This is because the common people are not the specialists for accepting or rejecting narrations so that we can say that what is widespread amongst them is considered as acceptable. As such, we find that scholars wrote a number of books regarding many of the famous *aḥādīth* that were widespread among the laity. One of these books is *Tamyīz al-Ṭayyib min al-Khabīth fīmā Yadūr 'alā Alsinat al-Nās min al-Ḥadīth* (Distinction of the Good from the Evil of Common Narrations Amongst the Speech of the People).

ومما اشتهر من الأحاديث عندهم (خير الأسماء ما حمد وعبد) وهذا مشتهر عند العامة على أنه حديث صحيح، وهو حديث لا أصل له، ولم يصح ذلك عن النبي صلى الله عليه وسلم، بل قال النبي صلى الله عليه وسلم: ((أحب الأسماء إلى الله عبد الله، وعبد الرحمن)).

An example of such widespread *ḥadīths* amongst them is, "The best of names is one that begins with Muḥammad or 'Abd."[40] This is famous amongst the common people and it is said to be a *ṣaḥīḥ* narration. However it is a *ḥadīth* which has no origin and it is not confirmed from the Prophet ﷺ. In fact, the Prophet ﷺ said, "The most beloved names to Allāh are 'Abdullāh and 'Abd al-Raḥmān."[41]

ومثله (حب الوطن من الإيمان) وهو مشهور عند العامة على أنه حديث صحيح،

---

40 *Al-Maqāsid al-Ḥasanah* page 103 and *al-Asrār al-Marfū'ah* page 193.

41 The book of Manners; Chapter: The forbiddance of having Abu 'l-Qāsim as a nickname 2/2132.

وهو حديث موضوع مكذوب، بل المعنى أيضا غير صحيح بل حب الوطن من التعصب.

Another example would be, "The love for one's country is part of faith,"[42] and it is popularly spread amongst the common people as being a *ṣaḥīḥ* narration. However it is a fabricated and untrue *ḥadīth*. In fact its meaning is incorrect, as the love for the country is from fanaticism.

ومثله حديث (يوم صومكم يوم نحركم) وهو مشهور عند العامة، على أنه حديث صحيح، وهو لا أصل له.

Another example is the narration, "The day of your fast is the day of your slaughter."[43] It is famous amongst the common people and held as a *ṣaḥīḥ* narration but there is no origin for it.

ومثله ما يقال (رابعة رجب غرة رمضان فيها تنحرون) وهو حديث منمق لا أصل له، ويعني أن اليوم الرابع لرجب، هو اليوم الأول لرمضان، وهو اليوم العاشر لذي الحجة، وهو باطل غير صحيح.

Likewise is the narration, "The fourth of Rajab is the start of Ramaḍān, in it you shall slaughter." I.e. the fourth day of the month of Rajab is the first day of Ramaḍān and the tenth day of Dhul Hijjah. It is an embellished *ḥadīth* with no origin and thus false and unsound.

والنوع الثاني هو المشهور عند العلماء فهذا يحتج به بعض العلماء وإن لم يكن له إسناد، ويقول: لأن اشتهاره عند أهل العلم، وقبولهم إياه وأخذهم به، يدل على أن له أصلا.

The second type is what is widespread amongst the scholars, and thus is depended upon by some scholars, even if it has no *isnād*. They reason that

42 *Kashf al-Khafā'*; volume 1 page 413, *Tadhkirat al-Mawḍū'āt* 11, and *al-Silsilat al-Ḍa'īfah* 36.
43 *Kashf al-Khafā'*; volume 2 page 211.

the popularity of the narration amongst the people of knowledge, their acceptance and taking it into consideration shows that there is origin for the narration.

ومن ذلك حديث (لا يقاد الوالد بالولد) يعني لا يقتل الوالد بالولد قصاصا، وهو مشهور عند العلماء، فمنهم من أخذ به، وقال لأن اشتهاره عند العلماء وتداولهم إياه واستدلالهم به يدل على أن له أصلا.

One such *ḥadīth* is: "There is no retaliation on the father who murdered his son."[44] I.e. the father is not executed as a form of *qiṣāṣ* (legal retribution) for killing his son. It is a well-known narration amongst the scholars and there are those who took it into consideration saying that due to its popularity amongst the scholars, its circulation amongst them and their deductions from it, it shows that the narration has an origin.

ومن العلماء من لم يعتبر بهذا.

There are scholars who did not take this narration into consideration.

ومنهم من فصل وقال: إن لم يخالف ظاهر النص فهو مقبول.

And there are those who elaborated and said that if the narration does not contradict the apparent meaning of a religious text, then it is acceptable.

أما إن خالف ظاهر النص فهو مردود، وهذا أقرب الأقوال الثلاثة وهو: أن ما اشتهر بين العلماء ينظر فيه، فإن لم يخالف نصا فهو مقبول، وإن خالف نصا فليس بمقبول.

As for the one that contradicts the apparent meaning of a religious text, it is rejected. And this the closest opinion to the truth, which is that the narration which is widespread amongst scholars has to be analysed; if it does

---

44 Recorded by al-Imām Aḥmad 1/49 and al-Tirmidhī; The Book of Blood Monies; Chapter: What comes regarding the man who killed his son, whether he is to be executed or not (1400).

not contradict a religious text then it can be accepted, and if it contradicts a religious text then it cannot be accepted.

مثلا (لا يقاد الوالد بالولد) مخالف لظاهر النص وهو قوله تعالى: ﴿**وكتبنا عليهم فيها أن النفس بالنفس**﴾ [المائدة: ٤٥] . الآية. بل ويخالف قوله تعالى: ﴿**يا أيها الذين آمنوا كتب عليكم القصاص في القتلى الحر بالحر**﴾ [البقرة: ١٧٨] الآية. وقوله صلى الله عليه وسلم: ((لا يحل دم امرئ مسلم إلا بإحدى ثلاث: النفس بالنفس ...)). الحديث.

For instance, the narration, "There is no retribution on the father who murdered his son" contradicts with the apparent meaning of a text, which is the ayah: **{And We ordained for them therein a life for a life.}**[45] In fact, it is also contradictory with the ayah, **{O you who have believed, prescribed for you is legal retribution for those murdered – the free for the free.}**[46] And the *ḥadīth*, "The blood of the Muslim man is not permissible except due to three reasons: a life for a life..."[47]

۞۞۞

المتن

(١٣) مُعَنْعَنٌ كَعَنْ سَعِيدٍ عَنْ كَرَمْ وَمُبْهَمٌ مَا فِيهِ رَاوٍ لَمْ يُسَمّْ

(13) Muʿanʿan is like "from Saʿīd from Karam,"
Mubham is that in which a narrator hasn't been named.

الشرح

المعنعن مأخوذٌ من كلمة (عن) وهو: ما أُدي بصيغة عن.

45 Al-Mā'idah: 45
46 Al-Baqarah: 178
47 Recorded by al-Bukhārī; The Book of Blood Monies; Chapter: The verse: "life for a life" (6878) and Muslim; The Book of Oaths; Chapter: What permits the blood of the Muslim 25 (1676).

Al-mu'an'an is taken from the word *'an,* and it is what is transmitted with the format "from so-and-so".

وهذا هو القسم الحادي عشر، من أقسام الحديث المذكورة في هذا النظم مثل أن يقول: عن نافع عن ابن عمر - رضي الله عنهما - ومثل أن يقول: حدثني فلان، عن فلان، عن فلان، عن فلان.

And this is the eleventh category from the classifications of *ḥadīth* mentioned in this poem. An example is to say: "*'An* (from) Nāfi, *'an* (from) Ibn 'Umar ﵄." Another example would be to say: "*Ḥadathanā fulān* (So and so informed me), *'an fulān* (from so and so), *'an fulān* (from so and so), *'an fulān* (from so and so)."

واقتصر المؤلف على التعريف بالمثال؛ لأن التعريف بالمثال جائز، إذ أن المقصود بالتعريف هو إيضاح المعرَّف، والمثال قد يُغني عن الحد، والمثال الذي ذكره المؤلف هو (عن سعيد عن كرم) فيقول أروي هذا الحديث عن سعيد عن كرم، هذا هو المعنعن.

The author sufficed in its definition with the illustration of an example. This is because the definition by example is permissible, as the aim of defining something is to clarify the defined and providing the example may suffice from doing so. The example that the author gave is, "From Sa'īd from Karam" thus he said, "I narrated this *ḥadīth* from Sa'īd from Karam" and this is the *mu'an'an*.

وهناك نوع آخر مثله وهو المؤنن، وهو ما روي بلفظ (أن)، مثل أن يقول: حدثني فلان أن فلاناً قال: أن فلاناً قال ... إلخ.

There is another type of narration which is called *al-mu'annan.* It is that which is narrated with the word *anna* (that). An example is to say, "*Ḥadathanā fulān* (so and so told me) *anna fulān qāla* (that so-and-so said) *anna fulān qāla* (that so-and-so said) [... to the end]."

وحكم المعنعن والمؤنن هو: الاتصال، إلا ممن عُرف بالتدليس، فإنه لا يُحكم باتصاله إلا بعد أن يُصرح بالسماع في موضع آخر. ومن ثم نحتاج إلى معرفة المدلسين، وذلك لكي تستطيع أن تعرف الحديث إذا جاء بلفظ (عن)، وكان عن مدلس فإنه لا يُحكم له بالاتصال، لأن المدلس قد يُسقط الراوي الذي بينه وبين المذكور تدليساً، لأن الراوي الذي أسقطه قد يكون ضعيفاً في روايته، أو في دينه، فيُسقطه حتى يظهر السند بمظهر الصحيح، فهذا لا نحمله على الاتصال ونخشى من تدليسه، وهذا من احتياط أهل العلم لسنة النبي صلى الله عليه وسلّم، ومن نعمة الله تعالى على هذه الأمة حيث إنهم كانوا يتحرزون أشد التحرز فيما يُنسب إلى النبي صلى الله عليه وسلّم.

And the ruling for the *mu'an'an* and *mu'annan* is that the chain is connected except if it includes a narrator who is known to make *tadlīs* (deception). In this case it is not considered as being connected until it is made explicit in another place that the hearing occurred. Hence, we need to know the *mudallisīn* (those who perform *al-tadlīs*) so that we are capable of identifying a *ḥadīth* as not being connected when it comes with the word *'an* and it is narrated from a *mudallis* (singular of *mudallisūn*). This is because the deceiver may have abandoned a narrator between him and the one mentioned in the chain as a form of deception due to the weakness of the abandoned narrator in his narration or his religion, and hence the abandonment was to give the *sanad* an appearance of authenticity. Therefore, we do not consider it as being connected as we fear from his deception. And this is the cautiousness of the people of knowledge when it comes to the Sunnah of the Prophet ﷺ and one of Allāh's Blessings that is bestowed upon this nation is that the scholars were very reserved in attributing anything to the Prophet ﷺ.

وقوله: (ومبهم ما فيه راو لم يسم).

The author's statement: "*Mubhām* is that in which a narrator hasn't been named."

والمبهم هو: الذي فيه راو لم يسم، وهذا هو القسم الثاني عشر من أقسام الحديث المذكورة في هذا النظم.

The *mubham* (ambiguous) narration is one that has an unidentified narrator and this is the twelfth category from the classifications of *ḥadīth* mentioned in this poem.

مثل أن يقول: حدثني رجل، قال: حدثني فلانٌ عن فلان عن فلان، فإننا نسمي هذا الحديث مبهماً، لأنه أُبهم فيه الراوي، وكذلك إذا قال: حدثني الثقة فإنه أيضاً يكون مبهماً، لأننا لا ندري من هو هذا الثقة فقد يكون ثقة عند المحدث، وليس بثقة عند غيره.

An example would be to say: "A man told me and he said, 'So-and-so told me from so-and-so from so-and-so.'" We term this *ḥadīth* as *mubham* because a narrator in the chain is unknown. Likewise if he were to say, "The trustworthy person told me", it is also considered as *mubham* because we do not know who this trustworthy person is; he could be reliable in the eyes of the scholar but not trustworthy according to others.

وكذلك إذا قال: حدثني من أثق به، فهذا أيضاً يكون مبهماً.

Similarly if he were to say, "Someone I trust told me", this is also considered as *mubham*.

وكذلك إذا قال: حدثني صاحب هذه الدار فإنه يكون مبهماً ما لم يكن صاحب الدار معروفاً.

If he were to say, "The owner of this residence told me", it is considered as *mubham* as well, so long as the owner of the house is not known.

إذاً فالمبهم هو: كل ما فيه راوٍ لم يُسم، أما ما كان الحديث فيه عن رجل لم يسمَّ مثل حديث أنسٍ - رضي الله عنه - قال: دخل أعرابي يوم الجمعة والنبي صلى

الله عليه وسلّم يخطب ... الحديث، فالأعرابي هنا مبهم، لكنه لا يدخل في التعريف الذي معنا، لأن الأعرابي هنا لم يحدث بالحديث، ولكنه تُحدِّث عنه.

Therefore, the *mubham* is everything that has an unnamed narrator. As for the *ḥadīth* which includes a man who is not named e.g. the *ḥadīth* of Anas ﷺ who said, "A Bedouin man entered the *masjid* on a Friday when the Prophet ﷺ was delivering his sermon ..."[48] The Bedouin here is unknown but the narration is not considered to fall under the term we are discussing here because the Bedouin did not narrate a *ḥadīth*, rather he was spoken about.

إذاً فقوله (ما فيه راوٍ لم يُسمّ) معناه أي: ما كان في السند راوٍ لم يسمّ.

Hence the author's statement, "That in which a narrator hasn't been named" refers to the instance when a narrator in the *sanad* is not named.

وحكم المبهم أن حديثه لا يُقبل، حتى يُعلم من هو هذا المبهم، وذلك لجهالتنا بحال هذا المبهم، إلا المبهم من الصحابة فإن إبهامه لا يضر، لأن الصحابة كلهم عدولٌ ثقاتٌ بشهادة الله تعالى لهم في قوله تعالى: ﴿وَكُلًّا وَعَدَ اللَّهُ الْحُسْنَىٰ وَاللَّهُ بِمَا تَعْمَلُونَ خَبِيرٌ﴾ [الحديد: ١٠] . وتزكيته إياهم في قوله تعالى: ﴿مُّحَمَّدٌ رَّسُولُ اللَّهِ وَالَّذِينَ مَعَهُ أَشِدَّاءُ عَلَى الْكُفَّارِ رُحَمَاءُ بَيْنَهُمْ﴾ [الفتح: ٢٩] . وقوله: ﴿ وَالسَّابِقُونَ الْأَوَّلُونَ مِنَ الْمُهَاجِرِينَ وَالْأَنصَارِ وَالَّذِينَ اتَّبَعُوهُم بِإِحْسَانٍ رَّضِيَ اللَّهُ عَنْهُمْ وَرَضُوا عَنْهُ﴾ [التوبة: ١٠٠] .

The ruling of *mubham* is that the *ḥadīth* is not acceptable until the identity of this *mubham* narrator is ascertained. This is because we do not know the status of this ambiguous person. However an exception is the *mubham* narrator from amongst the companions, for his ambiguity does not cause any harm. This is because all of the companions are righteous and trustworthy

48 Recorded by al-Bukhārī; The Book of Seeking Rain; Chapter: The seeking of rain on a Friday (1014) and Muslim; The Book of Seeking Rain; Chapter: Supplications during the seeking of rain 8 (897).

with Allāh's testimony in the ayah: **{But to all Allāh has promised the best [reward].}**[49] And His commendation in the ayah: **{Muhammad is the Messenger of Allāh; and those with him are forceful against the disbelievers, merciful among themselves.}**[50] As well as the ayah: **{And the first forerunners [in the faith] among the Muhājirīn and the Anṣār and those who followed them with good conduct – Allāh is pleased with them and they are pleased with Him.}**[51]

إذاً فحكم الحديث المبهم أنه موقوف حتى يتبين من هو هذا المبهم إلا الصحابة رضوان الله عليهم فإن المبهم منهم مقبول كما سبق بيانه.

Therefore, the ruling of the *mubham* narration is that it is put on hold until the unknown narrator is identified, except for the companions, as the ambiguous amongst them are acceptable, as discussed earlier.

۞۞۞

المتن

(١٤) وَكُلُّ مَا قَلَّتْ رِجَالُهُ عَلاَ   وَضِدُّهُ ذَاكَ الَّذِي قَدْ نَزَلاَ

(14) That which has few narrators shall arise,
And its opposite is the one which shall descend.

الشرح

هذان قسمان من أقسام الحديث وهما الثالث عشر والرابع عشر مما ذُكر في هذا النظم وهما العالي، والنازل.

These are two categories of the classifications of *ḥadīth*, which are the thirteenth and fourteenth mentioned in this poem. They are called *al-ʿālī* (high graded) and *al-nāzil* (low graded).

---

49 Al-Ḥadīd: 10
50 Al-Fatḥ: 29
51 Al-Tawbah: 100

وعلو الإسناد ونزوله من وصف الإسناد.

The highness of a chain or its lowness is a description of the *isnād*.

وينقسم العلو إلى قسمين:

And there are two types of highly graded chains:

١ - علو عدد، وهو ما عرّفه المؤلف بقوله (ما قلت رجاله ... إلخ) فكل ما قل رجال السند فيه فهو عالٍ، وكل ما كثر رجال السند فيه فهو نازل، وذلك لأنه إذا قلّ عدد الرجال، قلت الوسائط، وكلما قلت الوسائط ضعف احتمال الخطأ، ويتضح هذا بالمثال:

Firstly: The highness in terms of numbers, and it is as defined by the author in his statement, "That which has few narrators ..." As such, every *sanad* that has a lower quantity of narrators is considered as highly graded, while every *sanad* that has a higher quantity of narrators is considered as lowly graded. This is because a lower number of narrators leads to fewer intermediaries, and the fewer the intermediaries that are present lowers the risk of mistakes. This becomes clear via an example:

فإذا كان الرواة زيداً، عن عمرو، عن بكر، فالخطأ يحتمل في الأول، ويحتمل في الثاني، ويحتمل في الثالث، فالاحتمالات ثلاثة، وإذا كانوا زيداً، عن عمرو، عن بكر، عن خالد، عن سفيان، صار عندنا خمسة احتمالات، ومعلوم أنه كلما قل احتمال الخطأ كان أقرب إلى القبول.

If the narrators were Zayd from ʿAmr from Bakr, the risk of making mistakes can occur at the first, the second and the third narrator. Thus there are three possibilities. And if they were Zayd from ʿAmr from Bakr from Khālid from Sufyān, then there are five possibilities. It is known that the lower the risk of making mistakes, the closer the matter is to being accepted.

فإذا رُوي الحديث بسند بينه وبين الراوي خمسة، ورُوي من طريق آخر بينه وبين

الراوي ثلاثة، فالثاني هو العالي، والأول هو النازل، لأن احتمال الخطأ في الثلاثة أقل من احتمال الخطأ في الخمسة.

Thus, if the *ḥadīth* was narrated with a *sanad* having five individuals between the narration and the narrator, and in another route there are three individuals between the narration and the narrator, then the second is termed as *al-ʿālī* and the first is called *al-nāzil*. This is due to the reduced possibility of making mistakes when there are three intermediaries compared to five.

وهل يلزم من علو السند عدداً أن يكون أصحَّ من النازل؟

Does the highness of the *sanad* in terms of numbers imply that it is more sound than that of *al-nāzil*?

نقول: لا يلزم ذلك، لأن هذا العدد القليل من الرواة قد يكون الرواة فيه ضعفاء، ويكون في العدد الكثير الرواة فيه ثقات أثبات، فلا يلزم من علو الإسناد عدداً، أن يكون العالي أصح، لأن اعتبار حال الرجال أمرٌ مهم.

We say that it does not imply as such because the one with fewer numbers may include weak narrators whereas the one with more numbers may include trustworthy and steadfast narrators. Hence, the highly graded *sanad* in terms of numbers does not lead us to conclude that the *ʿālī* is more authentic, as the status of the narrators is an important matter to take into consideration.

٢ - علو صفة. وذلك بأن يكون رجال السند أثبت في الحفظ والعدالة من السند الآخر.

Secondly: The highness in terms of description. This is the *sanad* where the narrators are more firm in terms of memorisation and righteousness than the other *sanad*.

مثاله:

An example:

إذا روي الحديث من طريق عدد رجاله ثلاثة، وروي من طريق آخر عدد رجاله ثلاثة، لكن رجال الطريق الأول أضعف من الطريق الثاني في الحفظ، والعدالة، فالثاني بلا شك أقوى وأعلى من الطريق الأول.

If a *ḥadīth* were to be narrated through a route of three narrators, and it is also narrated through another route of three narrators, but the narrators of the first route are weaker in terms of memory and righteousness than that of the second, then undoubtedly the second is stronger and higher in grade than the first route.

ولو رُوي الحديث من طريق فيه أربعة رجال، وروي من طريق آخر فيه ثلاثة رجال، لكن الطريق الأول أثبت من الطريق الثاني في العدالة والحفظ، فالأول أعلى باعتبار حال الرواة.

And if a *ḥadīth* were to be narrated through a route of four narrators, and the same *ḥadīth* is also narrated through another route of three narrators. If the first route is firmer in terms of memory and righteousness than that of the second, then the first is higher in grade in terms of the status of the narrators.

يعني أن الأول أعلى علو صفة، والثاني أعلى علو عدد، ففي هذه الحالة أيهما نقدم؟

So if the first is higher in terms of description while the second is higher in terms of numbers, which of the two situations should we give more priority?

نقول: نقدم الأول وهو العلو في الصفة، لأن العلو في الصفة هو الذي يُعتمد عليه في صحة الحديث، لأن العدد قد يكون مثلاً ثلاثة رواة وكلهم ثقات، فيكون الحديث صحيحاً، وقد يكون العدد عشرين راوياً، لكن كلهم ضعفاء، فلا يكون الحديث صحيحاً.

We say that we prefer the first, which is the highness in terms of description. This is because it is the one that is taken into consideration for the authentication of the *ḥadīth,* as the numbers may be for example three narrators and all of them are reliable thus the narration is *ṣaḥīḥ*, and the numbers may be twenty narrators but all of them are weak thus the *ḥadīth* is not *ṣaḥīḥ*.

إذاً فالعلو ينقسم إلى قسمين:

Therefore, there are two categories in terms of the highness of an *isnād*:

١ - علو العدد وهو: ما كان فيه عدد الرجال أقل.

1. Highness in terms of number: There are fewer numbers of narrators.

٢ - علو الصفة وهو: ما كان حال الرجال فيه أقوى وأعلى من جهة الحفظ والعدالة.

2. Highness in terms of description: In which the statuses of the narrators are stronger and higher in terms of memorisation and righteousness.

والمؤلف رحمه الله لم يتكلم عن علو الصفة وإنما تكلم عن علو العدد.

And the author did not speak about the highness in terms of description and only spoke about the highness in terms of numbers.

المتن

(١٥) وَمَا أَضَفْتَهُ إِلَى الأَصْحَابِ مِنْ قَولٍ وَفِعْلٍ فَهْوَ مَوْقُوفٌ زُكِنْ

(15) And whatever you attributed to the companions such as,
A statement or an action is known as mawqūf.

الشرح

هذا هو القسم الخامس عشر من أقسام الحديث المذكورة في هذا النظم وهو

الموقوف.

This is the fifteenth category from the classifications of *ḥadīth* mentioned in the poem, and it is called *al-mawqūf*.

قوله (ما) شرطية.

The word *mā* (whatever) is a conditional preposition.

(أضفته إلى الأصحاب) أي ما أضفته أيها الراوي إلى الأصحاب.

"Attributed to the *aṣḥāb* (companions)" i.e. whatever the narrator attributes to the *aṣḥāb*.

والأصحاب جمع صحبٍ، وصَحْبٌ اسم جمع صاحب.

Aṣḥāb is the plural of *ṣaḥb*, and *ṣaḥb* is the plural noun of *ṣāḥib* (companion).

والمراد بالأصحاب هنا: أصحاب النبي صلى الله عليه وسلّم.

And *aṣḥāb* here refers to the companions of the Prophet ﷺ.

والصحابي هو: من اجتمع بالنبي صلى الله عليه وسلّم مؤمناً به، ومات على ذلك.

The companion is one who met with the Prophet ﷺ, believed in him and passed away upon it.

حتى ولو كان الاجتماع لحظة، وهذا من خصائص النبي صلى الله عليه وسلّم أن يكون صاحبه من اجتمع به ولو لحظة.

Even if the meeting was for a moment, and this is amongst the specific attributes of the Prophet ﷺ, that his companions include those who met him even for a moment.

أما غيره فلا يكون الصاحب صاحباً إلا بطول صحبة، أما مجرد أن يلاقيه في أي مكان، فلا يكون بذلك صاحباً له.

Other than those attributed to him ﷺ, a companion is not termed as such until the companionship occurs for a long period of time. As for someone who meets another individual for the first time at a location, he would not be considered as a companion of the other merely from this meeting.

ولابد في الصحابي أن يموت مؤمناً بالنبي صلى الله عليه وسلّم حتى ولو ارتد عن الإسلام ثم رجع إليه مرة أخرى، فهو صحابي على الصحيح من أقوال أهل العلم.

It is a criterion for a companion to pass away as a believer of the Prophet ﷺ. Even if he were to renounce Islām and then return to embrace it once again, in this case he is still considered as a companion according to the correct opinion amongst the scholars.

إذاً فما أضفته إلى الصحابة - رضوان الله تعالى عليهم - فإنه يسمى عند المحدثين موقوفاً.

That which is attributed to a companion is termed by the scholars of *ḥadīth* as *mawqūf*.

وقوله (زُكِنْ) يعني عُلِم.

And the author's word *"zukin"* means known.

وقوله (من قول وفعل). يُستثنى من ذلك ما ثبت له حكم الرفع، من قول الصحابي أو فعله، فإنه يكون مرفوعاً حُكماً، ولو كان من فعل الصحابي، كصلاة علي رضي الله عنه في الكسوف ثلاث ركوعات في كل ركعة، فهذا مرفوعٌ حُكماً، لأن عدد الركوعات في ركعة واحدة، أمرٌ يتوقف فيه على الشرع، ولا مجال للاجتهاد فيه، وكذلك لو تحدث الصحابي عن أمر من أمور المستقبل، أو أمور الغيب، فإنه يُحكم له بالرفع، لأن أمور الغيب ليس للرأي فيها مجال.

The author's statement, "A statement or an action": The exceptions of *al-mawqūf* are the narrations which are ruled to be *al-marfū'*. Whether it is the speech of the companion or his action, it has the ruling of *marfū'* even if it is his action, such as the prayer of 'Alī ﵁ whereby he made three bows in every unit of the solar eclipse prayer. This is because, the number of bows in a unit of prayer is a matter bound by the Islamic law and there is no room for *ijtihād* in it. Similar is the case for the speech of the companions regarding the matters that shall happen in the future or the unseen. These are given the ruling of *marfū'* due to the fact that there is no room for logical reasoning in the matters of the unseen.

۞۞۞

المتن

(١٦) وَمُـرْسَلٌ مِنْهُ الصَّحَابِيُّ سَقَطْ ... ...

(16) And al-mursal, from it the companion was omitted,

الشرح

هذا هو القسم السادس عشر من أقسام الحديث المذكورة في هذا النظم وهو المرسل.

This is the sixteenth category of the classifications of *ḥadīth* mentioned in the poem and it is called *al-mursal* (the released chain).

والمرسل في اللغة: المطلق، ومنه أرسل الناقة في المرعى، أي أطلقها.

Linguistically, *al-mursal* means the one released. An example of its usage is the sentence, *"Arsala nāqata fi 'l-mar'ā"* which means he released the camel at the pasture.

وفي الاصطلاح عرفه الناظم بأنه: ما سقط منه الصحابي.

In terms of terminology, the author defined it as the narration where the companion was omitted from it.

وعرفه بعض العلماء بأنه: ما رفعه التابعي أو الصحابي الذي لم يسمع من النبي صلى الله عليه وسلّم وهذا التعريف أدق؛ لأن ظاهر كلام المؤلف أنه إذا ذكر الصحابي فليس بمرسل، ولو كان الصحابي لم يسمع من النبي صلى الله عليه وعلى آله وسلم، كمحمد بن أبي بكر - رضي الله عنهما - الذي ولد في حجة الوداع وهذا ليس بجيد، فإن حديث الصحابي الذي لم يسمع من النبي صلى الله عليه وسلّم من قبيل المرسل عند المحققين.

And some scholars defined it as the attribution of a narration to the Prophet ﷺ by a *tābiʿī* or a companion who did not hear the narration from the Prophet himself. This definition is more precise because the apparent meaning of the author's speech is that if the name of the companion is mentioned, then it is not considered as *mursal* even if the companion did not hear from the Prophet ﷺ such as Muḥammad ibn Abī Bakr ؓ who was born during the Farewell Pilgrimage, and this is not a legitimate definition. As such, the *ḥadīth* of a companion who did not hear from the Prophet ﷺ is also categorised as *mursal* according to the *muḥaqqiqīn* (*ḥadīth* investigators).

والمرسل من أقسام الضعيف؛ لأن الواسطة بين النبي صلى الله عليه وسلّم وبين من رفعه مجهول إلا في المواضع التالية:

The *mursal* is one of the divisions of the weak narrations because the intermediary between the Prophet ﷺ and the one who attributed it to him is unknown. There are exceptions in a few situations:

الأول: إذا علم الواسطة بين النبي صلى الله عليه وسلّم ومن رفعه، فيحكم بما تقتضيه حاله.

Firstly: If the intermediary between the Prophet ﷺ and the one who attributed it to him ﷺ is known, then the ruling is according to the status of the intermediary.

الثاني: إذا كان الرافع له صحابيًا.

Secondly: If the one attributing it is a companion.

الثالث: إذا علم أن رافعه لا يرفعه إلا عن طريق صحابي.

Thirdly: If the one who made the attribution is known to always attribute through the route of a companion.

الرابع: إذا تلقته الأمة بالقبول.

Fourthly: If the Ummah has received the narration with acceptance.

المتن

(١٦) ... ...   وَقُلْ غَرِيبٌ مَا رَوَى رَاوٍ فَقَطْ

(16) And say that gharīb is that which was narrated by only one.

الشرح

هذا هو القسم السابع عشر من أقسام الحديث المذكورة في هذا النظم وهو الغريب.

This is the seventeenth category of the classifications of *ḥadīth* mentioned in the poem and it is called *al-gharīb* (the one-of-its-kind chain).

قوله: (وقُل غريبٌ ما روى راوٍ فقط) الغريب مشتق من الغربة، والغريب في البلد هو الذي ليس من أهلها.

The author's statement, "And say that *gharīb* is that which was narrated by only one": The word *al-gharīb* comes from *al-ghurbah* (strangeness). And the *gharīb* (stranger) in a country is one who is not its resident.

والغريب في الحديث هو: ما رواه راوٍ واحد فقط، حتى ولو كان الصحابي، فهو غريب، مثل أن لا نجد راو من الصحابة إلا ابن عباس - رضي الله عنهما - فهو

غريب، أو لم نجد راوياً من التابعين إلا قتادة فهو غريب.

And the term *gharīb* in the science of *ḥadīth* is the narration that was narrated by only one narrator. Even if it was a companion, it is considered as *gharīb*. For example if we do not find any other companion except Ibn 'Abbās ﷺ then it is considered as *gharīb*. Or if we do not find any other *tābi'ī* reporter except Qatādah, then it is considered as *gharīb*.

والغرابة إما أن تكون في: أول السند. أو في أثنائه. أو في آخره.

The state of *gharīb* may occur either at the beginning of the *sanad*, or in the middle, or at the end.

يعني قد يكون الحديث غريباً في آخر السند لم يروه إلا تابعي واحد عن الصحابة، ثم يرويه عنه عدد كبير، فيكون هذا غريباً في آخر السند، وفيما بعده قد يصل إلى حد التواتر، فحديث ((إنما الأعمال بالنيات ...)) من الغريب، لكنه غريب في طبقة الصحابة والتابعين، وأما بعد ذلك فقد انتشر انتشاراً عظيماً.

Which means that the *ḥadīth* may be *gharīb* at the end of the *sanad* whereby it is only narrated by one *tābi'ī* from a companion, followed by it being narrated by a large number of narrators. Thus this narration is *gharīb* at the end of the *sanad,* even if the ones after him may reach the level of *tawātur*. As such, the *ḥadīth*, "Indeed actions are according to intentions ..."[52] is considered as *gharīb*. It is *gharīb* at the levels of the companions and the *tābi'īn*. As for the levels after that, it was widely spread.

وقد يكون غريباً في أثنائه، رواه جماعة وانفرد به عنهم واحد، ثم رواه عن جماعة، وقد يكون غريباً في أوله انفرد به واحد عن جماعة.

The narration may also be *gharīb* in the middle, whereby it was narrated by a group of narrators followed by only one person and then a group of narrators. It could also be *gharīb* at the beginning, whereby only one narrator narrated it from a group of narrators.

52 Mentioned previously.

والغريب قد يكون صحيحاً، وقد يكون ضعيفاً، لكن الغالب على الغرائب أنها تكون ضعيفة.

And the *gharīb* narration may be *ṣaḥīḥ* or *ḍaʿīf*, but usually the *gharīb* narrations are taken to be *ḍaʿīf*.

المتن

(١٧) وَكُلُّ مَا لَمْ يَتَّصِلْ بِحَالِ   إِسْنَادُهُ مُنْقَطِعُ الأَوْصَالِ

(17) And all that is not connected in any instance,
Its chain has munqaṭiʿ (severed) ties.

الشرح

هذا هو القسم الثامن عشر من أقسام الحديث المذكورة في هذا النظم وهو المنقطع.

This is the eighteenth category of the classifications of *ḥadīth* mentioned in the poem and it is called *al-munqaṭiʿ* (disconnected).

قوله: (وكل ما).

The author's phrase, "And all":

أي كل حديث أو كل إسناد، لكن الظاهر أن مراده كل حديث بدليل قوله: (لم يتصل إسناده) أي أن كل حديث لم يتصل إسناده بأي حال من الأحوال فإنه يسمى منقطعاً، وهذا بالمعنى العام، فإذا كان الحديث قد رواه خمسة، الأول، عن الثاني، عن الثالث، عن الرابع، عن الخامس.

Which refers to either all *ḥadīths* or all *isnāds*, but the apparent meaning is that he is referring to the *ḥadīths*. The proof is that he said, "That is not connected ... its chain" i.e. that all *ḥadīths* with *isnāds* not connected in any state are called *al-munqaṭi'*. And this is the general meaning. As such, if the *ḥadīth* were to be narrated by five narrators; from the first, from the second, from the third, from the fourth, from the fifth.

ثم وجدناه مروياً عن الأول، عن الثالث، عن الرابع، عن الخامس فهو منقطع.

And then we found that it was narrated from the first, from the third, from the fourth, from the fifth, then it is considered to be *munqaṭi'*.

ولو وجدناه مروياً عن الثاني، عن الثالث، عن الرابع، عن الخامس فهو منقطع لأنه سقط أوله.

And if we found that it was narrated from the second, from the third, from the fourth, from the fifth, then it is also considered to be *munqaṭi'* as the first narrator was abandoned.

ولو رواه الأول، عن الثالث، عن الخامس فهو أيضاً منقطع.

And if it was narrated from the first, from the third, from the fifth, then it is also considered to be *munqaṭi'*.

ويقسم العلماء الانقطاع إلى أربعة أقسام:

The scholars classified the state of *munqaṭi'* into four divisions:

١ - أن يكون الانقطاع من أول السند.

1. The disconnection is from its beginning.

٢ - أن يكون الانقطاع من آخر السند.

2. The disconnection is from its end.

٣ - أن يكون الانقطاع من أثناء السند بواحد فقط.

3. The disconnection is by only one narrator from its middle.

٤ - أن يكون الانقطاع من أثناء السند باثنين فأكثر على التوالي.

4. The disconnection is by two or more narrators consecutively from its middle.

فأما القسم الأول وهو: إذا كان الانقطاع من أول السند فإنه يسمى معلقاً.

As for the first category, which is the disconnection from the beginning of the *sanad*, it is called *al-mu'allaq* (the hanged chain).

ووجه التسمية فيه: ظاهرة؛ لأنك إذا علقت شيئاً في السقف، وهو منقطع من أسفله فلن يصل إلى الأرض، فالمعلق ما حُذف منه أول إسناده.

And the logic behind its name is apparent because if you were to hang something from the ceiling, it is then disconnected from its lowest end and does not reach the ground. Therefore, the *mu'allaq* is what has the beginning of its chain omitted.

وهل المعلق من قسم الصحيح أو هو من قسم الضعيف؟

Is the *mu'allaq* one of the types of the *ṣaḥīḥ* or the *ḍa'īf* narrations?

نقول: هو من قسم الضعيف؛ لأن من شرط الصحيح، اتصال السند، لكن ما علقه البخاري جازماً به فهو صحيح عنده، وإن لم يكن على شرطه، وإنما قلنا صحيح عنده؛ لأنه يعلّقه مستدلاً به على الحكم، ولا يمكن أن يستدل على حُكم من أحكام الله تعالى، إلا بشيء صحيح عنده، لكنه ليس على شرطه، لأنه لو كان على شرطه، لساقه بسنده حتى يُعرف، مع أنه - رحمه الله تعالى - ربما يأتي به معلقاً في باب، ومتصلاً في باب آخر.

We say that it is one of the types of *ḍa'īf* narrations, as a requirement of the *ṣaḥīḥ* narration is the connection of its chain. However, whatever al-Bukhārī recorded as *mu'allaq* and he was emphatic about it, it is considered as *ṣaḥīḥ* according to him, even if it was not according to his conditions.

And we say that it is *ṣaḥīḥ* according to al-Bukhārī because he recorded it as *mu'allaq* and used it [as a valid evidence] to infer the rulings. Evidently it is not possible that he would conclude any of Allāh's rulings except by deriving from the sound narrations he possessed. However the narration did not meet al-Bukhārī's criteria, and if it had, he would have mentioned its *sanad* so that it is known, whilst bearing in mind that he would sometimes report a *ḥadīth* as *mu'allaq* in a chapter but *muttaṣil* (connected) in another.

وأما القسم الثاني وهو: أن يكون الانقطاع من آخر السند فهذا هو المرسل.

As for the second category, which is the disconnection from the end of the *sanad*, it is called *al-mursal* (the released chain).

وأما القسم الثالث وهو: أن يكون الانقطاع من أثناء السند برجل واحد فهذا يسمى منقطعاً في الاصطلاح، فالمنقطع عندهم هو ما حُذف من أثناء سنده راوٍ واحد فقط.

As for the third category, which is the disconnection by one narrator from the middle of the *sanad*, it is called *al-munqaṭi'* (the disconnected chain) in terms of nomenclature. Thus the *munqaṭi'* according to the scholars is that which has an omission of only a single narrator in the middle of its chain.

وأما القسم الرابع وهو: أن يكون الانقطاع من أثناء السند برجلين فأكثر على التوالي فهذا يسمى معضلاً.

As for the fourth category, wherein the disconnection is by two or more narrators consecutively from the middle of the *sanad*, it is called *al-mu'ḍal* (the impassable chain).

❁❁❁

ولهذا قال المؤلف رحمه الله:

And due to this, the author said:

المتن

(١٨) والْمُعْضَلُ الساقِطُ مِنْهُ اثْنَان ... ...

(18) And the mu'dal has two omitted from it,

الشرح

هذا هو القسم التاسع عشر من أقسام الحديث المذكورة في هذا وهو المعضل.

This is the nineteenth category of the classifications of *ḥadīth* mentioned in the poem, and it is called *al-mu'dal* (the impassable chain).

وقوله (المعضل) مبتدأ، و(الساقط) خبره. وقوله (الساقطُ منه اثنان) يعني على التوالي، لا على التفريق.

The author's words *"the mu'dal"* is the subject (Arabic grammar: *mubtada*) and "omitted" (*al-sāqitu*) is its predicate (Arabic grammar: *khabr*). And the phrase, "has two omitted from it" means consecutively and not separately.

فمثلاً: إذا كان السند هم الأول، والثاني، والثالث، والرابع وسقط الثاني والثالث فهذا يسمى معضلاً، لأنه سقط راويان على التوالي، وكذلك لو سقط ثلاثة فأكثر على التوالي.

For example, if the *sanad* comprises of the first, second, third and fourth narrators, and the second and third were omitted, then it is called *mu'dal* because two consecutive narrators were omitted. Similar is the case if three or more consecutive narrators were omitted.

وإذا سقط منه الثاني والرابع فهذا منقطع، لأنه وإن سقط منه راويان ولكنهما ليسا على التوالي.

If the second and fourth were abandoned, then this is called *munqaṭi'*. This is because even if two narrators were abandoned, they were not consecutive.

وإذا سقط منه الأول والأخير، فهذا معلقٌ مرسل، أي أنه معلقٌ باعتبار أول السند، ومرسلٌ باعتبار آخر السند.

And if the first and the last were abandoned, then it is *mu'allaq* and *mursal* at the same time i.e. *mu'allaq* in view of the abandonment at the beginning of the *sanad* and *mursal* in view of its end.

وكل هذه الأقسام تعتبر من أقسام الضعيف.

All these categories are taken to be types of *ḍa'īf* narrations.

وإذا وجدنا حديثين أحدهما معضل، والآخر منقطع، أو معلق، أو مرسل، فإن المعضل أشدُّ ضعفاً، لأنه سقط منه راويان على التوالي.

And if we found two narrations, one of which is *mu'ḍal* and the other may be *munqaṭi'*, *mu'allaq* or *mursal*, then the *mu'ḍal* is the weakest of all, because two of its consecutive narrators were abandoned.

۞۞۞

المتن

(١٨) ... ... وَمَا أَتَى مُدَلَّساً نَوْعَانِ

(18) That which comes as mudallas is of two types:

الشرح

وقوله (وما أتى مدلساً نوعان) هذا هو القسم العشرون من أقسام الحديث المذكورة في هذا النظم.

The statement: "That which comes as *mudallas* is of two types" brings us to the twentieth category of the classifications of *ḥadīth* mentioned in the poem.

ف(مدلساً) حال من فاعل أتى، و(نوعان) خبر المبتدأ، و(ما) اسم موصول بمعنى الذي، يعني والذي أتى مدلساً نوعان.

The word "*mudallas*" is the circumstance (Arabic grammar: *ḥāl*) of the doer (Arabic grammar: *fā'il*) of the verb "come". While "two types" (*naw'ān*) is the predicate for the subject. "What" (*mā*) is a relative pronoun (Arabic grammar: *ism mawṣūl*) with the meaning "the one that" i.e. the one that comes as *mudallas* is of two types.

وقوله (مدلساً) المدلس مأخوذ من التدليس، وأصله من الدُّلسة وهي الظلمة، والتدليس في البيع هو أن يُظهر المبيع بصفةٍ أحسن مما هو عليه في الواقع، مثل أن يصري اللبن في ضرع البهيمة، أو أن يصبغ الجدار بأصباغ يظنُّ الرائي أنّه جديد، وهو ليس كذلك.

The author's word, "*mudallas*": *Al-mudallas* (the deceived narration) comes from the word *al-tadlīs*. Its origin comes from the word *al-dulsah,* which means the darkness. And the act of *tadlīs* in trading is to display the goods in a manner that makes them seem better in quality than they really are, such as the accumulation of milk in the udders of livestock or to colour the wall with paint so that the one who sees it will think that it is new but in actual fact it is not.

أما التدليس في الحديث فينقسم إلى قسمين: كما قال المؤلف - رحمه الله - (وما أتى مدلساً نوعان)، وبعض العلماء يقسِّمه إلى ثلاثة أقسام.

As for *tadlīs* in the science of *ḥadīth*, it is divided into two categories as mentioned by the author: "That which comes as *mudallas* is of two types", while some scholars divided it into three categories.

أما على تقسيم المؤلف فهو قسمان:

As for the classification of the author, it is divided into two categories.

الأول: ذكره بقوله:

The first category is mentioned in the next couplet of the poem:

المتن

(١٩) الأَوَّلُ الإِسْقَاطُ لِلشَّيْخِ وَأَنْ يَنْقُلَ عَمَّنْ فَوقَهُ بِعَنْ وَأَنْ

(19) The first is omission of the shaykh and to,
Transmit from the one above him by using "an" and "an";

الشرح

وهذا تدليس التسوية، بان يسقط الراوي شيخه، ويروي عمن فوقه بصيغة ظاهرها الاتصال.

This is called *tadlīs al-taswiyah* whereby the narrator abandoned his *shaykh* (teacher) and narrated from the one above the teacher with a format that is made to appear connected.

كما لو قال: خالدٌ: إنّ عليًّا قال كذا وكذا، وبين خالد وعلي رجل اسمه محمد، وهو قد أسقط محمداً ولم يذكره، وقال إن عليًّا قال كذا وكذا.

Such as if Khālid were to say that ʿAlī said such-and-such, whereas between Khālid and ʿAlī is a narrator named Muḥammad. However Khālid had abandoned Muḥammad and did not mention his name, instead he said that ʿAlī said such-and-such.

فنقول هذا تدليس وهو في الحقيقة لم يكذب بل هو صادق، لكن هناك بعض الأسباب تحمل الراوي على التدليس: كأن يريد الراوي أن يخفي نفسه لئلا يُقال عنه أنه أخذ عن هذا الشيخ مثلاً، أو أخفى ذلك لغرض سياسي، أو لأنه يخشى على نفسه من سلطان أو نحوه، أو لغير ذلك من الأسباب الأخرى، أو لأجل أن الشيخ الذي أسقطه غير مقبول الرواية، إما لكونه ضعيف الحفظ، أو لكونه قليل

الدين، أو لأن شيخه الذي روى عنه أقل مرتبة منه، أو ما أشبه ذلك.

We say that this is an act of *tadlīs* and it is in actual fact not a form of lying, as he is speaking the truth. However there are a few reasons that cause the narrator to make *tadlīs*. Examples being to hide himself in a manner that it is not said that he studied from a particular *shaykh* for example, or to hide it for political reasons, or due to his fear of authorities or the like, or due to other reasons. Or perhaps because the *shaykh* he abandoned is someone whose narration is not acceptable, either due to the fact that he has poor memory or is weak in his religion, or maybe that his *shaykh* is of lower status than him etc.

المهم أن أغراض إسقاط الشيخ كثيرة غير محصورة، لكن أسوأها أن يكون الشيخ غير عدل، فيسقطه من أجل أن يصبح الحديث مقبولاً، لأن هذا يترتب عليه أحكام شرعية كثيرة، وربما يكون الحديث مكذوباً من قبل الشيخ الساقط.

Most importantly, the objectives behind the abandonment of the *shaykh* are many and limitless but the worst of them is where the *shaykh* is not righteous and the abandonment is so that the *ḥadīth* becomes acceptable. This is because it may have an impact on many of the legislative rulings and perhaps the *ḥadīth* may be fabricated by the abandoned *shaykh* himself.

ولا يقبل حديث المدلس، ولو كان الراوي ثقة، إلا إذا صرح بالتحديث وقال: حدثني فلان، أو سمعت فلاناً، فحينئذ يكون متصلاً.

The narration of the *mudallis* is not acceptable, even if the narrator is trustworthy, except if he made it obvious that he was told directly by saying: "So-and-so told me" or "I heard so-and-so", in which case it becomes connected.

القسم الثاني: تدليس الشيوخ: وهو ألا يُسقط الشيخ ولكن يصفه بأوصاف لا يعرف بها، وإليه الإشارة بقوله:

The second category is the *tadlīs* of *shuyūkh* (plural of *shaykh*), whereby the *shaykh* is not being abandoned but being described with characteristics that he was not known for, and the author pointed this out in his next couplet:

المتن

(٢٠) وَالثَّانِي لاَ يُسْقِطُهُ لَكِنْ يَصِفْ أَوْصَافَهُ بِمَا بِهِ لاَ يَنْعَرِفْ

(20) And in the second he does not omit him but he describes,
His characteristics with that by which he is not known.

الشرح

مثل أن يسمي أحد شيوخه باسم غير اسمه، أو بلقبٍ غير لقبه، وهو لا يمكن أن يُعرف إلا بذلك الذي لم يسمه به، أو يصفُهُ بصفةٍ عامة كمن يقول: حدثني من أنفه بين عينيه، أو حدثني من جلس للتحديث.

An example would be to identify one of his teachers with other than his name, or to call him with other than his nickname, while the *shaykh* cannot be identified except with the name that was omitted. Another example is to describe him with a general characteristic, such as the one who says, "The one whose nose is between his two eyes told me," or "The one who sat to narrate *ḥadīth* told me".

والأمر الذي دفع الراوي أن يفعل ذلك هو مثل الأغراض التي تقدمت في النوع الأول، لأنه يخفي اسم الشيخ حتى لا يوسم الحديث بالضعف، أو لأجل أن لا يرد الحديث، أو لأسباب أخرى.

And the reasons that cause the narrator to act in such a way are similar to the objectives that were mentioned earlier in the first category. The narrator may hide the *shaykh*'s name so that the *ḥadīth* isn't termed as *ḍaʿīf*, rejected or due to other reasons.

وهذا النوع كسابقه غير مقبول إلا إذا وصف من دلسه بما يعرف به فينظر في حاله.

And this type of *tadlīs* is not acceptable, just like the previous type. This is not the case if the one that was made *tadlīs* of is being described by what identifies him, in which case we look at his status.

وهل التدليس جائز أم حرام؟

Is the act of *tadlīs* permissible or prohibited?

نقول: الأصل فيه أنه حرام، لأنه من الغش، وقد قال النبي صلى الله عليه وسلّم: ((من غش فليس منا)) ولا سيما الغش في الشيء الذي ينسب إلى الرسول صلى الله عليه وسلّم، فهذا أعظم من الغش في البيع، وإذا كان النبي صلى الله عليه وسلّم قال لصاحب الطعام الذي أخفى ما أصابته السماء: ((من غش فليس منا)) فما بالك بمن يغش في سند الحديث، هذا يكون أعظم وأشد، ولكن ومع ذلك فقد كان يستعمله بعض التابعين، وغير التابعين، لأغراض حسنة، ولا يريدون بذلك الإساءة إلى سنة النبي صلى الله عليه وسلّم، ولا إلى الناس، وإنما يريدون بذلك بعض الأغراض الحسنة، ولكن هذا في الحقيقة لا يبرر لهم ما صنعوا، بل نقول: هم مجتهدون؛ لهم أجرهم على اجتهادهم، ولكن لو أصابوا وبينوا الأمر، لكان أولى وأحسن وأفضل.

We say that the *aṣl* (root principle) is that it is prohibited. This is because it is a form of cheating and the Prophet ﷺ said, "Whoever cheats is not from amongst us."[53] This is especially so if the cheating was regarding a matter that is attributed to the Messenger ﷺ, for this is worse than cheating in business. As the Prophet ﷺ told the trader wherein food wet by rain was being hidden, "Whoever cheats is not from amongst us", if a person were to cheat in the *sanad* of the *ḥadīth*; this would be greater and more serious. Even so, some of the *tābi'īn* or other than them may have used *tadlīs* for good reason, and they did not intend to wrong the Sunnah of the Prophet ﷺ or the people, but rather they intended to do so for some good reasons. However,

53 Recorded by Muslim; The Book of Faith; Chapter: His speech, prayers and blessings upon him: "Whoever cheated us ..." with the number 164 (102).

in actual fact, it does not rationalise what they have done. Rather we say that they are *mujtahidūn* (qualified to make independent reasoning), so they are rewarded for their reasoning, but if they were to be explicit and clarified the matter, then it would have been preferable and better.

المتن

(٢١) وَمَا يُخَالِفْ ثِقَةٌ بِهِ الْـمَلاَ فَالشَّاذُّ وَالْمَقْلُوبُ قِسمَانِ تَلاَ

(21) And when a trustworthy narrator contradicts the assembly,
It is al-shādh while al-maqlūb has two types that follow:

الشرح

وهذان هما الحادي والعشرون والثاني والعشرون من أقسام الحديث المذكورة في هذه المنظومة وهما: الشاذ، والمقلوب.

These two are the twenty first and twenty second categories of the classifications of *ḥadīth* mentioned in the poem and they are: *al-shādh* (contradictory) and *al-maqlūb* (inverted).

فالشاذ مأخوذ من الشذوذ، وهو الخروج عن القاعدة أو الخروج عن ما عليه الناس، وفي الحديث: ((عليكم بالجماعة فإن يد الله على الجماعة، ومن شذَّ شذَّ في النار)) يعني من خرج عنهم، فالشاذُّ هو الذي يخالف فيه الثقة الملأ (أي الجماعة)، ومعلوم أن الجماعة أقرب إلى الصواب من الواحد وأرجح، ولهذا يمكن أن نقول: إن المؤلف رحمه الله قال: (ما يخالف ثقة فيه الملأ) على سبيل المثال، وأن المراد بالقاعدة أن الشاذ هو: ما خالف فيه الثقة من هو أرجح منه عدداً، أو عدالة، أو ضبطاً.

As for *al-shādh*, it is taken from the word *al-shudhūth,* which means something removed from the general principle (*qā'idah*) or from the norm of the people. As in the *ḥadīth*, "Being in congregation is obligatory upon you as the Hand of Allāh is upon the congregation, and whoever excludes himself (*shadha*) shall be segregated (*shadha*) in the Hellfire,"[54] which refers to whoever diverted from them. As such, the *shādh* is when the trustworthy narrator contradicts the assembly (i.e. the congregation). It is known that the congregation is closer to being correct and stronger than one person. Due to this we can say that when the author said, "When a trustworthy narrator contradicts the assembly", he was giving an example, whereas in principle, the *shādh* is when the trustworthy narrator contradicts whoever is more correct than him in terms of numbers, righteousness or accuracy.

والمؤلف ذكر القسم الأول وهو: العدد لأن الملأ جماعة، وقد يقال: إن الملأ هم أشراف القوم كما قال الله تعالى: ﴿قَالَ الْمَلَأُ الَّذِينَ اسْتَكْبَرُوا مِن قَوْمِهِ﴾ [الأعراف: ٨٨]. ومعلوم أن الأشراف في علم الحديث هم الحفاظ العدول، فيكون كلامه شاملاً من هو أرجح عدداً، أو عدالة، أو حفظاً.

The author mentioned the first type, which is the numbers, because the assembly is a group. It is said that the assembly refers to the eminent ones of the people, as mentioned in the ayah: **{Said the eminent ones who were arrogant among his people.}**[55] It is known that the eminent ones in the science of *ḥadīth* are the righteous *ḥuffāẓ,* hence his statement is comprehensive, including whoever is more correct in terms of numbers, righteousness or memorisation.

مثال العدد: روى جماعة عن شيخهم حديثاً، ثم انفرد أحدهم برواية تخالف الجماعة وهو ثقة.

An example for numbers would be the case whereby a congregation narrate a *ḥadīth* from their *shaykh,* then one of them came with an isolated narration that contradicts the congregation and he is trustworthy.

54 Recorded by al-Ḥākim in his *Mustadrak* volume 1, page 199.
55 Al-A'rāf: 88

فنقول: إن هذه الرواية شاذة، لأنه خالف من هو أرجح منه، باعتبار العدد.

As such we say that this particular narration is *shādh* because the narrator contradicts the one who is more correct/stronger than him in terms of numbers.

ومثال الأرجح عدالة أو حفظاً معلوم.

Examples of the more correct/stronger narrator in terms of righteousness or memorisation are well-known.

نقول: الأول هو الراجح، والثاني هو الشاذ وهو حديث المرجوح.

We term the first narration, which is correct, as *al-rājiḥ* (the preponderant), and the second narration, which is incorrect, as *al-shādh* and *al-marjūḥ* (the subordinate).

ونُسمِّي الحديث الذي يقابل الشاذ بالمحفوظ.

And we call the *ḥadīth* which is the opposite of *al-shādh* as *al-maḥfūẓ* (the preserved).

ومثاله: حديث وضوء النبي صلى الله عليه وسلّم أنه توضأ، فأخذ لرأسه ماءً غير فضل يديه، أي لما أراد أن يمسح رأسه، أخذ ماءً فمسحه بماء غير فضل يديه، هكذا جاء في صحيح مسلم، وفي رواية ابن ماجة (أنه مسح أذنيه بماء غير فضل رأسه) فاختلفت الروايتان، فرواية مسلم أنه أخذ ماء جديداً لمسح الرأس غير ماء اليدين.

An example would be the *ḥadīth* of the Prophet's ablution, that he ﷺ made his *wuḍū* by taking water for his head other than the excess water for his arms[56] i.e. when he was about to wipe his head, he would take water and not just use the excess water from his arms. This was how it was narrated in *Ṣaḥīḥ Muslim*. In the narration of Ibn Mājah it stated that he ﷺ wiped

56 Recorded by Muslim; the Book of Purity; Chapter: Characteristics of the ablution no. 19 (236).

his ears with water that was not the excess from his head.[57] As such, the two narrations differ; as the narration of Muslim stated that he used new water for wiping his head and not the excess from washing his arms.

والثانية: أنه أخذ ماء جديداً لمسح الأذنين، غير ما مسح الرأس، قال ابن حجر في بلوغ المرام عن الأول إنه المحفوظ، يعني أن رواية مسلم هي المحفوظة، ورواية ابن ماجه تكون شاذة.

While the second narration stated that he used new water for wiping his two ears and not the excess from wiping his head. Ibn Ḥajar said in his book *Bulūgh al-Marām* that the first i.e. Muslim's narration is *maḥfūẓ* while Ibn Mājah's narration is *shādh*.

ولا يحكم بالمخالفة بمجرد ما ينقدح في ذهنه أنه مخالف، بل يجب أن يتأمل ويفكر وينظر ويحاول الجمع، لأنك إذا حكمت بالمخالفة، ثم قلت عن الثاني إنه شاذ فمعناه أنه غير مقبول، لأن من شرط الصحيح المقبول ألا يكون معللاً ولا شاذًّا، فإذا كان شاذًّا فإننا سنرده، فلا يجوز أن نرد الحديث المخالف بمجرد ما ينقدح في الذهن، فلابد من التأمل فإنه ربما يبدو مخالفاً، ولكن عند التأمل لا يكون مخالفاً فمثلاً: حديث ((اللهم رب هذه الدعوة التامة، والصلاة القائمة، آت محمداً الوسيلة والفضيلة، وابعثه مقاماً محموداً الذي وعدته))، ((إنك لا تخلف الميعاد)) بعض الناس قال إن زيادة (إنك لا تخلف الميعاد) شاذة، لأن أكثر الرواة رووه بدون هذه الزيادة، فتكون رواية من انفرد بها شاذة، لأنها مخالفة للثقات، وإن كان الراوي ثقة.

One should not regard the narrations as contradictory merely due to a variance that makes one think that there is a confliction. In fact, it is obligatory to ponder and think about it and try to combine the narrations. This is be-

57 I did not find it in the chapters of purity of *Sunan Ibn Mājah* but it is recorded by al-Bayhaqī 1/303 *ḥadīth* no. 719.

cause if you regard the narrations as conflicting, followed by ruling the second narration as *shādh*, it means that the second narration is not acceptable, as from the requirements of an acceptable *ṣaḥīḥ* narration is that it does not have a defect and that it isn't contradictory. If the narration is considered to be *shādh*, then we have to reject it and it is not permissible to reject a conflicting *ḥadīth* merely with what comes as a misapprehension in the mind. As such, it is a must to ponder upon it, as it may seem to be conflicting, but after some thought it is found not to be conflicting. For example, the *ḥadīth*, "O Allāh the Lord of this perfect call and the established prayer. Grant Muḥammad the intercession and favour, and raise him to the honoured position that You have promised him."[58] "Indeed You do not fail in Your promise."[59] Some people said that the additional phrase, "Indeed You do not fail in Your promise," is *shādh* because most of the narrators narrated it without this addition, and the isolated narration is considered to be contradictory because it conflicts with the trustworthy narrators, even though the narrator himself is trustworthy.

لكنه يمكن أن نقول: لا مخالفة هنا، لأن هذه الزيادة لا تنافي ما سبق، بحيث أنها لا تكذبه ولا تخصصه، وإنما تطبعه بطابع هو من دعاء المؤمنين كما قال الله عنهم ﴿رَبَّنَا وَآتِنَا مَا وَعَدْتَنَا عَلَىٰ رُسُلِكَ وَلَا تُخْزِنَا يَوْمَ الْقِيَامَةِ إِنَّكَ لَا تُخْلِفُ الْمِيعَادَ﴾ [آل عمران: ١٩٤] . وهنا تقول: وابعثه مقاماً محموداً الذي وعدته إنك لا تخلف الميعاد، نظير قول الله تعالى: ﴿وَلَا تُخْزِنَا يَوْمَ الْقِيَامَةِ إِنَّكَ لَا تُخْلِفُ الْمِيعَادَ﴾ فحينئذ يحتاج إلى أن نتثبت في مسألة الزيادة هل هي مخالفة أو غير مخالفة، أي أننا لا نتسرع بالقول بالمخالفة. لأن المخالفة تعني أنه لا يمكن الجمع، أما إذا أمكن الجمع فلا مخالفة.

However, it is possible for us to say that there is no conflict between the two narrations here. This is because the additional phrase does not contravene

58 Recorded by *al-Bukhārī*; The Book of Prayer Call; Chapter: The supplication upon hearing the call (614).

59 Al-Bayhaqī vol. 1 page 410, and our *shaykh* - may Allāh have mercy upon him and forgive him - regarded it as *ṣaḥīḥ* in *Majmūʿ al-Fatāwā* vol. 12 page 199.

the former by denying it or making it specific. Rather it ends the narration with a seal that is from the supplication of the believers, as Allāh mentioned in the ayah: **{Our Lord, and grant us what You promised us through Your Messengers and do not disgrace us on the Day of Resurrection. Indeed You do not fail in [Your] promise.}**[60] And here you say, "And raise him to the honoured position that You have promised him. Indeed You do not fail in Your promise." Which is parallel to the ayah: **{And do not disgrace us on the Day of Resurrection. Indeed You do not fail in [Your] promise.}** Therefore it is a need to confirm in the case of the addition if it is a confliction or not. This means that we do not rush to a conclusion that it is conflicting because this would entail that combination is not possible, whereas if it is possible to combine then there is no contradiction.

وهل يشترط في الشذوذ أن يكون في حديث واحد بمعنى أن يكون هذا الحديث رواه جماعة على وجه، ورواه فرد على وجهٍ يخالف الجماعة أو لا يشترط.

Is it a requirement for the *shudhūth* to be in one narration; meaning that this *ḥadīth* is narrated by a group of narrators in a certain way and an individual narrated it in a way that conflicts with the group, or is it not a requirement?

نقول: لا يشترط، يمكن أن يكون في حديث، وفي حديثين، هذا هو الذي يظهر لنا من تصرفات العلماء.

We say that it is not a requirement, as it may occur in a *ḥadīth* or two. This is made obvious to us from the actions of the scholars.

مثال ذلك: ما أخرج أصحاب السنن من حديث أبي هريرة رضي الله عنه أن النبي صلى الله عليه وسلّم قال: ((إذا انتصف شعبان فلا تصوموا)) وهذا الحديث صححه بعض العلماء، وقال: إنه يُكره الصيام تطوعاً إذا انتصف شعبان، إلا من كانت له عادةٌ فلا كراهة، وقال الإمام أحمد: لا يكره؛ لأن هذا الحديث شاذ، لأنه يخالف حديث أبي هريرة رضي الله عنه الذي في الصحيحين وهو قوله صلى

60 Āli ʿImrān: 194

الله عليه وسلّم: ((لا تقدموا رمضان بصوم يوم ولا يومين إلا رجلاً كان يصوم صوماً فليصمه)) وذلك لأن الحديث الثاني يدل على جواز الصيام قبل اليومين وهو أرجح من الأول.

An example for it is what was recorded by the authors of the *Sunan* from the *ḥadīth* of Abū Hurayrah ﵁ that the Prophet ﷺ said, "Do not fast when the half point of the month of Shaʿbān has passed."[61] Some scholars regarded this narration as *ṣaḥīḥ.* They said that it is discouraged to voluntarily fast after half of Shaʿbān has passed, except for the one who fasts due to it being a habitual practice. As for al-Imām Aḥmad, he said that there is no discouragement because this *ḥadīth* is *shādh,* as it conflicts with the *ḥadīth* of Abū Hurayrah ﵁ which is in the *Ṣaḥīḥayn* where he ﷺ said, "Do not precede Ramaḍān with fasting a day or two except for someone who has been fasting voluntarily, so he fasted."[62] This is because the second *ḥadīth* shows that it is permissible to fast before the two days and this is more correct than the first.

إذاً نفهم من هذا أن الشذوذ ليس شرطاً أن يكون في حديث واحد.

Therefore we understand that it is not a requirement for *shudhūth* to occur in one *ḥadīth*.

مثال آخر: ما أخرجه أبو داود في سننه عن النبي صلى الله عليه وسلّم أنه قال: ((لا تصوموا يوم السبت إلا فيما افترض عليكم)) فهذا الحديث يخالف الحديث الذي في الصحيحين وهو أن النبي صلى الله عليه وسلّم قالت له إحدى نسائه إنها صائمة هذا اليوم وكان يوم الجمعة، فقال لها: ((أصمت أمس؟)) قالت: لا، قال: ((أتصومين غداً؟))، قالت: لا، قال: ((فأفطري)) فقوله: ((أتصومين غداً؟)) وهو يوم السبت، يدل على جواز صيام يوم السبت، لذلك اختلف العلماء في صحة حديث النهي عن صيام يوم السبت على أقوال:

---

61 Mentioned previously.
62 Mentioned previously.

Another example is what was recorded by Abū Dawūd in his *Sunan* from the Prophet ﷺ, that he said, "Do not fast on Saturdays except those that are obligatory upon you."[63] As such, this narration contradicts the *ḥadīth* in the *Ṣaḥīḥayn* where the Prophet's ﷺ wife told him that she was fasting that day and it was on a Friday, so he asked her, "Did you fast yesterday?" She replied, "No." Then he asked, "Will you be fasting tomorrow?" She answered, "No." He said, "Break your fast then."[64] So his statement: "Will you be fasting tomorrow" which refers to a Saturday, shows that it is permissible to fast on a Saturday. Due to this, the scholars differ with regards to the soundness of the *ḥadīth* prohibiting the fasting on Saturdays to a few opinions:

١ - فمنهم من قال: إن الحديث منسوخ، وهذا القول ضعيف، لأن من شرط الحكم بالنسخ العلم بالتاريخ، وهنا لا نعلم التاريخ.

1. Amongst them were some who said that the *ḥadīth* was abrogated. However this is a weak opinion because one of the requirements of the abrogation ruling is that the chronological order of the narrations is known, whereas here we do not know the chronological order.

٢ - ومنهم من قال: بل الحديث شاذ؛ لأنه يخالف الحديث الذي في الصحيحين الذي يدل على جواز صيام يوم السبت.

2. Amongst them were some who said that the *ḥadīth* is *shādh*, because it conflicts with the narration which is in the *Ṣaḥīḥayn* that shows the permissibility of fasting on a Saturday.

٣ - ومنهم من حمله على وجه لا يخالف الحديث الذي في الصحيحين، وذلك بأن يُحمل النهي على إفراد يوم السبت بالصيام، وأما إذا صام يوماً قبله أو يوماً بعده فلا بأس، وهذا الأخير جمع بين الحديثين، وإذا أمكن الجمع فلا شذوذ، لأن من شرط الشذوذ المخالفة وهنا لا مخالفة، فقالوا: حديث النهي عن صوم

63 Mentioned previously.
64 Mentioned previously.

يوم السبت، محمولٌ على الإفراد، أما إذا جمع إليه ما قبله أو ما بعده فلا بأس حينئذ.

3. And there are those who considered it from the perspective that it does not contradict the narration in the *Ṣaḥīḥayn* by viewing the prohibition as being upon the singling out of fasting on a Saturday. As such, if the person fasts a day before or after then there is nothing wrong with it. And this last opinion is where the two narrations are combined, and if combination is possible then there is no *shudhūth,* as contradiction is a requirement of *shudhūth* and there is no conflict here. Thus they said that the prohibition of fasting on a Saturday is taken upon the singling out of the day, so if the person were to combine to it a day before or after, then there is no problem with it.

مثال ثالث: وردت أحاديث متعددة - لكن ليست في البخاري ومسلم - في النهي عن لبس الذهب المحلَّق مثل الخاتم والسوار ونحوه، ووردت أحاديث أخرى في الصحيحين وغيرهما تدل على جواز لبس الذهب المحلق، مثل ما في حديث جابر - رضي الله عنه - أن النبي صلى الله عليه وسلّم أمر النساء أن يتصدقن، فجعلن يلقين خواتيمهن، وخروصهن في ثوب بلال - رضي الله عنه - ثم أن النبي صلى الله عليه وسلّم لما رأى الرجل الذي عليه خاتم الذهب أخذه ورمى به، وقال: ((يعمدُ أحدكم إلى جمرة من النار فيلقيها في يده)).

Third example: There are a number of narrations (however, they were not recorded by Bukhārī or Muslim) regarding the prohibition of wearing gold in the form of circles such as rings, bracelets etc.[65] And there are other narrations in the *Ṣaḥīḥayn* and other sources that show the permissibility of wearing gold in the form of circles. For example, the *ḥadīth* of Jābir ﵁ that the Prophet ﷺ told the women to contribute to charity, then they threw their rings and earrings into the robe of Bilāl ﵁. Also, when the Prophet ﷺ saw a man who wore a gold ring, he took it from him, flung it and said: "One

65 *Musnad Imām Aḥmad* vol. 1 page 119 (138), and *Sunan al-Nasā'ī* vol. 8 page 545; The Book of Ornaments; Chapter: The gold ring.

of you desires a live ember from the Hellfire, and puts it on his hand."[66]

فمن العلماء من قال: إن النهي عن الذهب المحلق حجة يُعمل بها.

Thus there are some scholars who said that the prohibition of wearing gold in the form of circles is a valid argument with a basis behind it.

ومنهم من قال: إن النهي عن لبس الذهب المحلق شاذٌّ لا يعمل به، لأنه يخالف ما ثبت في الصحيحين وغيرهما من جواز لبس الذهب المحلّق، وهذا هو الذي سلكه شيخنا عبد العزيز بن عبد الله بن باز.

And there are those who said that the prohibition of wearing gold in the form of circles is *shādh* and not something that should be acted upon, as it contradicts what is confirmed in the *Ṣaḥīḥayn* and other *ḥadīth* collections which permit the wearing of gold in the form of circles. And this is the opinion that our *shaykh* ʿAbd al-ʿAzīz ibn ʿAbdullāh ibn Bāz upholds.

ومنهم من قال: إن الأحاديث الواردة في النهي في أول الأمر حين كان الناس في ضيق وفي شدة ثم بعد ذلك رُخِّص فيه.

And there are those who said that the *aḥādīth* that prohibit the wearing of circular gold were narrated during the early times when the people were in poverty and hardship and then it was legalised later on.

وإنما ضربت هذه الأمثلة الثلاثة للإشارة إلى أن الشذوذ لا يشترط أن يكون في حديث واحد، بل قد يكون في واحد، أو في اثنين، أو أكثر.

Thus, I provided these above examples to illustrate that it is not a criterion of the *shudhūth* to occur in one *ḥadīth*, but rather it could occur in one, two or more narrations.

إذاً عرفنا ما هو الشاذ، وما هو الذي يقابله، وهناك مخالفة أخرى لم يذكرها

66 Recorded by Muslim; The Book of Garments; Chapter: The prohibition of gold rings upon men, no. 52 (2090).

المؤلف وهي: إذا كان المخالف غير ثقة فإن حديثه يسمى منكراً.

Therefore we learned what is *shādh* and its opposite. There is another type of contradiction which the author did not mention. This is if the contradicting narrator were to be untrustworthy, then his narration would be called *al-munkar* (the denied).

والمنكر هو: ما خالف فيه الضعيف الثقة، وهو أسوأ من الشاذ، لأن المنكر المخالفة مع الضعف، والشاذ المخالفة فيه مع الثقة.

Al-munkar occurs when the weak narrator contradicts the trustworthy. It is worse than the *shādh* because the *munkar* is a contradiction with weakness whereas the *shādh* is a contradiction with trustworthiness.

ويقابل المنكر المعروف، إذاً فهي أربعة أقسام: (١) المحفوظ، (٢) الشاذ، (٣) المنكر، (٤) المعروف.

And the opposite of *al-munkar* is *al-ma'rūf* (the well-known). Therefore there are four categories: (i) *al-maḥfūẓ*, (ii) *al-shādh*, (iii) *al-munkar* and (iv) *al-ma'rūf*.

فالشاذ هو: ما رواه الثقة مخالفاً لمن هو أرجح منه.

As for *al-shādh*: It is what a trustworthy narrator narrates which contradicts another who is more correct/stronger than him.

والمنكر هو: ما رواه الضعيف مخالفاً للثقة.

And *al-munkar* is when a weak narrator narrates something that contradicts a trustworthy narrator.

والمحفوظ هو: ما رواه الأرجح مخالفاً لثقة دونه، وهو مقابل للشاذ.

Whereas *al-maḥfūẓ* is what a stronger narrator narrates that contradicts a trustworthy narrator of a lower grade than him, and it is the opposite of the *shādh*.

والمعروف هو: ما رواه الثقة مخالفاً للضعيف.

And *al-ma'rūf* is what a trustworthy narrator narrates that contradicts a weak narrator.

وقوله: (والمقلوبُ قسمان تلا) هذا تكملة للبيت يعني تلا في الذكر الشاذَّ، لكن هي ليس لها معنى، وإنما هي تكملة للبيت فقط، والمقلوب ينقسم إلى قسمين ذكرها في البيت الذي بعده.

The author's phrase, "While *al-maqlūb* has two types that follow" is the completion of the line i.e. it follows *al-shādh* in terms of the order mentioned. Its addition here is not due to it being connected to the *shādh* narration or for a specific reason, rather it is for the sake of completing the line. And *al-maqlūb* is divided into two categories, mentioned in the following couplet:

المتن

(٢٢) إِبْدَالُ رَاوٍ مَا بِرَاوٍ قِسْمُ   وَقَلْبُ إِسْنَادٍ لِمَتْنٍ قِسْمُ

(22) Substituting any narrator for a narrator is a category,
And exchanging a chain of a text is a category.

الشرح

قوله (إبدال راوٍ ما براوٍ).

The author's phrase, "Substituting a narrator for a narrator":

فـ(ما) هنا نكرة واصفة.

The word "*mā*" (some) here is an indefinite adjective.

ومعنى نكرة واصفة أي أنك تقدر ما بـ(أيّ) والتقدير إبدال راوٍ أي راوٍ، و(ما) تأتي

نكرة واصفة، وتأتي نكرة موصوفة كما في قوله تعالى: ﴿إِنَّ اللَّهَ نِعِمَّا يَعِظُكُمْ بِهِ﴾ ومثال النكرة الواصفة قول المؤلف (إبدال راوٍ ما).

And the meaning of an indefinite adjective is that you can decipher "*mā*" with "*ayyu*" (any). Thus the decipherment here is substituting any narrator. And "*mā*" comes in the form of an indefinite adjective or an indefinite adverb, such as in the ayah: **{Excellent is that which Allāh instructs you.}**[67] While the example of it being used as an indefinite adjective is the author's speech: "Substituting any narrator."

والمقلوب ينقسم إلى قسمين:

And *al-maqlūb* is classified into two categories:

القسم الأول: وهو ما ذكره المؤلف بقوله (إبدال راوٍ ما براوٍ قسمُ) وهو ما يُسمَّى بقلب الإسناد.

The first category is as mentioned by the author in his phrase, "Substituting any narrator for a narrator" and it is called *qalb al-isnād* (inversion of the chain).

مثلاً: إذا قال: حدثني يوسف عن يعقوب، فيقلبُ الإسناد ويقول: حدثني يعقوب عن يوسف، وهذا أكثر ما يقعُ خطأ، إما لنسيان أو غيره، لأنه لا توجد فائدة في تعمد ذلك.

An example is if someone were to say, "Yūsuf told me from Ya'qūb", and then the chain becomes inverted to, "Ya'qūb told me from Yūsuf". This mostly occurs mistakenly, either due to forgetfulness or other reasons because there is no benefit from intentionally doing so.

فإذا قال قائل ما الذي أعلمنا أن الإسناد مقلوب فقد يكون على الوضع الصحيح؟

And if someone were to ask: "What makes us think that the chain is inverted

67 Al-Nisā: 58

as it could be in its correct state?"

فنقول: نعلم أنه مقلوب، إذا جاء من طريق آخر أوثق على خلاف ما هو عليه، أو جاء من نفس الراوي الذي قَلَبَهُ في حال شبابه وحفظه، يكون قد ضبطه وحدَّث به على الوضع الصحيح، وفي حال كِبَرِه ونسيانه، يحدِّثُ بالحديث ويقلب إسناده، ففي هذه الحالة نعرف أن الأول هو الصحيح، والثاني هو المقلوب.

We say that we know that it is *maqlūb* if the narration comes from a different route that is more trustworthy in a way that conflicts what it is upon, or it comes from the same narrator who inverted it; during his youth and [time of strong] memorization he could have perfected it and thus narrated it in the correct manner, then during his old age and forgetfulness, he could have narrated the *ḥadīth* and inverted its chain. From this case we know that the first is correct and the second is *maqlūb*.

مثاله: إذا روى هذا الحديث بهذا الإسناد الصحيح رجلان، أحدهما أوثق من الآخر، فيأتي الذي ليس بأوثق من صاحبه ويقلب الإسناد، بأن يجعل التلميذ شيخاً والشيخ تلميذاً، فإننا نحكم في هذا الحديث بأنه مقلوب عليه لأنه قلب السند.

An example would be when there are two narrators who narrated a particular *ḥadīth* with a particular authentic *isnād*, one of the two is more trustworthy than the other, and the narrator who is not as trustworthy as his colleague came with an inverted chain by making the student as the teacher and the teacher as the student, then we regard this narration as *maqlūb* because he inverted the *sanad*.

ومثال آخر: هذا الحديث حدَّث به هذا الرجل في حال شبابه وحفظه على وجه، وحدَّث به بعد شيخوخته ونسيانه على وجهٍ آخر، فإننا نحكم على الثاني أنه مقلوب، وربما نطَّلع أيضاً على هذا من طريق آخر بحيث أننا نعرف أن الذي

جعله تلميذاً هو الشيخ، لأنه تقدم في عصره بمعرفة التاريخ.

Another example would be the case where an individual narrated a particular *ḥadīth* during his days of youth and memorisation in a particular order, and when he reached his old age and became forgetful, he narrated it in a different order; hence we regard the latter as *maqlūb*. We could also find this through another method whereby we know that the one who was named as the student is actually the *shaykh* because he is known to be earlier in terms of era through analysing history.

والمقلوب من قسم الضعيف، لأنه يدل على عدم ضبط الراوي.

And *maqlūb* is one of the categories of *ḍaʿīf* narrations because it shows the inaccuracy of the narrator.

القسم الثاني: وهو ما ذكره المؤلف بقوله (وقلب إسناد لمتن قسم) ويعني أن يُقلب إسناد المتن لمتن آخر.

The second category is what the author mentioned in his line, "And exchanging a chain of a text is a category." Meaning to exchange the *isnād* of a particular *matn* for another *matn*.

مثاله: رجل روى حديثاً: من طريق زيد، عن عمرو، عن خالد، وحديثاً آخر: من طريق بكر، عن سعد، عن حاتم، فجعل الإسناد الثاني للحديث الأول، وجعل الإسناد الأول للحديث الثاني، فهذا يُسمَّى قلب إسناد المتن، والغالب أنه يقعُ عمداً للاختبار، أي لأجل أن يُختبر المحدِّث.

An example of this is: A narrator narrates a *ḥadīth* through the route of Zayd from ʿAmr from Khālid, and another *ḥadīth* through the route of Bakr from Saʿd from Ḥātim. Then he attributed the *isnād* of the second *ḥadīth* to the first one, and the *isnād* of the first *ḥadīth* to the second one. Hence this is called *qalb isnād al-matn* (exchange of the chain of a text). Usually it occurred intentionally for the sake of a trial i.e. for the sake of testing the scholar of *ḥadīth*.

كما صنع أهل بغداد مع البخاري، وذلك لما علموا أنه قادم عليهم، اجتمعوا من العراق وما حوله وقالوا: نريد أن نختبر هذا الرجل، فوضعوا له مائة حديث ووضعوا لكل حديث إسناداً غير إسناده، وقلبوا الأسانيد ليختبروا البخاري - رحمه الله - وقالوا: كل واحد منكم عنده عشرة أحاديث يسأله عنها، ووضعوا عشرة رجال حفاظ أقوياء، فلما جاء البخاري - رحمه الله - واجتمع الناس، بدأوا يسوقون الأسانيد كلها حتى انتهوا منها، وكانوا كلما ساقوا إسناداً ومعه المتن قال البخاري: لا أعرفه، حتى أتموها كلها، فالعامة من الناس قالوا: هذا الرجل لا يعرف شيئاً، يُعرض عليه مائة حديث وهو يقول: لا أعرفه، يعني لا أعرف هذا السند لهذا الحديث، ثم قام - رحمه الله - بعد ذلك وساق كل حديث بإسناده الصحيح، حتى انتهى من المائة كلها، فعرفوا أن الرجل آية من آيات الله في الحفظ، فأقرُّوا وأذعنوا له.

This is like what the people of Baghdad did with al-Bukhārī, which occurred when they knew he was coming to them, so they came from Iraq and its surroundings to a gathering and said, "We would like to test this man." So they set one hundred *ḥadīth* and set for each *ḥadīth* an *isnād* which was not its chain and thus exchanged the chains in order to test al-Bukhārī and said, "Every one of you shall have ten *aḥadīth* to ask him about," and they appointed ten men who were strong in memorisation. When al-Bukhārī arrived, the people gathered and they began reporting all of the *asānīd* (chains) until they finished them, and every time an *isnād* was reported with a *matn* al-Bukhārī would say, "I do not know it" until they completed all of it. As such, the common people said that this man does not know anything; he was presented with a hundred *ḥadīth* but he said, "I do not know it," i.e. I do not know this *sanad* with this *ḥadīth*. Then he stood up afterwards and reported all the *ḥadīth* with their correct *isnāds* until he completed all one hundred. Henceforth the people knew that this man was one of the miracles of Allāh in terms of memorisation, thus they recognised and yielded to him.

فهذا نسميه قلب إسناد المتن يعني أن تركب إسناد متن على متن آخر، والغالب أنه لا يقع إلا للاختبار، وقد يقع غشًّا، بحيث يريد الرجل أن يُرَوِّج الحديث لكنْ يكون إسناده ساقطاً يعني كلهم ضعفاء مثلاً، فيأتي بإسناد حديث صحيح ويُركبه عليه، فهو نوع من التدليس، لكنه بطريق آخر.

Therefore, we call this *qalb isnād al-matn* i.e. to fix the chain of a text upon another text. Usually it does not occur except for the purpose of trial, and it may occur as a form of cheating whereby the narrator wishes to circulate a *ḥadīth* but its *isnād* is abandoned i.e. all of the narrators were weak for instance. So he would come with the *isnād* of an authentic narration and fix it upon it. This is a type of *tadlīs* but in a different way.

وهناك قسم آخر وهو قلب المتن: وهذا الذي يعتني به الفقهاء، وأما قلب الإسناد فيعتني به المحدثون، لأنهم ينظرون إلى السند هل هو صحيح؟ وهل يصح به الحديث أم لا.

There is another category which is *qalb al-matn* (inversion of the text). This is the one that the scholars of *fiqh* (jurisprudence) are concerned with. The scholars of *ḥadīth*, however, are concerned with *qalb al-isnād* because they pay more attention to the authenticity of the *sanad*, and whether the *ḥadīth* becomes *ṣaḥīḥ* with it or not.

وأما الفقهاء فيعتنون بقلب المتن، لأنه هو الذي يتغيَّر به الحكم، حيث إن هؤلاء ينظرون إلى الدلالة.

As for the scholars of *fiqh*, they emphasise paying attention to *qalb al-matn* because it is the one that changes the rulings, and they seek the meanings of the text.

وقلب المتن يحصل من بعض الرواة تنقلب عليهم المتون فيروون بعض الأحاديث على غير وجهها.

Qalb al-matn occurs from some of the narrators and thus the texts were inverted and they narrated some of the *aḥādīth* in a way that it is contrary to the actual form.

من ذلك مثلاً: حديث أبي هريرة رضي الله عنه أن النبي صلى الله عليه وسلّم قال: ((سبعة يظلهم الله في ظله يوم لا ظل إلا ظله . . .)) الحديث وفيه ((ورجل تصدق بصدقةٍ فأخفاها حتى لا تعلم شماله ما تنفق يمينه)) فقلبه بعض الرواة فقال: (حتى لا تعلم يمينه ما تنفق شماله) فهذا مقلوب، لأنه جعل اليمين شمالاً، والشمال يميناً.

One example of this is the *ḥadīth* of Abu Hurayrah ﵁ that the Prophet ﷺ said, "Seven whom Allāh will shade under His Shade on the Day when there is no shade except His Shade ..."[68] In the *ḥadīth* there is the statement, "And a man who gave charity discreetly until his left hand did not know what his right hand gave." Some of the narrators inverted the wording and said, "Until his right hand did not know what his left hand gave." This is considered to be *maqlūb* because he inverted the right for the left and the left for the right.

ومن ذلك الحديث الذي ثبت في صحيح البخاري (أنه يبقى في النار فضلٌ عمن دخلها، فينشئ الله لها أقواماً يدخلهم النار) فهذا الحديث منقلبٌ على الراوي وصوابه ((أنه يبقي في الجنة فضلٌ عمن دخلها من أهل الدنيا فينشئ الله لها أقواماً فيدخلهم الجنة)) الحديث.

Another example is the *ḥadīth* which is confirmed in *Ṣaḥīḥ al-Bukhārī*, "There is space left in the Hellfire after those whom have been sent into it, thus Allāh created nations and sent them into the Hellfire." This *ḥadīth* is inverted upon the narrator and the correct version of the *ḥadīth* is, "There is space left in the Paradise after the people of the earth have been sent into

68 Recorded by al-Bukhārī; The Book of *Zakah*; Chapter: Donations with the right hand (1423), (620), (1334), (5998) and (6308) and Muslim; The Book of *Zakah*; Chapter: The significance of giving donations discreetly 91 (1031), (1712).

it, thus Allāh created nations and sent them into the Paradise."[69]

وذلك لأنه - أي إنشاء أقوام للنار - ينافي كمال عدل الله تعالى إذ كيف يمكن أن يُنشأ الله تعالى أقواماً للعذاب، ولأنه ينافي الحديث الصحيح ((لا يزال يُلقى في النار وهي تقول هل من مزيد، حتى يضع الله تعالى عليها قدمه فينزوي بعضها إلى بعض وتقول: قط قط)).

This is because the creation of the nations for Hellfire denies the perfect justice of Allāh, i.e. how could Allāh create nations for the sake of punishment. Also due to the fact that this denies the authentic *ḥadīth*, "The people will continue to be thrown into Hellfire as it keeps saying, 'Is there any more?' until Allāh puts His Foot over it, causing its different sides to come close to each other and it will say, 'Enough! Enough!'[70]

ومثال آخر: حديث أبي هريرة رضي الله عنه أن النبي صلى الله عليه وسلّم قال: ((إذا سجد أحدكم فلا يبرك كما يبرك البعير وليضع يديه قبل ركبتيه)) انقلب هذا الحديث على الراوي فقال: (وليضع يديه قبل ركبتيه) والصواب: ((وليضع ركبتيه قبل يديه)) وإنما قلنا ذلك لأن هذا التفريع يخالف أول الحديث، فأول الحديث ((فلا يبرك كما يبرك البعير)) فالنهي عن التشبه بالبعير في صفة السجود ((فلا يبرك كما يبرك)) ونحن إذا شاهدنا البعير نراه إذا برك، فإنه يقدم يديه قبل ركبتيه، حيث إنه أول ما يبرك ينزل مقدمه قبل مؤخره، وأنت إذا قدمت يديك نزل مقدمك قبل مؤخرك، فأشبهت بروك البعير.

Another example would be the *ḥadīth* of Abu Hurayrah ﵁ that the Prophet ﷺ said, "If one of you were to make the prostration do not kneel like the kneeling of the camel, rather one is to place his hands before his knees."[71]

---

69 Mentioned previously.

70 Recorded by al-Bukhārī; The Book of *Tawḥīd* and Muslim; The Book of Paradise; Chapter: the verse: "And He is the Exalted in Might, the Wise" (7384)

71 Recorded by al-Imām Aḥmad vol. 2 page 381, Abū Dawūd; The Book of Prayers;

This *ḥadīth* was inverted by one of the narrators in the phrase, "place his hands before his knees," as the correct narration is, "place his knees before his hands." Indeed we say this because this part of the *ḥadīth* conflicts with the first part of the *ḥadīth* whereby it says, "Do not kneel like the kneeling of the camel." Thus the prohibition regarding the resemblance of the camel in the characteristics of the *sujūd* is, "Do not kneel like the kneeling." We witness that the camel, when it is about to kneel, descends with its front legs first before the knees of its hind legs whereby the front part of its body descends before the back. And if you were to descend with your hands first, the upper part of your body shall descend before your lower part, then you have resembled the kneeling of the camel.

فإذا قيل: (وليضع يديه قبل ركبتيه) صار لا يناسب أول الحديث، والذي يناسبه (وليضع ركبتيه قبل يديه)، وقد ظن بعض العلماء أن الحديث ليس فيه قلب، وقال: إن ركبة البعير في يديه، ونحن نُسلِّم أن ركبة البعير في يديه.

And if it was said, "To place his hands before his knees", it becomes irrelevant to the first part of the *ḥadīth*, and the one which is relevant to it is, "To place his knees before his hands." Some scholars thought that there is no inversion in the *ḥadīth*, stating that the knees of the camel are also present in its forelegs, and so we agree that the knee of the camel is present on the forelegs.

ولكن الحديث لم يقل فيه الرسول صلى الله عليه وسلّم: فلا يبرك على ما يبرك عليه البعير، فإنه لو قال كذلك لقلنا: لا تبرك على الركبتين لأن البعير يبرك على ركبتيه، لكن النبي صلى الله عليه وسلّم قال: ((فلا يبرك كما)) والكاف هنا للتشبيه، وبين العبارتين فرق.

However, the Messenger ﷺ did not mention in the *ḥadīth*, "Do not kneel upon what the camel kneels upon." If he did say as such, then we would say

Chapter: How he placed his knees before his two hands (840) and al-Nasā'ī; The Book of Prayers; Chapter: What comes in contact with the ground first of the human in his prostration (1092).

not to kneel upon the knees because the camel descends upon its knees. On the contrary, the Prophet ﷺ said, "Do not kneel like the", and the preposition *kāf* (like) here is for the purpose of comparison, and between the two phrases is a difference in meaning.

فإذا عرفنا أن مدلول قوله ((فلا يبرك كما يبرك البعير)) أي لا يقدِّم يديه فينزل مقدمه قبل مؤخره، ولأن النزول في السجود بالركبتين، هو الوضع الطبيعي.

We say that the meaning of his statement, "Do not kneel like the kneeling of the camel," is to not place your hands first in a manner that will cause your upper body to descend before your lower body. This is due to the fact that the descent for prostration is via the knees, which is the natural posture.

ففي الوضع الطبيعي أول ما ينزل إلى الأرض هو ما يلي الأرض وهو الركبة ثم اليد ثم الجبهة والأنف.

Thus, the normal order of what descends is what is closest to the ground, which is the knees, followed by the hands and then the forehead and the nose.[72]

۞۞۞

المتن

٢٣ - وَالْفَرْدُ مَا قَيَّدْتَهُ بِثِقَةِ أَوْ جَمْعٍ أَوْ قَصْرٍ عَلَى رِوَايَةِ

(23) And al-fard is what you limit to a trustworthy narrator,
Or a group or a restriction upon a particular narration.

الشرح

هذا هو الثالث والعشرون من أقسام الحديث المذكورة في هذه المنظومة، وهو الفرد، وذكر الناظم له ثلاثة أنواع.

72 Our *shaykh* - may Allāh have mercy upon him and forgive him - made the conclusion of this issue in *Majmū' al-Fatāwā* vol. 13, pages 175-179.

This is the twenty third category of the classifications of *ḥadīth* mentioned in the poem, which is *al-fard* (unique narrations) and the author mentioned three types of it:

١ - ما قُيد بثقة.

1. What is limited to a trustworthy narrator.

٢ - ما قُيد بجمع.

2. What is limited to a group.

٣ - ما قُيد برواية.

3. What is limited to a narration.

فما هو الفرد؟

So, what is *al-fard*?

نقول: الفرد هو أن ينفرد الراوي بالحديث، يعني أن يروي الحديث رجلٌ فرد.

We say that *al-fard* is that a *ḥadīth* is unique to a narrator i.e. the *ḥadīth* is narrated by one narrator.

والغالب على الأفراد الضعف، لكن بعضها صحيح متلقى بالقبول، لكن الغالب على الأفراد أنها ضعيفة، لاسيما فيما بعد القرون الثلاثة، لأنه بعد القرون الثلاثة، كثر الرواة فتجد الشيخ الواحد عنده ستمائة راوي. فإذا انفرد عنه راوٍ واحد دون غيره فإن هذا يوجب الشك، فكيف يخفى هذا الحديث على هذا العدد الكثير، ولا يرويه إلا واحد فقط.

Usually the *afrād* (plural of *fard*) are weak narrations, though some of them are *ṣaḥīḥ* and received acceptance. However, usually the ruling for the *fard* is that it is *ḍaʿīf*, especially if it was narrated after the first three generations because after them the narrators increased, and so it could be found that a single *shaykh* may have six hundred narrators under him. Thus, if he had only one narrator and no one else, then this leads to doubt; how could he have hidden this *ḥadīth* from a large number and no one narrated it except only one person?

لكن في عهد الصحابة تكثر الفردية، وكذلك في عهد التابعين لكنها أقل من عهد الصحابة، لانتشار التابعين وكثرتهم، وفي عهد تابع التابعين تكثر الفردية لكنها أقل من عهد التابعين.

However, during the era of the companions, there were many *fard* narrations. Likewise during the time of the *tabiʿīn,* but it occurred less than in the time of the companions due to the spread/prevalence of the *tābiʿīn* and their large numbers. And in the time of the *tābiʿ al-tābiʿīn* (followers of the successors) there were many *fard* narrations but it was less than that in the time of the *tābiʿīn*.

إذاً فالفردُ من قبيل الضعيف غالباً.

Therefore, the *fard* is typically from the *ḍaʿīf* narrations.

وأنواعه ثلاثة وهي:

It has three types and they are:

١ - ما قُيِّدَ بثقة، أي ما انفرد به ثقة، ولم يروه غيره، لكنه لا يخالف غيره، مثل حديث عمر بن الخطاب رضي الله عنه ((إنما الأعمال بالنيات، وإنما لكل امرئ ما نوى)) فقد حصل الإفراد فيه، في ثلاث طبقات من رواته، ومع ذلك فهو صحيح، لأنه انفرد به الثقة عن الثقة عن الثقة، فهذا يُسمى فرداً، ويسمى غريباً.

1. What is limited to a trustworthy narrator i.e. what is unique to a trustworthy narrator and no one else narrated it, but it does not conflict with the others. An example is the *ḥadīth* of ʿUmar ibn al-Khaṭṭāb ﷺ: "Indeed actions are according to intentions, and indeed for every man is what he

intended."[73] Indeed it was unique to him and in three levels of its narrators. Even so, it is *ṣaḥīḥ* because it is unique to a trustworthy narrator, from a trustworthy narrator, from a trustworthy narrator. Thus this is called *fard* or *gharīb*.

٢ - ما قُيدَ بجمعٍ، ومراده بالجمع أهل البلد، أو أهل القرية، أو القبيلة أو ما أشبه ذلك، فإذا انفرد بهذا الحديث عن أهل هذا البلد شخص واحد، بمعنى أن يقال: تفرد فلان برواية هذا الحديث عن الشاميين، أو تفرد فلان برواية هذا الحديث عن الحجازيين، أو ما أشبه ذلك، فهنا فردٌ لكنه ليس فرداً مطلقاً، بل هو في بلد معين، وقد انفرد به من بين المحدثين من أهل هذا البلد.

2. What is limited to a group and "group" refers to the people of a certain country, village, tribe or its likes. If a *ḥadīth* is reported by one person from the people of a certain country, meaning to say that the narration of this *ḥadīth* by a person is exclusive amongst the people of Shām, or it is exclusive to the people of Ḥijāz etc then it is considered to be *fard* but not in its absolute sense. Rather it is *fard* to a particular country, and it may be unique amongst the scholars of the *ḥadīth* from the people of this country.

فمثلاً إذا قدَّرنا أن المحدثين في الشام ألف محدث، فروى هذا الحديث منهم واحد، ولم يروه سواه.

For example, if we assume that there are one thousand scholars of *ḥadīth* in Greater Syria and one of them narrated this *ḥadīth* and there was no one else who narrated it except him.

فنقول: هذا فرد لكن هل هو فرد مطلقاً؟

Then we say that this is *fard*, but is it *fard muṭlaq* (unique absolutely)?

بل فرد نسبي، نسبي أي: بالنسبة لأهل الشام.

Rather it is *fard nisbī* (relatively unique) i.e. in relation to the people of

73 Mentioned previously.

Shām.

وللفرد المقيد بالجمع معنى آخر وهو: أن ينفرد به أهل بلد ما، بروايته عن فلان، فيقال: تفرد به أهل الشام عن فلان.

There is another meaning for the *fard* which is restricted to a group and it is that the narration from so-and-so is exclusive to the people of some country. Thus to say, for example, that the people of Greater Syria exclusively narrated from so-and-so.

٣ - وقوله (أو قصر على رواية).

3. The author's phrase, "Or a restriction upon a particular narration":

القصر على الرواية هي أن يقال مثلاً: لم يروِ هذا الحديث بهذا المعنى إلا فلان، يعني أن هذا الحديث بهذا المعنى لم يروه إلا شخص واحد عن فلان، فتجد أن القصر في الرواية فقط، وإلا فالحديث من طرق أخرى مشهور، وطرقه كثيرة.

The restriction upon a certain narration is to say that no one narrated this *ḥadīth* with this meaning except so-and-so, i.e. that this *ḥadīth* with this meaning was not narrated by anyone else except one person from so-and-so. Thus you find that the restriction is upon the narration only but the actual *ḥadīth* is well-known from other routes and its chains are numerous.

وإنما قسَّم المؤلف الفرد إلى هذا التقسيم: ليبين أن الفرد قد يكون فرداً نسبيًّا، وقد يكون فرداً مطلقاً، فإذا كان هذا الحديث لم يُروَ إلا من طريق واحد بالنسبة لأهل الشام، أو أي بلد فهو فردٌ نسبي.

Indeed the author divided *al-fard* into these divisions to explain that the uniqueness could occur comparatively *(fard nisbi)* or absolutely *(fard muṭlaq)*. If the *ḥadīth* was not narrated except from one route in relation to the people of Shām or any other country, then it is called *fard nisbī*.

وكذلك بالنسبة للشيخ فلو قال: تفرَّد به فلان عن هذا الشيخ فإنه يُسمى فرداً

نسبيًّا، والفرد النسبي غرابته نسبية، والفرد المطلق غرابته مطلقة، والفرد النسبي أقرب إلى الصحة، لأنه قد يكون فرداً بالنسبة لهؤلاء، ولكنه بالنسبة إلى غيرهم مشهور أو عزيز، أي مروي بعدة طرق.

And likewise if it was in relation to a certain *shaykh*; if it was said that so-and-so was unique in narrating from this *shaykh*, then it is also *fard nisbī*. The uniqueness of *fard nisbī* is relative while the uniqueness of *fard muṭlaq* is unrestricted. And the *fard nisbī* is closer to soundness because it could be unique in relation to those people but in relation to other than them, it may be *mash-hūr* or *ʿazīz* i.e. narrated from a number of routes.

المتن

(٢٤) وَمَا بِعِلَّةٍ غُمُوضٌ أَوْ خَفَا مُعَلَّلٌ عِنْدَهُمُ قَدْ عُرِفَا

(24) And that which has an obscure or hidden defect,
Is known to them as muʿallal.

الشرح

هذا هو القسم الرابع والعشرون من أقسام الحديث المذكورة في النظم وهو المعلول أو المعلل.

This is the twenty fourth category of the classifications of *ḥadīth* mentioned in the poem, which is *al-maʿlūl* or *muʿallal* (the narration with a hidden defect).

يقال: (الحديث المعلل)، ويُقال: (الحديث الُمعَلّ)، ويقال الحديث المعلول، كل هذه الاصطلاحات لعلماء الحديث ولا شك أن أقربها للصواب من حيث اللغة هو (المُعَلُّ)، لأن وزن مُعَلّ الصرفي هو مُفْعَل، وذلك لأن اللام مشددة، فتكون عن حرفين أولهما ساكن، وإذا نظرنا إلى الاشتقاق وجدنا أن هذا هو

الصواب، لأنه مأخوذ من أعلّه يُعلُّه فهو مُعَلّ مثل أقره يقره فهو مقرّ.

It is said that, "The *ḥadīth* is *mu'allal,*" or, "The *ḥadīth* is *mu'all,*" or, "The *ḥadīth* is *ma'lūl.*" All of these terminologies are from the scholars of *ḥadīth*. And there is no doubt that the most accurate of them linguistically is *al-mu'all.* This is because the morphological structure (i.e. in the Arabic language science of *sarf*) for *mu'all* is *muf'al,* and that is due to the consonant *lām* being emphasised (having a *shaddah* above it), thus it becomes two letters, the first having a *sukūn*. When we look at its etymology (study of the source of the word) we shall find that this is the precise derivation because it is derived from *a'allahu yu'illuhu* (he spoiled it) and thus it is called *mu'all* (the thing spoiled). Another example to make this clearer is the word *aqarrahu yuqirruhu* (he admitted it); therefore it is called *muqarr* (the thing admitted).

والذين قالوا إنه معلول أخذوه من علّة مثل شدَّهُ فهو مشدودٌ، فيسمونه معلولاً، لأنه مأخوذٌ من الفعل الثلاثي.

Whereas those who said that it is *ma'lūl* derived it from *'illah* (ailing) like in the case of the word *shaddahu* (he tied it) and thus it becomes *mashdūd* (tightened). So they named it *ma'lūl* (the ill) as it was derived from a three-letter verb.

والذين يقولون (مُعَلَّل) أخذوه من علَّله، فهو معلل مثل قوّمه فهو مقوّم، والصواب: كما سبق (المُعَلّ).

And those who termed it as *mu'allal* derived it from the word *'allalahu* (he regarded it as defective) so it is *mu'allal* (defective). Just like *qawwamahu* (he straightened it) so it is *muqawwam* (straightened). And the correct opinion is *al-mu'all,* as previously mentioned.

فنقول: المعلُّ هو الحديث الذي يكون ظاهره الصحة، ولكنه بعد البحث عنه يتبين أن فيه علة قادحة، لكنها خفية.

Thus we say that *al-mu'all* is the *ḥadīth* which is apparently *ṣaḥīḥ* but after doing research, it is found to have a dispraise worthy defect which is discreet.

مثال ذلك: أن يُروى الحديث على أنه مرفوع إلى النبي صلى الله عليه وسلّم باتصال السند، ويكون هذا هو المعروف المتداول عند المحدثين، ثم يأتي أحدُ الحفاظ ويقول هذا الحديث فيه علة قادحة وهي أن الحفاظ رووه منقطعاً، فتكون فيه علة ضعف، وهي الانقطاع، بينما المعروف بين الناس أن الحديث متصلٌ.

Its example is to narrate a *ḥadīth* as *marfū'* to the Prophet ﷺ with a connected *sanad* and this narration is popular and circulated amongst the scholars of *ḥadīth*. Then one of the *ḥuffāẓ* came and said that this *ḥadīth* has an *'illah qādihah* (dispraise worthy defect) and that the *ḥuffāẓ* narrated it as *munqaṭi'*. Thus it possesses a defect of the weak narrations which is the disconnection of the *sanad*, though it is popular amongst the people that the *ḥadīth* is connected.

قال الحافظ ابن حجر - رحمه الله - في شرح النخبة: وهذا القسم من أغمض أنواع الحديث، لأنه لا يطَّلع عليه إلا أهل العلم النقاد الذين يبحثون الأحاديث بأسانيدها ومتونها.

Al-Ḥāfiẓ Ibn Ḥajar said in his book *Sharḥ al-Nukhbah*, "This category is from the deepest types of *ḥadīth,* as no one can detect it except the critics amongst the people of knowledge who studied the chains and texts of the narrations vigorously."

وابن حجر يقول دائماً في بلوغ المرام: أُعلَّ بالإرسال، أو أُعلَّ بالوقف، وهكذا.

And Ibn Ḥajar would frequently say in *Bulūgh al-Marām*, "Defective due to being *mursal,*" or "Defective due to being *mawqūf,*" etc.

فإذا قال ذلك فارجع إلى السند وانظر فيه من رواه؟

Thus, when he says this, we have to analyse the *isnād* and look at who were the narrators.

ولهذا اشترطوا في الصحيح أن يكون سالماً من الشذوذ والعلة القادحة، والمعلُّ من أقسام علم المصطلح وهو مهمٌّ جداً لطالب علم الحديث حيث إن معرفته تفيده فائدة كبيرة؛ لأنه قد يقرأ حديثاً ظاهره الصحة، وهو غير صحيح.

Due to this, it has been made a requirement for *ṣaḥīḥ* narrations to be free from *shudhūth* and *'illah qādihah*. Therefore, the *mu'all* is one of the divisions of the science of *mustalah*, and it is of extreme importance for the students of *ḥadīth*. Possessing knowledge of it is of great benefit because one could read a *ḥadīth* which seems to be *ṣaḥīḥ* but it is not.

۞۞۞

المتن

(٢٥) وَذُو اخْتِلَافٍ سَنَدٍ أَوْ مَتْنِ مُضْطَرِبٌ عِنْدَ أُهَيلِ الْفَنِّ

(25) And that which has a discrepancy in a chain or text is,
Muḍṭarib according to the people of the art.

الشرح

وهذا هو الخامس والعشرون من أقسام الحديث المذكورة في هذا النظم وهو المضطرب.

This is the twenty fifth category of the classifications of *ḥadīth* mentioned in the poem, which is *al-muḍṭarib* (the narration with *ikhtilāf* in its *isnād* or *matn*).

والاضطراب معناه في اللغة: الاختلاف.

The word *iḍṭirāb* means "difference" (*ikhtilāf*) linguistically.

والمضطرب في الاصطلاح: هو الذي اختلف الرواة في سنده، أو متنه، على وجه لا يمكن فيه الجمع ولا الترجيح.

As for *al-muḍṭarib* in *muṣṭalāḥ al-ḥadīth*: It is the one that the narrators differ regarding its *sanad* or *matn* in such a way that it is neither possible to combine them nor gain preponderance (*tarjīh*).

فالاختلاف في السند مثل: أن يرويه بعضهم متصلاً، وبعضهم يرويه منقطعاً.

As for the difference in the *sanad*; an example would be where some of the narrators narrated the *ḥadīth* as *muttaṣil*, whilst others narrated it as *munqaṭi'*.

والاختلاف في المتن مثل: أن يرويه بعضهم على أنه مرفوع، وبعضهم على أنه موقوف، أو يرويه على وجه يخالف الآخر بدون ترجيح، ولا جمع.

And as for the difference in the *matn*; an example would be where some of them narrated it as *marfū'*, while others narrated it as *mawqūf* or they narrated it in a different manner without *tarjīḥ* (gaining preponderance) or *jam'* (combining).

فإن أمكن الجمع فلا اضطراب.

As such, if combination is possible, then there is no *iḍṭirāb*.

وإن أمكن الترجيح أخذنا بالراجح ولا اضطراب.

And if outweighing (*tarjīḥ*) is possible, then we take to the preponderant and thus there is no *iḍṭirāb*.

وإذا كان الاختلاف لا يعود لأصل المعنى فلا اضطراب أيضاً.

And if the difference is not based on the fundamental meaning, then there is no *idtirāb* in this case as well.

مثال الذي يمكن فيه الجمع: حديث حج النبي صلى الله عليه وسلّم، فإن حج النبي صلى الله عليه وسلّم، اختلف فيه الرواة على وجوه متعددة.

An example of where combination is possible is the *ḥadīth* of the Prophet's

ﷺ Ḥajj, as the narrators differ in a number of ways.

فمنهم من قال: إنه حجَّ قارناً.

Some of them said that he performed the Ḥajj in the manner of *qirān*.

ومنهم من قال: إنه حجَّ مفرداً.

And some said that he performed it in the manner of *ifrād*.

ومنهم من قال: إنه حجَّ متمتعاً.

While others said that he performed it in the manner of *tamattuʿ*.

ففي حديث عائشة - رضي الله عنها - قالت: خرجنا مع النبي صلى الله عليه وسلّم عام حجة الوداع فمنا من أهلَّ بحج، ومنَّا من أهل بعمرة، ومنَّا من أهلَّ بحج وعمرة، وأهلَّ رسول الله صلى الله عليه وسلّم بالحج.

In the *ḥadīth* of ʿĀ'ishah ﵂ she said, "We travelled with the Prophet ﷺ in the year of the Farewell Ḥajj. Some of us exited the state of *iḥrām* with a Ḥajj, while some with an ʿUmrah and some with a Ḥajj and an ʿUmrah. And the Prophet ﷺ performed the *tahallul* with the Ḥajj."[74]

وفي حديث ابن عمر وغيره - رضي الله عنهم - أنه حجَّ متمتعاً، وفي بعض الأحاديث أنه حج قارناً.

Whereas in the *ḥadīth* of Ibn ʿUmar ﵄ and the other companions, he performed the Ḥajj as *tamattuʿ*[75] and in some of the *aḥādīth*; he performed it as *qirān*.[76]

---

74 Recorded by al-Bukhārī; The Book of Pilgrimage; Chapter: The *tamattuʿ*, the *qirān* and the *ifrād* (1562) and Muslim; The Book of Pilgrimage; Chapter: The ways of pilgrimage 118 (1211).

75 Recorded by al-Bukhārī; The Book of Pilgrimage; Chapter: Those who herded camels with them (1691) and Muslim; The Book of Pilgrimage; Chapter: The obligation of slaughter upon the *mutamattiʿ* 174 (1227).

76 Recorded by al-Bukhārī; The Book of Pilgrimage; Chapter: The speech of the

فهذا الاختلاف إذا نظرنا إليه قلنا في بادىء الأمر: إن الحديث مضطرب، وإذا حكمنا بالاضطراب، بقيت حجة النبي صلى الله عليه وسلّم مشكلة، فلا ندري هل حج مفرداً، أم متمتعاً، أم قارناً؟

As such, if we look at this difference in the beginning (i.e. without analysis), we would say that the *ḥadīth* is *muḍṭarib*. And as we rule it as *idtirāb*, then the pilgrimage of the Prophet ﷺ remains an unsolved problem. Thus we do not know if the Prophet ﷺ performed it as *tamattu*ʿ, *qirān* or *ifrād*.

وعند التأمل: نرى أن الجمع ممكن يندفع به الاضطراب.

However, after contemplation we see that combination is possible to expel the *iḍṭirāb*.

وللجمع بين هذه الروايات وجهان:

There are two ways to combine these narrations:

١ - الوجه الأول: أن من روى أنه أهلَّ بالحج مفرداً، أراد إفراد الأعمال، يعني أنه لم يزد على عمل المفرد.

1. The first perspective is that those who narrated that he made the *tahallul* with the *ifrād* pilgrimage refer to the state of *ifrād* of the rites, i.e. that he did not go beyond the rites of the one performing the *ifrād* pilgrimage.

وعمل المفرد هو: أنه إذا وصل إلى مكة طاف طواف القدوم، ثم سعى للحج، وإذا كان يوم العيد طاف طواف الإفاضة فقط ولم يسع، وإذا أراد أن يخرج طاف طواف الوداع وخرج.

And the *ifrād* rites are such that upon arriving in Makkah, one would perform the arrival circling (of the Kaʿbah), followed by the *saʿī* (going between Ṣafā and Marwah) for Ḥajj. On the day of Eid, one performs only the *ṭawāf*

Prophet ﷺ: al-ʿAqīq is a blessed valley (1534) and Muslim; The Book of Pilgrimage; Chapter: The exit of the Prophet ﷺ from the state of *iḥrām* and his sacrifice 214 (1251).

al-ifāḍah (the circling performed on the 10th of Dhul Ḥijjah) and not the *sa'ī*. And when one intends to leave Makkah, he performs the farewell circling and then leaves.

ومن روى أنه متمتع: أراد أنه جمع بين العمرة والحج في سفر واحد، فتمتع بسقوط أحد السفرين.

While those who narrated that he performed the *tamattu'* form of Ḥajj refer to him coupling the 'Umrah and Ḥajj in one journey, thus enjoying the privilege of abandoning one of the two journeys.

ومن روى أنه قرن بين الحج والعمرة فهذا هو الواقع.

And those who narrated that he performed *qirān* by integrating the Ḥajj and 'Umrah, then this is the actual case.

قال الإمام أحمد: لا أشك أن النبي صلى الله عليه وسلّم كان قارناً، والمتعة أحب إلّي.

Al-Imām Aḥmad said, "There is no doubt to me that the Prophet ﷺ performed *qirān*, and the *tamattu'* is more preferred to me."

٢ - الوجه الثاني: أنه أحرم أولاً بالحج ثم أدخل العمرة عليه، فصار مفرداً باعتبار أول إحرامه، وقارناً باعتبار ثاني الحال، ولكن هذا لا يصح على أصول مذهب الإمام أحمد، لأن من أصوله أنه لا يصح إدخال العمرة على الحج، وإنما الذي يصح هو العكس.

2. The second perspective is that he entered the state of *iḥrām* for Ḥajj initially and then inserted the 'Umrah into it. Thus he entered into the state of *ifrād* in terms of his initial *ihrām*, and the state of *qirān* in the second case. However, this is not correct according to the fundamentals of al-Imām Aḥmad's *madhhab*. This is because, one of his *usūl* is that it is not permissible to insert the 'Umrah into the Ḥajj, and indeed it is permissible only to do the opposite.

قال شيخ الإسلام ابن تيمية مقرراً الوجه الأول: من روى أنه مفرد، فقد أراد أعمال الحج.

Shaykh al-Islām Ibn Taymiyyāh said, whilst confirming the first perspective, "Whoever narrated that he ﷺ performed the *ifrād* pilgrimage, refers to his performance of the rites of the Ḥajj.

ومن قال إنه متمتع: فقد أراد أنه أتى بعمرة وحج في سفر واحد، فتمتع بسقوط أحد السفرين عنه، لأنه لولا أنه أتى بالعمرة والحج، لكان قد أتى بعمرة في سفر، وبالحج في سفر آخر، فيكون تمتعه بكونه أسقط أحد السفرين، لأنه سافر سفراً واحداً، وقرن بين العمرة والحج فتمتع بذلك.

And whoever said that he ﷺ performed the *tamattu'* pilgrimage, then he refers to the fact that he ﷺ came with an 'Umrah and a Ḥajj in one journey and thus enjoyed the privilege of abandoning one of the two journeys upon it. This is due to the fact that if he were to perform the 'Umrah and the Ḥajj, then he would have performed the 'Umrah in one journey and the Ḥajj in another. Thus the state of *tamattu'* was due to his abandonment of one of the two journeys as he only set out once and combined the 'Umrah and Ḥajj. And as such, he enjoyed this privilege.

وأما من قال: إنه كان قارناً فهذا هو الواقع، أي أنه كان قارناً، لأننا لا نشك أن الرسول صلى الله عليه وسلّم لم يحل من العمرة، بل بقي على إحرامه لكونه قد ساق الهدي. اه.

As for whoever states that he was in the state of *qirān*, then this is the reality. He was in the state of *qirān* because there is no doubt that the Messenger ﷺ did not exit the state of *iḥrām* from the 'Umrah. In fact he remained in the state of *iḥrām* as he brought with him his animal sacrifice."

ثم نرجع إلى الحج فنقول: الأنساك ثلاثة:

Now, we return to the topic of Ḥajj. We say that there are three types of rites:

١ - الإفراد.

1. *Al-ifrād*.

٢ - التمتع.

2. *Al-tamattu'*.

٣ - القِران.

3. *Al-qirān*.

(١) فالإفراد هو: أن يحرم الإنسان بالحج وحده من الميقات، ويقول: لبيك اللهم حجًّا، ثم إذا وصل إلى مكة فإنه يطوف طواف القدوم، ويسعى للحج، ويبقى على إحرامه إلى أن يتم الحج، وفي يوم العيد يطوف طواف الإفاضة، وعند السفر يطوف طواف الوداع.

1. As for *al-ifrād*, it is such that a person enters the state of *iḥrām* for Ḥajj on its own from the *mīqāt* and says, "*Labbayk allāhhumma ḥajjā*," (O Allāh I answer your call for Ḥajj) followed by performing the *ṭawāf al-qudūm* and the *sa'ī* for Ḥajj upon arrival in Makkah. He shall remain in the state of *iḥrām* until he completes his Ḥajj. On the Day of Eid he shall perform the *ṭawāf al-ifāḍah*. Upon leaving he performs the *ṭawāf al-wadā'*.

(٢) والقران هو: أن يحرم بالعمرة والحج معاً من الميقات، ويقول: لبيك اللهم عمرة وحجًّا، فإذا وصل إلى مكة طاف طواف القدوم وسعى للعمرة والحج، ثم يبقى على إحرامه، ويوم العيد يطوف طواف الإفاضة، وعند السفر يطوف طواف الوداع. ففعله كفعل المفرد لكن تختلف النية.

2. As for *al-qirān*, it is such that a person enters the state of *iḥrām* for 'Umrah and Ḥajj combined from the *mīqāt* and says, "*Labbayk allāhumma 'umratan wa ḥajjā*" (O Allāh I answer your call for 'Umrah and Ḥajj).

When he arrives in Makkah he performs the *ṭawāf al-qudūm* and the *sa'ī* for 'Umrah and Ḥajj. Then he shall remain in the state of *iḥrām*. On the day of Eid, he shall perform the *ṭawāf al-ifāḍah* and upon leaving he shall perform the *ṭawāf al-wadā'*. Thus his rites are similar to that of *al-ifrād* but the intention is different.

(٣) أما التمتع فهو أن يحرم من الميقات بالعمرة، ثم إذا وصل إلى مكة، يطوف ويسعى ويقصِّر، لأنها عمرة، ثم يحل من إحرامه ويلبس ثيابه ويتحلَّل تحللاً كاملاً، ثم في اليوم الثامن من شهر ذي الحجة يحرم بالحج، وفي يوم العيد يطوف طواف الإفاضة ويسعى للحج، وعند السفر يطوف للوداع.

3. As for *al-tamattu'*, it is such that a person enters the state of *iḥrām* for 'Umrah from the *mīqāt*. Then, when he arrives at Makkah he shall perform the *ṭawāf*, the *sa'ī* and shorten his hair as he is performing 'Umrah. As such, he shall exit from the state of *iḥrām* completely and may wear his clothes. Then on the eighth day of Dhul Ḥijjah he shall enter the state of *iḥrām* for Ḥajj, and on the day of Eid he shall perform the *ṭawāf al-ifāḍah* and the *sa'ī* for Ḥajj. And upon leaving he shall perform the *ṭawāf al-wadā'*.

وإذا لم يمكن الجمع بين الروايات، عملنا بالترجيح فنأخذ بالراجح، ويندفع الاضطراب.

If the combination of the narrations is not possible, we shall work upon outweighing one of the narrations and take the most correct opinion and abandon the *muḍṭarib*.

مثاله: حديث بريرة - رضي الله عنها - حين أعتقتها عائشة رضي الله عنها، ثم خيرها رسول الله صلى الله عليه وسلّم على أن تبقى مع زوجها، أو أن تفسخ نكاحها منه.

Its example would be the *ḥadīth* of Barīrah ﷺ when she was freed from slavery by 'Ā'ishah ﷺ; the Prophet ﷺ gave her the choice to remain with her husband or to annul the marriage from him.[77]

ففي بعض روايات الحديث أن زوجها - وهو مغيث - كان حرًّا. وفي بعض الروايات أنه كان عبداً.

In some of the narrations, it was stated that her husband Mughīth was a free man. And in some he was said to be a slave.

إذاً في الحديث اختلاف والحديث واحد، والجمع غير ممكن فنعمل بالترجيح.

Thus, there is a discrepancy in the *ḥadīth* though the *ḥadīth* is one. Combination (*al-jamʿ*) is not possible thus we work upon outweighing one of the narrations (*tarjīḥ*).

والراجح: أنه كان عبداً، فإذا كان هو الراجح، إذاً نلغي المرجوح، ونأخذ بالراجح، ويكون الراجح هذا سالماً من الاضطراب، لأنه راجح.

And the correct opinion is that he was a slave. If this is the correct opinion, then we shall abandon the incorrect opinion and take the correct one, and this correct opinion shall be free from *iḍṭirāb* because it is the *rājiḥ* (correct opinion).

وإذا لم يكن الاختلاف في أصل المعنى، فلا اضطراب، بأن يكون أمراً جانبيًّا.

And if there is no discrepancy in the fundamental meaning, then there is no *iḍṭirāb*, and it is seen as a secondary matter.

مثل: اختلاف الرواة في ثمن جمل جابر - رضي الله عنه - واختلاف الرواة في حديث فضالة بن عبيد في ثمن القلادة التي فيها ذهب وخرز، هل اشتراها باثني عشر ديناراً، أو بأكثر من ذلك أو بأقل.

Example: The narrators differ regarding the price of the camel belonging

77 Recorded by al-Bukhārī; The Book of Freeing Slaves; Chapter: Selling of the right guardianship, and Muslim; The Book of Freeing Slaves; Chapter: The prohibition of selling the right of guardianship.

to Jābir[78] ﷺ and the narrators in the *ḥadīth* of Fuḍālah ibn ʿUbayd differ regarding the price of the necklace containing gold and pearls, whether he purchased it with twelve dinars or more or less than that.[79]

فنقول: هذا الاختلاف لا يضر، لأنه لا يعود إلى أصل المعنى، وهو بيع الذهب بالذهب، لأنهم كلهم متفقون على أنها قلادة فيها ذهب وخرز، وكانت قد بيعت بدنانير، ولكن كم عدد هذه الدنانير؟

Thus, we say that this difference has no impact because it does not go back to the fundamental meaning of the *ḥadīth*, which is the selling of gold for gold, as all of them agreed upon the fact that the necklace had gold and pearls, and was sold for gold coins. The difference is merely regarding the amount of gold coins that it was sold for.

قد اختلف فيها الرواة، ولكن هذا الاختلاف لا يضر.

The narrators differed upon it, but this is a difference that has no affect.

وكذلك حديث جابر - رضي الله عنه - فقد اتفق الرواة على أن الرسول صلى الله عليه وسلّم اشتراه، وأن جابراً اشترط أن يركبه إلى الميدنة، ولكن اختلفوا في مقدار الثمن، فنقول: إن هذا الاختلاف لا يضر، لأنه لا يعود إلى أصل المعنى الذي سيق من أجله الحديث.

Similarly in the *ḥadīth* of Jābir ﷺ, the narrators agreed upon the fact that the Prophet ﷺ brought his camel and that Jābir laid the condition that he would ride it to Madīnah, but they differed upon its price. Thus we say that this difference has no affect because it does not go back to the fundamental purport of the *ḥadīth* of which it was narrated for.

وحكم الحديث المضطرب هو: الضعف، لأن اضطراب الرواة فيه على هذا الوجه يدل على أنهم لم يضبطوه، ومعلوم أن الحديث إذا لم يكن مضبوطاً، فهو

78 Mentioned previously.
79 Mentioned previously.

من قسم الضعيف.

The ruling of the *muḍṭarib* narration is that it is *ḍaʿīf*, because the discrepancy of the narrators in this manner shows that they were not precise in its narration. And it is known that if the *ḥadīth* is not precise, then it is one of the types of *ḍaʿīf* narrations.

وقوله (مضطربٌ عند أُهيل الفن).

The author's phrase, "*Muḍṭarib* according to the people of the art":

قد يقول قائل: لماذا صغر كلمة (أهل) وهل ينبغي أن يصغر أهل العلم؟

It may be asked, "Why is the word *ahl* in its *taṣghīr* (diminutive) form and should one diminish the people of knowledge?"

فنقول: إن المؤلف اضطرَّه النظم إلى التصغير، ولهذا يُعتبر التصغير من تمام البيت فقط، وإلا كان عليه أن يقول: عند أهل الفن.

We say that the author was in need of the *taṣghīr* form due to the [structuring of the] poem. As such, the *tasghīr* is considered only as a means of completing the line. If not, he would have said, "To the *ahl* (people) of the art" .

فإذا قال قائل: الفنُّ عندنا غير محمودٍ عُرفاً؟

And if someone were to say, "Art (*al-fann*) is known to be not praiseworthy to us":

فنقول: إن المراد بالفن عند العلماء، هو الصنف.

We say that the scholars refer to *al-fann* as the category of knowledge.

قال الشاعر:

A poet once said:

تمنيتَ أن تمسي فقيهاً مناظراً   بغير عناء والجنون فنون

You wish to become a scholar of fiqh with insight overnight,
Without any pain while madness has different arts.

يعني أن الذي يتمنى أن يُمسي فقيهاً مناظراً بغير تعب فإنه مجنون، والجنون أصناف من جملتها أن يقول القائل: أريد أن أكون فقيهاً مناظراً، وأنا نائم على الفراش.

Meaning that the one who wishes to be a scholar of *fiqh* able to give opinions on issues overnight without enduring the required fatigue, he is considered to be *majnūn* (mad). And madness has different types, one of which is if someone were to say, "I want to be a scholar of *fiqh* with deep insight whilst I sleep on my mattress."

۞۞۞

المتن

(٢٦) وَالْمُدْرَجَاتُ فِي الْحَدِيثِ مَا أَتَتْ مِنْ بَعْضِ أَلْفَاظِ الرُّوَاةِ اتَّصَلَتْ

(26) Insertions in the ḥadīth are what came,
From some of the words of the narrators that were connected.

الشرح

هذا هو السادس والعشرون من أقسام الحديث المذكورة في هذا النظم وهو المدرج.

This is the twenty sixth category of the classifications of *ḥadīth* mentioned in the poem which is *al-mudraj* (the insertion).

والحديث المدرج هو: ما أدخله أحد الرواة في الحديث بدون بيان، ولهذا سُمي مدرجاً، لأنه أُدرج في الحديث دون أن يبين الحديث من هذا المدرج، فالمدرج إذاً ليس من كلام النبي صلى الله عليه وسلّم، ولكنه من كلام الرواة، ويأتي به

الراوي أحياناً، إما تفسيراً لكلمة في الحديث، أو لغير ذلك من الأسباب.

The *ḥadīth* which is *mudraj* is where one of the narrators inserted something into the *ḥadīth* without distinguishing it. Due to this, it is termed as *mudraj* (inserted), because it was inserted into the *ḥadīth* without differentiating the narration from the insertion. Thus the *mudraj* is not from the speech of the Prophet ﷺ but from the speech of the narrators. Sometimes the narrator brings it either to explain a word in the *ḥadīth* or for other reasons.

ويكون الإدراج أحياناً:

The *mudraj* sometimes occur:

في أول الحديث.

In the beginning of the *ḥadīth*.

وأحياناً يكون في وسطه.

Or sometimes in the middle of it.

وأحياناً يكون في آخره.

And sometimes at the end.

مثاله في أول الحديث: حديث أبي هريرة - رضي الله عنه - قال: (أسبغوا الوضوء، ويلٌ للأعقاب من النار) فالمرفوع هو قوله: ((ويل للأعقاب من النار)) وأما قوله (أسبغوا الوضوء) فهو من كلام أبي هريرة - رضي الله عنه - والذي يقرأ الحديث يظن أن الكل، هو من كلام النبي صلى الله عليه وسلّم لأنه لم يُبين ذلك.

An example of the occurrence in the beginning of the *ḥadīth*: The *ḥadīth* of Abū Hurayrah ﷺ where he said, "Perform the ablution thoroughly. Woe to the heels from the Hellfire."[80] The *marfūʿ* is his statement, "Woe to the

80 Recorded by al-Bukhārī; The Book of Ablutions; Chapter: Washing of the heels (165) and Muslim; The Book of Purity; Chapter: The obligation of washing the two

heels from the Hellfire." As for the statement: "Perform the ablution thoroughly", it is from the speech of Abū Hurairah ﵁. And the one who reads this *ḥadīth* may think that all are from the speech of the Prophet ﷺ because it was not made clear as such.

ومثال الإدراج في وسط الحديث: حديث الزهري عن عائشة - رضي الله عنها - في كيفية نزول الوحي - يعني أوّل ما أُوحي إلى النبي صلى الله عليه وسلّم - فقالت: (كان النبي صلى الله عليه وسلّم يتحنَّثُ في غار حراء الليالي ذوات العدد، والتحنُّث التعبد ...) الحديث.

As for the example of *idrāj* (state of *mudraj*) in the middle of the *ḥadīth*: The narration of al-Zuhrī on the authority of 'Ā'ishah ﵂ regarding the description of the revelation i.e. what was revealed to the Prophet ﷺ during the beginning of his Prophethood. She said, "The Prophet ﷺ used to go in the state of *al-ḥinth* to the cave of Ḥirā' for a number of nights, and the state of *al-ḥinth* is a state of worship [... to the end of the *ḥadīth*.]"[81]

والذي يسمع هذا الحديث يظن أن التفسير من عائشة - رضي الله عنها - في قولها (والتحنث التعبد) والواقع أن التفسير من الزهري - رحمه الله - وهو الآن مدرج في الحديث بدون بيان منه أنه مدرج، وهذا الإدراج يُراد به التفسير، والتفسير هنا لابد منه؛ لأن الحنث في الأصل هو الإثم، كما قال تعالى: ﴿وَكَانُوا يُصِرُّونَ عَلَى الْحِنْثِ الْعَظِيمِ﴾. [الواقعة: ٤٦]. وإذا لم يُبين معنى التحنث لاشتبه بالإثم، ولكن النبي صلى الله عليه وسلّم كان يتعبد، والتعبُّد مزيلٌ للحنث الذي هو الإثم، فهو من باب تسمية الشيء بضده.

The one who hears this *ḥadīth* may think that the explanation is from 'Ā'ishah's ﵂ speech, "And the state of *al-ḥinth* is a state of worship." How-

feet 30 (240).

81 Recorded by al-Bukhārī; The Book of the Commencement of Revelations; Chapter: How revelation first started (3) and Muslim; The Book of Faith; Chapter: The commencement of revelations 252 (160).

ever, the explanation is actually from al-Zuhrī and it is now an addition in the *ḥadīth* without clarification from him that it has been inserted. And this type of *idrāj* is intended to be an explanation, and the explanation here is a must because *al-ḥinth* is originally considered to be a sin, as it was mentioned in the ayah: **{And they used to persist in *al-hinth al-'aẓīm* (the great violation i.e. *shirk*).}**[82] If the meaning of *al-ḥinth* is not made clear, then it could be confused with the wrongdoing. However, the Prophet ﷺ was in the state of worship, and worship is the remover of *al-ḥinth* (which is wrongdoing). This is from the manner of naming something with its opposite.

مثال الإدراج في آخر الحديث: حديث أبي هريرة - رضي الله عنه - أن النبي صلى الله عليه وسلّم قال: ((إن أمتي يُدعون يوم القيامة غُرًّا محجلين من أثر الوضوء، فمن استطاع منكم أن يُطيل غرته وتحجيله فليفعل))، فهذا الحديث إذا قرأته فإنك تظن أنه من قول الرسول صلى الله عليه وسلّم، ولكن الواقع أن الجملة الأخير ليست من كلام النبي صلى الله عليه وسلّم وهو قوله: (فمن استطاع منكم أن يطيل غرته وتحجيله فليفعل) بل هي مدرجة من كلام أبي هريرة - رضي الله عنه - والذي من كلامه صلى الله عليه وسلّم: ((إن أمتي يُدعون يوم القيامة غُرًّا محجلين من أثر الوضوء)).

And an example of *idrāj* at the end of the *ḥadīth*: The *ḥadīth* of Abū Hurayrah ﷺ in which he narrated that the Prophet ﷺ said, "Verily on the Day of Resurrection, my followers will be called *al-ghurr al-muhajjalīn* from the trace of ablution. So whoever amongst you can extend the area of his *ghurr* (whiteness on his forehead) and *tahjīl* (the whiteness on his limbs) should do so."[83] As such, if you were to read this *ḥadīth*, you would think that it is from the speech of the Messenger ﷺ. However, the last sentence,

82 Al-Wāqi'ah: 46

83 Recorded by al-Bukhārī; The Book of Ablutions; Chapter: The virtues of ablution and *al-ghurr al-muhajjalūn* from the traces of ablution (136) and Muslim; The Book of Purity; Chapter: The recommendation to extend the *ghurr* and the *tahjīl* during ablution 35 (246).

"So whoever amongst you can extend the area of his *ghurr* (whiteness on his forehead) and *tahjīl* (the whiteness on his limbs) should do so," is actually not from the speech of the Prophet ﷺ. In fact it is *mudraj* from the speech of Abu Hurayrah ؓ, whereas the part from the Prophet's speech is: "Verily on the Day of Resurrection, my followers will be called as *al-ghurr al-muhajjalūn* from the trace of ablution."

أما الجملة الأخيرة فقد أدرجها أبو هريرة - رضي الله عنه - تفقهاً منه في الحديث، ولهذا قال ابن القيم - رحمه الله - في النونية:

As for the last sentence, Abu Hurayrah inserted it due to his understanding from the *ḥadīth*. Due to this, Ibn al-Qayyim said in his *Nūniyyah*:

وأبو هريرة قال ذا من كيسه فغدا يميزه أولو العرفان

And Abu Hurayrah said this from his understanding,
So tomorrow the people of knowledge shall differentiate it.

ويعرف الإدراج بأمور:

The insertion is identified through a number of ways:

١ - بالنص، حيث يأتي من طريق آخر ويُبين أنه مدرج.

1. Via text (*al-naṣ*): Whereby it comes from another route and this makes it clear that it is *mudraj*.

٢ - باستحالة أن يكون النبي صلى الله عليه وسلّم قد قاله، وذلك لظهور خطأ فيه، أو قرينة تدل على أنه لا يمكن أن يكون من كلام النبي صلى الله عليه وسلّم.

2. The impossibility that the statement is from the Prophet ﷺ and this occurs due to an apparent mistake in it or another indication that shows that it is not possible to be from the speech of the Prophet ﷺ.

٣ - بنص من أحد الحفَّاظ الأئمة يبين فيه أن هذا مدرج.

3. An explicit text of one of the leading *ḥuffāẓ* that clarifies in it that this is *mudraj*.

ما هو حكم الإدراج؟

What is the ruling of *idrāj*?

نقول: إن كان يتغير المعنى بالإدراج فإنه لا يجوز إلا ببيانه.

We say that if the meaning changes due to the *idrāj*, then it is not permissible except with explanation.

وإن كان لا يتغير به المعنى مثل: حديث الزهري (والتحنُّث التعبُّد) فإنه لا بأس به، وذلك لأنه لا يعارض الحديث المرفوع، وإذا كان لا يعارضه فلا مانع من أن يُذكر على سبيل التفسير والإيضاح.

And if the meaning does not change, such as the *ḥadīth* of al-Zuhrī, "And *al-ḥinth* is a state of worship", then there is nothing wrong with it. This is because it does not oppose the *ḥadīth* which is *marfūʿ*, and if it does not contradict it, then there is no objection for it to be mentioned as a form of explanation and clarification.

وإذا تبين الإدراج فإنه لا يكون حجة، لأنه ليس من قول النبي صلى الله عليه وسلّم فلا يحتج به.

And when the *idrāj* is made clear, it is not used as an evidence. This is because it is not from the statements of the Prophet ﷺ and thus it is not taken as an argument.

وقوله (من بعض ألفاظ الرواة اتصلت) فكلمة (اتصلت) جملة حالية من فاعل أتت، يعني ما أتت متصلة في الحديث بدون بيان.

The author's phrase, "From some of the words of the narrators that were connected": The word "connected" is a *jumlah ḥālīyah* (circumstantial sentence) from the *fāʿil* (doer) of the verb "came". So the meaning is: What came connected in the *ḥadīth* without identification [of it being distinct.]

المتن

(٢٧) وَمَا رَوَى كُلُّ قَرِينٍ عَنْ أَخِهْ مُدَبَّجٌ فَاعْرِفْهُ حَقّاً وَانْتَخِهْ

(27) And what was narrated by every qarīn from his associate,
Is mudabbaj, know it well and be proud of it.

الشرح

هذا هو القسم السابع والعشرون من أقسام الحديث المذكورة في هذا النظم وهو المدبج.

This is the twenty seventh category of the classifications of *ḥadīth* mentioned in the poem, which *is al-mudabbaj* (narration from associates).

وعرفه بقوله: وما روى ... الخ.

And the author defined it with his statement, "And what was narrated by every *qarīn* from his associate."

والقرين هو: المصاحب لمن روى عنه، الموافِق له في السنن، أو في الأخذ عن الشيخ.

The *qarīn* (peer) is he who accompanied the one whom he narrated from, was close to him in terms of age or in narrating from the same *shaykh*.

فإذا قيل: فلان قرينٌ لفلان، أي مشاركٌ له، إما في السن، أو في الأخذ عن الشيخ الذي رويا عنه، مثل: أن يكون حضورهما للشيخ متقارباً مثلاً في سنةٍ

واحدة، وما أشبه ذلك.

If it was said that so-and-so is the *qarīn* for so-and-so, i.e. he is an associate of the other, either in terms of age or in narrating from the same teacher whom both narrated from. An example of this is that the period when they studied under the *shaykh* was close, such as in the same year etc.

فالأقران إذا روى أحدهم عن الآخر، فإن ذلك يسمى عند المحدثين رواية الأقران، ولهذا تجد في كتب الرجال أنهم يقولون: وروايته عن فلان من رواية الأقران، أي أنه اشترك معه في السنّ، أو في الأخذ عن الشيخ، فإن روى كل منهما عن الآخر فهو (مُدبَّج).

Thus when a peer narrates from the other, the scholars of *ḥadīth* termed this as *riwāyat al-aqrān* (narration of the peers). Due to this, you shall find in the books of narrators that they say, "And his narration from so-and-so is *riwāyat al-aqrān*," i.e. that he is similar to him in age or in taking from the same *shaykh*. If each of them narrated from the other, then it is called *mudabbaj*.

فمثلاً: أنا رويتُ عن قريني حديث ((إنما الأعمال بالنيات)) وهو روى عني حديث ((لا يقبل الله صلاة أحدكم إذا أحدث حتى يتوضأ)) فهذا يكون مُدَبَّجاً، أو يروي عني نفس الحديث الذي رويته أنا، وأكون أنا قد رويته عنه من طريق، وهو رواه عني من طرق آخر، فهذا يسمى أيضاً مُدَبَّجاً.

An example would be that I narrated the *ḥadīth*, "Indeed actions are according to intentions" from my peer, and he narrated the *ḥadīth*, "Allāh does not accept the prayer of any one of you if he were to be in the state of impurity until he performs the ablution" from me. Hence this is *mudabbaj*. Alternatively if he were to narrate the same *ḥadīth* that I narrated; and I narrated it from him through a route, while he narrated from me through another route, this is also called *mudabbaj*.

وما وجه كونه مُدَبَّجاً؟

What is the reason for calling this *muddabaj*?

قالوا: إنه مأخوذ من ديباجة الوجه، أي جانب الوجه، لأن كل قرين يلتفت إلى صاحبه ليحدثه فيلتفت إليه صاحبه ليحدثه، فيكون قد قابله بديباجة وجهه، وبالطبع فإن هذا الاشتقاق اصطلاحي، وإلا لقلنا إن كل حديث بين اثنين يتجه فيه أحدهما إلى الآخر فإنه يسمى مدبَّجاً، لكن علماء المصطلح خصوه، ولا مشاحة في الاصطلاح.

Scholars said that it is taken from *dibājat al-wajh* (meaning *jānib al-wajh* or the side of the face) as each one of the peers turns to his associate in order for the other to narrate to him, therefore each one faces the other with the side of his face. Of course this derivation is in terms of terminology, otherwise we could say that every *ḥadīth* between two narrators where one of them turned to the other in it is called *mudabbaj*. However the scholars of the terminologies of *ḥadīth* were more specific with it, and there is no argument in terminology.

ورواية المدبج هو: أن يروي كل قرين عن قرينه، إما حديثاً واحداً، أو أكثر من حديث.

Thus the *mudabbaj* narration is whereby each *qarīn* narrated from the other, be it in one *ḥadīth* or more.

والفرق بينهما أن المدبَّج يُحدِّث كل منهما عن الآخر. أما الأقران فأحدهما يحدث عن الآخر فقط بدون أن يحدث عنه صاحبه.

And the difference between the two terminologies is that the *mudabbaj* is whereby each one narrated from the other whereas *al-aqrān* is when only one of them narrated from the other.

المتن

(٢٨) مُتَّفِقٌ لَفْظاً وَخَطاً مُتَّفِقْ وَضِدُّهُ فِيمَا ذَكَرْنَا الْمُفْتَرِقْ

(28) Identical in pronunciation and writing is muttafiq,
While the opposite of what we mentioned is muftariq.

الشرح

هذان هما القسم الثامن والعشرون من أقسام الحديث المذكورة في هذا النظم وهو: المتفق والمفترق.

These two are the twenty eighth category of the classifications of *ḥadīth* mentioned in the poem, which is *al-muttafiq* (identical names of narrators) and *al-muftariq* (different personalities).

وهما في الحقيقة قسم واحد، خلافاً لما يظهر من كلام المؤلف - رحمه الله - حيث جعلهما قسمين وهذا القسم يتعلق بالرواة، وهو ما إذا وجدنا اسمين متفقين لفظاً وخطًّا، لكنهما مفترقان ذاتاً أي أن الاسم واحد والمسمى اثنان فأكثر.

And these two are in actual fact considered as one category, which is contrary to the apparent appearance given by the statement of the author where he divided them into two categories. This classification is related to the narrators; and it is about us finding two names that are identical in terms of pronunciation and writing, but they are two different personalities i.e. two or more persons with one name.

وهذا العلم نحتاج إليه لئلا يقع الاشتباه، فمثلاً: كلمة عباس اسم لرجل مقبول الرواية، وهو اسم لرجل آخر غير مقبول الرواية، فهذا يسمى المتفق والمفترق.

We require this knowledge so as to avoid confusion. For example, the word 'Abbās is the name of a narrator whose narration is acceptable, and it is also the name of another person whose narration is not acceptable. Thus this is called *al-muttafiq* and *al-muftariq*.

فإذا رأينا مثلاً أن الحافظ يقول: حدثني عباس وهو أحد شيوخه، وهو ثقة، ثم يقول مرة أخرى حدثني عباس وهو أيضاً من شيوخه ولكنه ليس بثقة، ثم يأتي هذا الحديث ولا ندري أي العباسين هو، فيبقى الحديث عندنا مشكوكاً في صحته، ويسمَّى عند أهل الفن بالمتفق والمفترق.

As such, if we saw, for example, al-Ḥāfiẓ saying "'Abbās told me", and this is one of his teachers who was reliable, and saying "'Abbās told me" on another occasion, and this is also one of his teachers but he was not reliable. Thus the *ḥadīth* comes as such and we do not know which one of the two 'Abbās he is referring to. Therefore the soundness of the *ḥadīth* remains doubtful to us. This is called *al-muttafiq* and *al-muftariq* according to the scholars.

ووجه التسمية ظاهر: وهو الاتفاق بحسب اللفظ والخط، والافتراق بحسب المسمى.

The reasoning for this nomenclature is apparent, that is the state of *ittifāq* (congruency) in terms of pronunciation and writing, and the state of *iftirāq* (divergence) in terms of the identified.

والعلم بهذا أمر ضروري، لأنهما إذا اختلفا في التوثيق صار الحديث محل توقف، حتى يتبين من هذا، فإن كان كل منهما ثقة، وقد لاقى كل منهما المحدِّث فإنه لا يضر لأن الحديث سيبقى صحيحاً.

Knowing this is an important matter, because if both narrators differ in terms of trustworthiness, then the evaluation of the *ḥadīth* is put to a halt until this is clarified. If each one of the two is trustworthy, and both have met the narrator, then there is no issue as the status of the *ḥadīth* will remain as *ṣaḥīḥ*.

فالمتفق والمفترق يتعلق بالرواة لا بالمتون، وإذا كان يتعلق بالرواة فإنه يُنظر إذا كان هذا المتفق والمفترق كل منهما ثقة، فإنه لا يضر، وإذا كان أحدهما ثقة

والآخر ضعيفاً فإنه حينئذ محل توقف، ولا يحكم بصحة الحديث، ولا ضعفه حتى يتبين الافتراق والاتفاق.

Therefore, the *muttafiq* and the *muftariq* are connected to the narrators and not the text. Since it is related to the narrators, we have to look at the *muttafiq* and the *muftariq*; if each one of them is reliable, then there is no effect, and if one of them is reliable while the other is weak, then the evaluation of the *ḥadīth* is put to a halt, and we do not rule the *ḥadīth* as *ṣaḥīḥ* or *ḍaʿīf* until the *muttafiq* and the *muftariq* are clarified.

المتن

(٢٩) مُؤْتَلِفٌ مُتَّفِقُ الْخَطِّ فَقَطْ وَضِدُّهُ مُخْتَلِفٌ فَاخْشَ الْغَلَطْ

(29) Muʾtalif is similar only in writing,
And its opposite is mukhtalif, so beware of mistakes.

الشرح

هذا هو القسم التاسع والعشرون من أقسام الحديث المذكورة في هذا النظم وهو المؤتلف والمختلف.

This is the twenty ninth category of the classifications of *ḥadīth* mentioned in the poem, which is *al-muʾtalif* (similar in writing) and *al-mukhtalif* (different in pronunciation).

والمؤتلف والمختلف هو: الذي اتفق خطًّا ولكنه اختلف لفظاً، مثل: عباس وعياش، وخياط وحباط، وما أشبه ذلك.

The *muʾtalif* and *mukhtalif* is one that is similar in terms of writing but has a different pronunciation, such as ʿAbbās and ʿAyyāsh, Khayāṭ and Ḥabāt etc.

يعني أن اللفظ في تركيب الكلمة واحد، لكن تختلف في النطق، فهذا يسمى مؤتلفاً مختلفاً.

I.e. the writing in terms of the word structure is one, but the difference is in the pronunciation; so this is called *mu'talif* and *mukhtalif*.

وسُمي مؤتلفاً لإتلافه خطًّا، وسُمي مختلفاً لاختلافه نطقاً، وهو أيضاً في نفس الوقت مفترق لاختلافه عيناً وذاتاً.

It is called *mu'talif* due to the state of *i'tilāf* (conformity) in terms of writing, and called *mukhtalif* due to its state of *ikhtilāf* (difference) in terms of pronunciation. At the same time, it is also called *muftariq* due to the difference in persons and selves.

فالأشخاص متعددون في المتفق والمفترق، والمؤتلف والمختلف، ولكن الكلام على الأسماء إن كانت مختلفة فسمِّه مؤتلفاً مختلفاً، وإن كانت متفقة فسمِّه متفقاً مفترقاً، وهذا اصطلاح، واصطلاح المحدثين أمرٌ لا يُنازَعون عليه، لأنه يقال: لا مشاحة في الاصطلاح.

As such, the personalities are numerous in the *muttafiq* and the *muftariq* as well as the *mu'talif* and the *mukhlatif*. However in the topic of names; if they are different, then they are classified as *mu'talif* and *mukhlatif*, whereas if they are the same, then they are classified as *muttafiq* and the *muftariq*. This is the proper terminology, and there is no dispute in terminology of the scholars of *ḥadīth* because it is said that there is no argument in defining terminologies.

إذا ما هي الفائدة من معرفة هذا القسم من أقسام الحديث؟

As such, what is the benefit from knowing these categories from the classifications of *ḥadīth*?

نقول: الفائدة لئلا يشتبه الأشخاص، فمثلاً: إذا كان عندنا عشرة رجال كلهم

يُسمَّون بـ(عباس) فلابد أن نعرف من هو عباس، لأنه قد يكون أحدهم ضعيفاً:

We say that the benefit is to avoid the arising of confusion amongst people. For example, if we have ten narrators all of them by the name of ʿAbbās, we have to know which ʿAbbās was referred to as one of them could be a weak narrator:

إما لسوء حفظه.

(i) Either due to his weak memory,

وإما لنقص في عدالته، وإما لغير ذلك.

(ii) Or due to his lack of righteousness or other reasons.

فلابد أن نعرف من عباس هذا، لأجل أن نعرف هل هو مقبول الرواية، أو غير مقبول الرواية، وهذا الباب قد أُلِّف فيه كثير من العلماء وتكلموا فيه، وعلى رأسهم الحافظ ابن حجر - رحمه الله -.

Thus it is a must to know who this ʿAbbās is in order to determine whether his narration is acceptable or not. Many scholars—amongst the leading from them is al-Ḥāfiẓ Ibn Ḥajar—have written books and spoken about this matter.

فإذا قال قائل: بأي طريق نميز هذا من هذا؟

So if someone were to ask: "How do we differentiate one from another?"

فنقول: أما المؤتلف والمختلف فتمييزه يسير؛ لأنه مختلف في النطق، ولا يكون فيه اشتباه في الواقع، إلا إذا سلكنا طريق المتقدمين في عدم الإعجام.

We say: As for *mu'talif* and *mukhtalif*, the differentiation is easy because of the difference in the pronunciation and there is no confusion in reality unless we follow the way of the predecessors in the absence of *iʿjām*.

والإعجام هو: عدم تنقيط الحروف.

And *al-i'jām* is the absence of dots from the Arabic letters.

فمثلاً: عند المتقدمين كانت كلمة (عباس - وعيَّاش) واحدة لأنها كانت لا تُشكل ولا تُنقط، أما عند المتأخرين فإن الباب يقلُّ فيه الاشتباه، لأنهم يُعجمون الكلمات.

An example would be the words 'Abbās and 'Ayyāsh, which were regarded as one to the predecessors due to the absence of dots and vowels. As for the contemporary scholars, the confusion rarely occurs in this matter as they dot the words.

أما المتفق والمفترق فهو صعب، حتى في زمن المتأخرين، لأن تعيين المراد تحتاج إلى بحث دقيق في معرفة الشخص بعينه، ووصفه تماماً.

As for *muttafiq* and *muftariq*, it is difficult even in the time of the later scholars because identifying the narrator whom was referred to requires in-depth research to specify the person in particular and his full description.

فصار إذاً فائدة معرفة هذا الباب هو: تعيين الراوي، للحكم عليه بقبول روايته أو بردّها، والمرجع في ذلك الكتب المؤلفة في هذا الباب، ومما يُعين على تعيين الرجل معرفة شيوخه الذين يروي عنهم، وكذلك معرفة طلابه، الذين يروون عنه.

Therefore the benefit of learning this chapter is to identify the narrator in order to rule him as someone whose narration is acceptable or not. As such, the reference for this is the books that were written in this field, and from that which helps in identifying the narrator is the knowledge of his teachers from whom he narrated from as well as his students who narrated from him.

المتن

(٣٠) وَالْـمُنْكَرُ الْفَرْدُ بِهِ رَاوٍ غَدَا تَعْدِيلُهُ لاَ يَحْمِلُ التَّفَرُّدَا

(30) Munkar is the singular narration by a narrator,
Whose standding does not allow for a singular narration.

الشرح

هذا هو القسم الثلاثون من أقسام الحديث المذكورة في هذا النظم وهو المنكر.

This is the thirtieth category of the classifications of *ḥadīth* mentioned in the poem, which *is al-munkar* (the rejected narration).

وقد اختلف المحدثون في تعريف المنكر: فقيل: إن المنكر هو ما رواه الضعيف مخالفاً للثقة.

The scholars differ in the definition of *munkar*. It is said that it is what was narrated by a weak narrator which contradicted that of a reliable narrator.

مثل: أن يروي الحديث ثقةٌ على وجه، ويرويه رجل ضعيف على وجه آخر، حتى وإن كانا الراويان تلميذين لشيخ واحد.

An example would be a *ḥadīth* narrated by a reliable narrator in a certain way whilst a weak one narrated it in another way even though the two narrators were students of the same *shaykh*.

وقال بعضهم في تعريف المنكر: هو ما انفرد به واحد، لا يحتمل قبوله إذا تفرَّد. وهذا ما ذهب إليه الناظم.

And some scholars defined the *munkar* as what was exclusive to one narrator wherein there is no possibility of accepting it if he was the sole narrator. And this is how the author defined it.

وعلى هذا التعريف يكون المنكر هو الغريب، الذي لا يحتمل تفرد من انفرد به، وهو مردود حتى لو فُرض أن له شواهد من جنسه، فإنه لا يرتقي إلى درجة

الحسن، وذلك لأن الضعف فيه متناهي، والتعريف الأول هو الذي مشى عليه الحافظ ابن حجر رحمه الله في كتابه نخبة الفِكر.

Upon this definition, the *munkar* is taken to be the *gharīb* which has no possibility of soundness due to the singularity of the sole narrator, and it is rejected, even if it has other supporting evidences of its type, so it does not move up to the grade of *al-ḥasan*. This is because the weakness in it has reached its peak. As for the first definition, it was the one adopted by al-Ḥāfiz Ibn Ḥajar in his book *Nukhbat al-Fikar*.

المتن

(٣١) مَتْرُوكُـهُ مَا وَاحِدٌ بِـهِ انْـفَرَدْ وَأَجْمَعُواْ لِضَعْفِـهِ فَهُوَ كَرَدّ

(31) Matrūk is that in which there is a solitary narrator,
And they agreed upon its weakness like the rejected.

الشرح

هذا هو القسم الحادي والثلاثون من أقسام الحديث المذكورة في هذا النظم وهو المتروك، وقد عرفه الناظم بقوله:

This is the thirty first category of the classifications of *ḥadīth* mentioned in the poem and it is called *al-matrūk* (the abandoned sole narration).

(ما واحدٌ به انفرد) يعني أن المتروك هو ما انفرد به واحد، أجمعوا على ضعفه.

The meaning of the author's statement is that the *matrūk* is what was exclusive to one narrator, and they agreed upon his weakness.

والضمير في (أجمعوا) يعود على المحدثين.

The pronoun in, "They agreed upon" refers to the scholars of *ḥadīth*.

قوله (فهو كردّ) أي هو مردود، والكاف زائدة من حيث المعنى.

And his words, "Like the rejected" means it is rejected. And the letter *kāf* (like) is an additional preposition in terms of the meaning.

فالمتروك كما عرفه المؤلف، هو: الذي رواه ضعيفٌ أجمع العلماء على ضعفه.

Thus, the *matrūk* as defined by the author is the narration by a weak narrator whom the scholars have agreed upon regarding his weakness.

فخرج به: ما رواه غير الضعيف فليس بمتروك، وما رواه الضعيف الذي اختلفوا في تضعيفه.

As such, the exception would be what was narrated by one who was not regarded as weak. In this case it is not termed as *matrūk*. Likewise is the case for what was narrated by an individual whom the scholars differed in opinion with regarding his weakness.

هذا هو ما ذهب إليه المؤلف.

And this is the definition that the author adopted.

وقال بعض العلماء ومنهم ابن حجر في النخبة: إن المتروك هو ما رواه راوٍ متهمٌ بالكذب.

Some scholars said, amongst them being Ibn Ḥajar in his text *al-Nukhbah*, that the *matrūk* is what was narrated by someone who was accused of lying.

فمثلاً: إذا وجدنا في التهذيب لابن حجر، عن شخصٍ من الرواة، قال فيه: أجمعوا على ضعفه، فإننا نسمي حديثه متروكاً إذا انفرد به، لأنهم أجمعوا على ضعفه.

For example; if we found in the book *al-Tahdhīb* by Ibn Ḥajar that he said that the scholars agreed upon the weakness of one of the narrators, then we call his narration as *matrūk* if he was the sole narrator, as the scholars agreed upon his weakness.

وإذا وجدنا فيه قوله: وقد اتهم بالكذب فنسميه متروكاً أيضاً، لأن المتهم بالكذب حديثه كالموضوع، ولا نجزم بأنه موضوع، ولكن كونه متهماً بالكذب، ينزل حديثه إلى درجة تقرُب من الوضع.

And if we found in it that he said that the narrator was accused of lying, then we shall call it as *matrūk* also because the *ḥadīth* of the one who is being accused of lying is considered to be like the *mawḍū'* (fabricated) narration. We are not affirmative with the particular narration being fabricated, but the fact that he was accused of lying degrades his narration close to the state of fabrication.

المتن

(٣٢) وَالْكَذِبُ الْمُخْتَلَقُ الْمَصْنُوعُ عَلَى النَّبِي فَذَلِكَ الْمَوْضُوعُ

(32) And the lie which was fabricated and created,
Upon the Prophet is thus al-mawḍū'.

الشرح

هذا هو القسم الثاني والثلاثون من أقسام الحديث المذكورة في هذا النظم وهو الموضوع.

This is the thirty second category of the classifications of *ḥadīth* mentioned in the poem, which is *al-mawḍū'* (fabricated narration).

وقد عرفه المؤلف بقوله: والكذب المختلق ... الخ.

The author has defined it with his statement, "And the lie which was fabricated..." until the end of the quote.

يعني هو: الذي اصطنعه بعض الناس، ونسبه إلى النبي صلى الله عليه وسلّم، فإننا نسميه موضوعاً في الاصطلاح.

I.e. it is that which was created by some people and attributed to the Prophet ﷺ so we call it *mawḍūʿ* terminologically.

وكلمة موضوع هل تعني أن العلماء وضعوه ولم يلقوا له بالاً، أم أن راويه وضعه على النبي صلى الله عليه وسلّم؟

And the word "*mawḍūʿ*" (placed/made-up); does it refer to the scholars placing it [in their books] and not paying attention to [its authenticity] or that the narrator made it up in the name of the Prophet ﷺ?

نقول: هو في الحقيقة يشملهما جميعاً، فالعلماء وضعوه ولم يلقوا له أي بالٍ، وهو موضوع أي وضعه راويه على النبي صلى الله عليه وسلّم.

We say that in actual fact, it encompasses both statements. As such, the scholars reported it without giving any regard to its status, and it is *mawḍūʿ*, i.e. the narrator made it up and attributed it to the Prophet ﷺ.

والأحاديث الموضوعة كثيرة ألَّف فيها العلماء تآليف منفردة، وتكلموا على بعضها على وجه الخصوص، ومما أُلف في هذا الباب كتاب (اللآلئ المصنوعة في الأحاديث الموضوعة) ومنها (الفوائد المجموعة في الأحاديث الموضوعة) للشوكاني، ومنها (الموضوعات) لابن الجوزي، إلا أن ابن الجوزي - رحمه الله - يتساهل في إطلاق الوضع على الحديث، حتى إنهم ذكروا أنه ساق حديثاً رواه مسلم في صحيحه وقال إنه موضوع! ولهذا يُقال: (لا عبرة بوضع ابن الجوزي، ولا بتصحيح الحاكم، ولا بإجماع ابن المنذر) لأن هؤلاء يتساهلون، مع أن ابن المنذر تتبعته فوجدته أن له أشياء مما نقل فيه الإجماع ويقول: لا نعلم فيه خلافاً، وإذا قال ذلك فقد أبرأ ذمته أمام الله تعالى.

In regards to fabricated *aḥādīth,* the scholars wrote many separate books on them and spoke about some of the narrations specifically. Amongst the books that were written for this purpose are: *al-Lāli' al-Maṣnū'ah fi 'l-Aḥādīth al-Mawḍū'ah*, *al-Fawā'id al-Majmū'ah fi 'l-Aḥādīth al-Mawḍū'ah* by al-Shawkānī and *al-Mawḍū'āt* by Ibn al-Jawzī. However Ibn al-Jawzī was very quick in giving the ruling of fabrication upon the *ḥadīth,* to the extent that the scholars said that he reported a *ḥadīth* which was recorded by Muslim and ruled it as being *mawḍū'!* As such, it was said that, "There is no consequence in Ibn al-Jawzī's ruling of *mawḍū'*, al-Ḥākim's ruling of *ṣaḥīḥ* and Ibn al-Mundhir's reporting of *ijmā'* (consensus)." This is because all of them were quick to give these attributes to narrations. In fact, I have analysed Ibn al-Mundhir's work and found points wherein he transmitted a consensus on them and stated, "And we do not know of any difference of opinion." And when he says this (i.e. limiting his ruling to his own knowledge), he freed himself of responsibility in front of Allāh ﷻ.

والأحاديث الموضوعة لها أسباب:

There are many reasons for the fabrication of *aḥādīth*:

منها التعصب لمذهب أو لطائفة، أو على مذهب أو على طائفة، مثل آل البيت؛ فإن الرافضة أكذب الناس على رسول الله صلى الله عليه وسلّم، لأنهم لا يستطيعون أن يُروجوا مذهبهم إلا بالكذب، إذ أنَّ مذهبهم باطل، كما ذكر ذلك شيخ الإسلام - رحمه الله - عنهم.

Amongst them is fanaticism for or against the *madhhabs* (schools of thought) or for groups e.g. the *Ahl al-Bayt* (family of the Prophet ﷺ). The *Rāfiḍah* are the worst of the liars upon the Prophet ﷺ because they are unable to support their ideology except through lying. Thus their school of thought is false, as Shaykh al-Islām [Ibn Taymiyyah] mentioned about them.

وهناك أحاديث كثيرة رويت في ذم بني أمية، وأكثر من وضعها الرافضة، لأن بني

أمية كان بينهم، وبين علي بن أبي طالب - رضي الله عنه - حروب وفتن.

There are also many narrations that dispraise the *Banī Umayyah*, and most of it was fabricated by the *Rāfiḍah* because the Umayyads and ʿAlī ibn Abī Ṭālib ﷺ were at war and engulfed in tribulations.

والموضوع مردود، والتحدث به حرام، إلا من تحدّث به من أجل أن يبين أنه موضوع فإنه يجب عليه أن يبين ذلك لناس، ووضع الحديث على رسول الله صلى الله عليه وسلّم من كبائر الذنوب لقول النبي صلى الله عليه وسلّم: ((من كذب عليّ متعمداً فليتبوأ مقعده من النار))، وثبت عنه أنه قال: ((من حدَّث عني بحديث يرى أنه كذب فهو أحدُ الكاذبين)).

And the *mawḍūʿ* narration is rejected and the mention of it is prohibited except in the case of mentioning it in order to clarify that it is a fabricated *ḥadīth*. So it is obligatory upon the narrator to explain this to the common people. And the fabrication of *ḥadīth* upon the Prophet ﷺ is one of the major sins, due to the narration, "Whosoever intentionally lies upon me, let him take his place in the Hellfire."[84] And it is established from him that he said, "Whosoever narrated from me a *ḥadīth* of which he knew was a lie, then he is one of the liars."[85]

وإذا أردت أن تسوق حديثاً للناس، وتُبين لهم أنه موضوع ومكذوب على النبي صلى الله عليه وسلّم، فلابد أن تذكره بصيغة التمريض (قيل ويُروى ويُذكر) ونحو ذلك، لكي لا تنسبه إلى النبي صلى الله عليه وسلّم بصيغة الجزم، لأنه إن فعلت ذلك أوقعت السامع في الإيهام.

If you were to report this type of *ḥadīth* to the people and clarify to them that it is *mawḍūʿ* and a lie attributed to the Prophet ﷺ, it is a must to report it in a passive form, such as using, "It was said", "It was narrated", "It was mentioned" and their likes so as not to attribute it to the Prophet ﷺ in an

84 Mentioned previously.
85 Mentioned previously.

affirmative manner. The reason is that if you did the latter, then you may cause a misconception to the audience.

ومن الأمور المهمة التي ينبغي أن ننبه عليها: ما يفعله الزمخشري في تفسيره من تصديره السورة التي يفسرها، أو ختمها بأحاديث ضعيفة جداً أو موضوعة، في فضل تلك السورة، ولكن الله يسر للحافظ ابن حجر رحمه الله فخرَّج أحاديث تفسير (الكشَّاف) للزمخشري وبين الصحيح من الضعيف من الموضوع.

Amongst the important matters that we must bring attention to is al-Zamakhsharī's method in his *tafsīr* book where he would begin or end the *sūrah* that he was commenting upon by reporting *aḥādīth* regarding the virtues of the *sūrah* which were very weak or fabricated. However, Allāh facilitated al-Ḥāfiz Ibn Ḥajar in making the *takhrīj* (extraction/research of the chains of narration) of the narrations in the *tafsīr* work *al-Kashāf* by al-Zamakhsharī and explained which were *ṣaḥīḥ*, *ḍaʿīf* and *mawḍūʿ*.

المتن

٣٣ - وَقَدْ أَتَتْ كَالْجَوْهَرِ الْمَكْنُونِ   سَمَّيْتُهَا مَنْظُومَةَ الْبَيْقُونِي

(33) Indeed it came like a hidden gem,
Which I have entitled "The Poem of al-Bayqūnī".

الشرح

قوله: (أتت) الضميُر يعود على هذه المنظومة.

The author's statement, "It came"; the pronoun (*damīr*) refers to this poem.

وقوله (كالجوهر المكنون) أي مثل الجوهر، فالكاف للتشبيه.

And his statement, "Like a hidden gem" means it came like the example of a hidden gem, thus the preposition *kāf* (like) is for the sake of comparison.

و(أتت) فعل ماضي، وفاعله مستتر، و(كالجوهر) منصوبة على الحال، أي: أتت مثل الجوهر.

The verb "came" is in the past tense, with its doer hidden, whilst the phrase, "Like a gem" (*kal-jawhar*) is accusative, as it is a situational i.e. it came like the parable of a gem.

وقوله (المكنون) أي المحفوظ عن الشمس، وعن الرياح، والغبار فيكون دائماً نضراً مشرقاً.

His statement, "hidden" i.e. kept away from the sun, the wind and the dust. As such it shall always be shining lustrously.

وقوله (منظومة البيقوني) نسبها إليه، لأنه هو الذي نظمها.

And his statement, "*The Poem of al-Bayqūnī*"; he attributed the poem to himself as he was the one who composed it.

المتن

(٣٤) فَوْقَ الثَّلاثِينَ بِأَرْبَعٍ أَتَتْ أَقْسَامُهَا تَمَّتْ بِخَيْرٍ خُتِمَتْ

(34) It came with four above thirty,
Its sections, concluded and sealed with goodness.

قوله (فوق الثلاثين بأربعٍ أتت) أي أنها أتت أربعة وثلاثين بيتاً.

The author's line, "It came with four above thirty" i.e. it came in thirty four couplets.

وقوله (أبياتها ثم بخير خُتمت) يعني أن أبيات هذه المنظومة جاءت فوق الثلاثين بأربع ثم خُتمت بخير.

And his statement, "Its sections, concluded and sealed with goodness": i.e.

that the couplets of this poem came four above thirty and then were concluded with goodness.

وإلى هنا ينتهي - بفضل الله تعالى - هذا الشرح،

نسأل الله تعالى أن يتقبل منا صالح الأعمال،

وأن يغفر الزلل والخطأ إنه سميع مجيب.

والله أعلم، وصلى الله وسلم وبارك

على نبينا وإمامنا محمد بن عبد الله

وعلى آله وأصحابه وأتباعه

بإحسان إلى يوم الدين.

This commentary ends here, with the grace of Allāh ﷻ,

On a Monday night, the 10th of *Jamād al-Akhīr* 1412 H (1991 CE).

We ask Allāh ﷻ to accept from us our pious deeds,

And to forgive our imperfections and mistakes as He is hearing and answering.

Allāh knows best, and may His salutations, peace and blessings be upon our Prophet and Leader Muḥammad ibn ʻAbdillāh.

As well as upon his family, companions and followers,

With wellness until the Day of Judgement.